"This is a superb book! It is rare to have a solidly evangelical author address Islam and Muslims objectively yet fairly, but maintain an uncompromising imperative to befriend Muslims and share the lifesaving good news of Jesus with them. This work does just that. Matthew Bennett's thorough, professional, straightforward (and easy-to-read!) approach places just what we need at our fingertips."
—Ant Greenham, Southeastern Baptist Theological Seminary

"*40 Questions About Islam* is the best one-stop introduction to Islam written by an evangelical Christian. In it, Matthew Bennett provides concise and reliable answers to the most important questions people have about Islam and Muslims, encouraging Christians all the while to relate lovingly, respectfully, and evangelistically to their Muslim neighbors. Recommended highly and without reservation."
—Bruce Riley Ashford, Provost, Professor of Theology & Culture, Southeastern Baptist Theological Seminary

"With the rise of Islam around the world, now is the time for Christians to become more conversant and more committed to gospel conversations with Muslims. I have had the unique privilege of observing Dr. Bennett engage Muslims in person about the critical differences between Christianity and Islam. *40 Questions About Islam* is the work of scholar-practitioner who is committed to loving and sharing the gospel with Muslims around the world. This book helps equip Christians to converse with their Muslim neighbors, co-workers, and friends about the truth."
—Paul Akin, Dean of the Billy Graham School, The Southern Baptist Theological Seminary

"Matthew Aaron Bennett is a careful scholar, thorough researcher, and thoughtful missiologist. His discussion of Islam does not merely develop from a host of books anyone may read, but rather from his many years of experience in loving and connecting with Muslims. With a great joy, I welcome the publication of his *40 Questions About Islam.*"
—Ayman S. Ibrahim, Bill and Connie Jenkins Associate Professor of Islamic Studies, The Southern Baptist Theological Seminary

"In an age when far too many Christians don't recognize the clear differences between Christianity and Islam, Matthew Bennett has done us all a great service by writing this accessible, well-researched, and comprehensive volume exploring the complex ideologies of Islam through the framework of 40 questions. Exploring the theology, practice, writings, and mission of Islam, Bennett frames our understanding of this growing religion in such a way that it properly equips readers to take the Christian gospel to their Muslim neighbors."
—Dustin W. Benge, Provost and Professor, Union School of Theology

40 QUESTIONS SERIES

40 Questions Angels, Demons, and Spirtual Warfare
John R. Gilhooly

40 Questions About Baptism and the Lord's Supper
John S. Hammett

40 Questions About Calvinism
Shawn D. Wright

40 Questions About Christians and Biblical Law
Thomas R. Schreiner

40 Questions About Church Membership and Discipline
Jeremy M. Kimble

40 Questions About Creation and Evolution
Kenneth D. Keathley and Mark F. Rooker

40 Questions About Elders and Deacons
Benjamin L. Merkle

40 Questions About Heaven and Hell
Alan W. Gomes

40 Questions About Interpreting the Bible
Robert L. Plummer

40 Questions About Islam
Matthew Aaron Bennett

40 Questions About Salvation
Matthew Barrettt

40 Questions About the End Times
Eckhard Schnabel

40 Questions About the Great Comission
Daniel L. Akin, Benjamin L. Merkle, and George G. Robinson

40 Questions About the Historical Jesus
C. Marvin Pate

40 QUESTIONS ABOUT
Islam

Matthew Aaron Bennett

Benjamin L. Merkle, Series Editor

40 Questions About Islam
© 2020 Matthew Aaron Bennett

Published by Kregel Academic, an imprint of Kregel Publications, 2450 Oak Industrial Dr. NE, Grand Rapids, MI 49505-6020.

This book is a title in the 40 Questions Series edited by Benjamin L. Merkle.

All Scripture quotations, unless otherwise indicated, are from The Holy Bible, English Standard Version, copyright © 2001 by Crossway Bibles, a division of Good News Publishers. Used by permission. All rights reserved.

All quotations of the Qur'an, unless otherwise indicated, are from A. J. Droge, trans., *The Qur'an: A New Annotated Translation*. Bristol, CT: Equinox, 2015.

The Hebrew font, NewJerusalemU, and the Greek font, GraecaU, are available from www.linguistsoftware.com/lgku.htm, +1-425-775-1130.

ISBN 978-0-8254-4622-1

Printed in the United States of America

20 21 22 23 24 / 5 4 3 2 1

To Emily,
my loving wife, my best friend,
and my wise co-laborer in the gospel.

Contents

Part 5: The Qur'an and the Bible

Part 6: The Development of Contemporary Critical Scholarship

Part 7: The Christian Gospel and the Followers of Islam

Acknowledgements

As with any project of this nature, I am indebted to a number of people who have contributed to its completion. From the more personal side of things, my wife Emily encouraged me along the way and labored through early draft chapters with patience and creative criticism. My dear friend and ministry partner Chris Watkins was also one who served to critique chapters along the way. I'm grateful to both of you for your patience and insight.

Likewise, on the academic side, I want to express my gratitude to Ayman Ibrahim, Ant Greenham, and Scott Bridger who did me the great service of reading through the manuscript and offering feedback. I am also grateful for colleagues such as J. R. Gilhooly, Anthony Moore, and Dan DeWitt at Cedarville University who read through various chapters and helped me write with greater clarity. Their critique has certainly helped me to avoid a number of missteps, though obviously any way in which this book is yet wanting is solely my responsibility.

As for the publishing process, working with Ben Merkle has been an absolute joy and privilege. Thank you, Ben, for your editing work and your encouragement of the project along the way. Of course, I am indebted to Kregel Publications for the chance they've given me to put together what I hope will be a helpful resource for those seeking to better understand some of the worldview of their Muslim friends and neighbors.

Finally, lest it go without saying, I am grateful to the Triune God who would make himself known to an undeserving creation in the gospel of Jesus the Messiah. May this book glorify him alone while encouraging readers to extend his boundless love and his beautiful gospel to their Muslim friends in meaningful ways.

Introduction

If you are reading this book, I am assuming that your personal interest in learning about Islam may arise from a number of motivations. It may be that you are taking a class on Islam, or that you are encountering confusing reports about Islam in the news. Perhaps your interest has been piqued because you are noticing a growing Muslim population in your community. Or perhaps it is because you either already have some Muslim friends or anticipate developing relationships with Muslim neighbors. Regardless of your motivation, it is a true privilege to play a small part in helping you develop an understanding of the complex and intriguing world of Islam.

I have spent significant time living in Muslim-majority countries, and I have also made Muslim friends in my home country of the United States. Many of those friends from various parts of the world have left an indelible impression on my life. Our conversations regarding our respective faiths have been formative and informative, and I am hopeful that you will experience the same things in dialogue with your Muslim friends. I also trust that this book will help to shed light on why conversations can be strained over certain issues or can even reach points of impasse.

Before jumping into our subject matter, it is important to note a few things about this book and my posture as its author. First, I want to make the reader aware of my intentions for the book. Speaking of someone else's faith will inevitably involve entanglements with one's own beliefs, and it is helpful to know where I am coming from as you engage this material. Second, I need to address the scope of this book along with its limitations. Finally, I want to provide a brief note about how one might use this book most effectively.

Posture and Aims

In the field of Islamic studies, for just about every sentence one writes, a dissenting opinion might be found. Perhaps even more tangibly, conversation with one's Muslim neighbors will also reveal a wide diversity of beliefs, practices, and opinions. I hope that the reader will recognize that no matter how much research one conducts about the Islamic faith, one will never have a conversation with the embodiment of Islam. Islam is a system or family of beliefs. Muslims, on the other hand, are individual human beings, filtering their faith and practice through the lens of their own experiences, concerns, values, and desires.

Thus, while it is essential to have a basic understanding of Islamic teaching, this book is more concerned with helping us ask informed questions of our conversation partners. Reader who finish this book will be better positioned to ask those questions but should not think that they are sufficiently informed of what their friends believe. In other words, this book intends to lay a basic foundation to aid us in asking well-informed questions of our friends who are practicing Islam.

Finally, the reader should be aware of the fact that, as an evangelical Christian, I believe that what Islam teaches is irreconcilable with the gospel of Jesus. With that in mind, I write not only as one who desires the reader to understand Muslim beliefs and to develop a love and compassion for Muslims, but also as one who longs for readers to engage in presenting the gospel to their Muslim friends. In presenting Islamic history, thought, and theology, I have sought to be fair and objective, yet I cannot claim objectivity or dispassionate concern in my desire to see Muslims understand the biblical gospel and place their faith in Christ.

Limitations and Scope

The title of this book can be deceptive. First, it might indicate to some readers that forty questions suffice to cover the basics of Islam. To the contrary, writing the list of questions alone was sufficient to reveal the impossibility of addressing the breadth—let alone the depth—of a topic so vast. This book intends, then, to serve as something of a primer on Islam, introducing the reader to some of the most pertinent topics. As a primer, this book requires a focus on some of the most widely held beliefs in Islam, to the unfortunate exclusion of many minority opinions or dissenting discussions in the academy. Wherever possible, though, I have tried to be sensitive to these issues by directing the reader to further resources in the footnotes.

Second, the title of the book might also be read to imply that Islam is monolithic. In light of the diversity of Islamic expressions, however, some argue that it would be better to speak of "Islams" in the plural so as to avoid such confusion. As Evelyne Reisacher points out, though, it may be better yet to speak of the manifold expressions of Islam in terms of bearing "family resemblance" to one another rather than to discuss Islam in either a universal sense or as a multiplicity of distinct "Islams."[1] This book should be understood as an attempt to trace common family lines, then, rather than definitively describing the nuances of every expression of Islam.

---

1. Evelyne Reisacher, "Defining Islam and Muslim Societies in Missiological Discourse," *Dynamics of Muslim Worlds* (Downers Grove, IL: IVP Academic, 2017), 241. Reisacher herself attributes this phraseology to Clifford Geertz.

How to Use This Book

With these two potential misunderstandings noted, my hope is that the convenient format of the 40 Questions Series will allow this work to serve as a quick reference for students, pastors, and those hoping to better understand their Muslim friends. Though the material in each section often builds upon previous questions, one need not read from cover to cover to understand the basic content of each chapter. As such, one should be able to consult the table of contents for specific questions that are of special interest and read each chapter as a stand-alone answer.

Statements made throughout these seven sections intend to be representative of a confessional Islamic perspective. When reading each chapter, however, the reader is advised to consider the section in which the chapter is situated. For example, when consulting a question within the sixth section, the reader should be aware that the answers given arise from critical scholarship and are not representative of mainline Islamic belief.

Likewise, the second and third sections deal with sources of authority and theology. These sections address issues over which there is significant intramural disagreement within the world of Islam. In various places I have tried to include perspectives from Shia and other minority expressions of Islam. When pressed for space, however, I have opted to highlight the Sunni position, since Sunnis reportedly make up more than 85 percent of the world's Muslim population. Thus, unless otherwise stated, the reader might assume this book is written from a Sunni perspective.

A Note regarding Arabic Transliteration

When presenting a phonetic equivalent of a non-English language originating in a non-English alphabet, an author has a number of choices to make. One can attempt to render the language using non-alphabet characters which, while perhaps more precise, remain meaningless to readers unacquainted with the original language. Or one can forego an attempt at precision for the purpose of increased readability. In the present work, I have opted to take the latter approach. Thus, the Arabic words and names that one encounters in this book have been adapted to promote readability, though the reader may encounter alternative spellings in other books on related topics.

Abbreviations

CE	Common Era: designator for dates according to the Gregorian calendar
CCQ	*Cambridge Companion to the Qur'an*
ESV	English Standard Version
IJFM	*International Journal of Frontier Missiology*
Sira	Ibn Hisham's recollection of Ibn Ishaq's biography of Muhammad, *Sirat Rasul Allah*

PART 1

The Traditional History of Islam

Where Did Islam Come From?

*Today I have perfected your religion for you, and
have completed my blessing on you, and I have
approved Islam for you as a religion.*
~Qur'an 5:3

Recently I found myself walking down a popular street in a well-known town in the southeast of the United States. Curio shops filled with trinkets and T-shirts lined the streets, and smells of various fried foods and candies wafted out to the sidewalks, enticing customers to enter and indulge. Some might call this a tourist trap.

While I was walking, an image in one of the shops caught my eye. It was one of several pictures of celebrities on display, but this one was unique in that it appeared to be moving. Upon closer inspection, I discovered that it was a poster including three images of the same celebrity at different points in his career. Depending upon what angle the viewer was approaching the poster, this celebrity showed up as either a young, up-and-coming heartthrob, a middle-aged success, or an aging, overweight has-been. Thus, as passersby glanced toward the window, their changing perspectives caused the images—and consequently, their impressions of the celebrity—to change.

Much like tourists passing by this poster, the angle of our approach to the study of Islam will determine the image produced by our inquiries. This is perhaps nowhere better illustrated than in giving an answer to our first question, "Where did Islam come from?" On the surface this appears to be merely a historical inquiry with but one basic answer, providing a suitable introduction to the book. Yet, as we consider three different angles of approach common among scholars, a more robust impression forms, allowing us to better answer subsequent questions.

For a Christian motivated to understand and minister to their Muslim friends, then, this tri-perspectival approach will provide an orientation to a more holistic investigation of Islam and its adherents. This chapter will treat these three approaches under the following headings: (1) an Orientalist approach, (2) a critical approach, and (3) a confessional approach. Like the tourists viewing the poster of the celebrity from several perspectives, these three angles of approach to Islamic origins will provide distinct yet helpful windows into the whole picture.

An Orientalist Approach: Muhammad's Ministry

The first image of Islam to confront us comes by approaching the question of Islamic origins from the perspective of Orientalist scholars. This nomenclature developed in the eighteenth century to describe scholars and artists involved in depicting eastern lands, including the Middle East.[1] Much of the popular material available in English takes this perspective, describing the religion of Islam as a cultural artifact of the East.

In contrast to confessional approaches to Islamic history that tout the virtues of Muhammad's religious message and assume God's blessing as the reason for Islamic expansion, Orientalists study the development of Islam as a mere sociological phenomenon. This secular approach excises the supernatural references within the reported accounts while yet depending upon the remaining information as reliable history. In so doing, Orientalists are left to sift through the traditional material in order to offer alternative explanations of how, apart from appeal to divine favor, seventh-century Arabia produced a global religion in less than two centuries.

According to the traditional material, the Arabian Peninsula of Muhammad's day was rife with intertribal conflict. Desire for a unified Arab state existed, though disunity prevailed at nearly every level of society. Seventh-century Arabia was in want of leadership and reform.

Muhammad's ministry began in Mecca, the regional center of polytheistic religious practice. The simple monotheism at the core of Muhammad's message, while not initially well received, provided a unifying bond with which the diversity of polytheism could not contend. Having gathered a modest following in Mecca, Muhammad relocated to Medina, where he proved influential as a political and social reformer.

---

1. The term "Orientalist" is admittedly problematic due to unavoidable echoes of colonialism. The word has been used to distinguish supposedly lesser forms of culture in the east from the supposedly superior cultures of the occident. Yet, it is prolific enough within the literature discussing Islam to merit retaining it here.

Shortly after Muhammad's move, Medina and Mecca entered into a state of war with one another. While the war continued to exacerbate the divisions of the peninsula, Muhammad's ability to strategically unify the Medinan population politically and militarily allowed him, and consequently his religious message, to rise in power and prominence.

For most Orientalists, then, Muhammad and the religion that followed him was successful on the basis of his ability to forge a common identity for his Arab kin. In the words of prolific author Bernard Lewis,

> From what is known of the circumstances of the time, it is clear that the deeds performed by Muhammad or ascribed to him served to revive and redirect currents that already existed among the Arabs of his time. The fact that his death was followed by a new burst of activity instead of by collapse shows that his career was the answer to a great political, social, and moral need. . . . Muhammad had aroused and redirected the latent forces of an Arab national revival and expansion.[2]

In other words, as we approach the question of Islamic origins from the perspective of the Orientalist scholar, we see Muhammad as a unifying reformer whose religious message was carried on the wings of his political savvy. Islam was born as a result of Muhammad's leadership and Arab nationalist desire.

A Critical Approach: Muhammad's Successors

One of the true wonders of the Islamic faith is its rapid expansion. Reportedly having begun in an isolated region on the Arabian Peninsula, in less than two centuries Islam had spread to what is now southern France in the west, and to what is now western India in the east. Yet if one follows the traditional accounts, upon his death Muhammad had not clearly provided his followers with instructions for appointing a successor, let alone a codified means of practicing Islam in the far-flung corners of the empire as the centuries progressed.[3]

How did this fledgling faith, left by its iconic leader in such an early stage of development, come to dominate such a wide region? One major issue that critical scholars have identified is that the material available to inform us of Muhammad's life does not pass the test of historical criticism.[4] While it is perhaps the text that exerts the most influence on the practice of Islam, the

---

2. Bernard Lewis, *The Arabs in History* (New York: Oxford University Press, 1993), 46.
3. Lewis, *Arabs in History*, 48. In fact, different claims regarding Muhammad's appointment of a successor is the basis for the split between Shia and Sunni Muslims and will be treated in Question 5.
4. See Gabriel Said Reynolds, *The Emergence of Islam: Classical Traditions in Contemporary Perspective* (Minneapolis: Fortress, 2012), 135–38.

traditional biography of Muhammad's life—to say nothing of the body of traditions known as the *hadith*—is unattested, late, and prone to bias.[5] Since Muhammad's biography is the primary source of information regarding the life and ministry of the Arab prophet, skeptical scholars question how much one can truly know about this man named Muhammad.[6]

Furthermore, beyond the dearth of acceptable literary evidence for a traditional understanding of Islamic origins, archeological evidence does not lend its support to the Muslim account. For example, the first apparently Muslim reference to Muhammad to be connected to any recognizable form of Islamic theology is found on an inscription on the Dome of the Rock in Jerusalem, dating to 691 CE, nearly sixty years after Muhammad's death.[7] After the date of this inscription, the archeological record reports frequent appearance of inscriptions, epitaphs, and documents bearing Islamic theological themes. However, that the first sixty years are silent leads some scholars to conclude that later Arab leaders were responsible for crafting a religious message and tying it to a character named Muhammad in order to unify the broad empire under a common identity.[8]

Unsatisfied with the supernatural explanation for Islam's explosive growth given by Muslims, and unconvinced by the traditional account of Muhammad's life, historical-critical scholars offer an alternative approach to Islamic origins. Instead of attempting to recreate a historical sketch of a man named Muhammad, critical scholars are keen to find Islamic origins in the political developments of later Arab rulers. Thus, as we approach the picture of Islamic origins from the vantage of critical scholarship, Islam did not precede Arab expansion, but was produced as an ideological bond, born and shaped in response to the Arab conquests.

---

5. For more details on the scholarly critique of traditional accounts of Muhammad's life, see Question 33.
6. Furthermore, there are scholarly works that deny that a character named Muhammad as described in the traditional material ever existed. Cf. Karl-Heinz Ohlig, "From *Muhammad* to Jesus Prophet of the Arabs: The Personalization of a Christological Epithet," in *Early Islam: A Critical Reconstruction based on Contemporary Sources*, ed. Karl-Heinz Ohlig (Amherst, NY: Prometheus, 2014), 251–307. For further treatment, see Question 33.
7. Though references to Muhammad as the leader of the Arabs appear in the early part of the eighth century, at least one author has challenged this idea, claiming that these references are linguistic misunderstandings of Arabic references to heterodox understandings of Jesus. See Christoph Luxenberg, "A New Interpretation of the Arabic Inscription in Jerusalem's Dome of the Rock," in *The Hidden Origins of Islam*, eds. Karl-Heinz Ohlig and Gerd-R. Puin (Amherst, NY: Prometheus, 2010), 125–52. Here, Luxenberg also counters prevailing scholarly opinion, making the case that even the Dome of the Rock inscription need not be understood as Islamic theology, but might actually be a form of Syriac Christian Christology.
8. See Yahuda D. Nevo, "Towards a Prehistory of Islam," in *What the Koran Really Says*, ed. Ibn Warraq (Amherst, NY: Prometheus, 2002), 131–69. Nevo states, "In short, the state decided, as a political act, to adopt Muhammadanism as its official creed."

A Confessional Approach: Muhammad's Predecessors

It is likely obvious that faithful Muslims reject the conclusions of critical scholars discussed above. Like the Orientalists, those who personally confess Islam are typically inclined to accept the traditional material as historically accurate. Yet in contrast, confessional approaches retain the supernatural elements that Orientalists dismiss, understanding Muhammad to be the mouthpiece of God, whose blessing accounts for the success of Islamic expansion.

However, despite adhering to the traditional material, from the confessional Muslim perspective, Islam does not actually begin with Muhammad. Rather, according to Islamic theology, submission to God is the original form of worship prescribed by all of the prophets since Adam.[9] Islamic scholar Mark Anderson highlights this idea, writing, "Every prophet before Muhammad is said to have pointed to the path of *islam*, since that is both the ideal for which we were created and our sole route of recovery from lostness."[10] In other words, Adam was a prototypical Muslim who foreshadowed the faith that Muhammad recovered and perfected.

While the claim that Islam precedes Muhammad is made variously throughout the Qur'an, perhaps no character is more centrally utilized to emphasize this idea than Abraham, of whom it is said in Qur'an 3:67, "Abraham was not a Jew, nor a Christian, but he was a *hanif*, a Muslim. He was not one of the idolaters." Therefore, by exalting Abraham as an embryonic exemplar of Islamic faith who preceded both Judaism and Christianity, the Qur'an lays claim to roots much more ancient than Muhammad.

Thus, for confessional Muslims, the source of Islamic origins is not the product of Arab political strategy, nor is it wholly tied to the dynamic leadership of Muhammad. Rather, Islam originates at the dawn of creation and, through Muhammad's call, humanity is given the opportunity to return to the one true expression of divine religion. A confessional perspective on the question of Islamic origins reveals a picture of Islam as the original religion, beginning when God first commanded submission from his creation.

Summary

Like the tourists glancing at the poster mentioned in the introduction, the preceding paragraphs have shown how drastically one's approach to Islam will affect the picture that emerges. In the same way that the three pictures of the celebrity tell a fuller story of his career than any individual picture does, so do the three perspectives on Islamic origins allow for a more robust investigation into the question, "What is Islam?" Each approach reveals an image

---

9. John Kaltner and Younus Mirza, *The Bible and the Qur'an: Biblical Figures in Islamic Tradition* (New York: T&T Clark, 2018), 16–19.

10. Mark Robert Anderson, *The Qur'an in Context: A Christian Exploration* (Downers Grove, IL: IVP Academic, 2016), 83.

that evokes a distinct impression about the faith and will affect the various answers given to the rest of the questions contained in this book. Yet, for the purposes of this book, each picture, perspective, and impression provides helpful insight for our holistic investigation of Islam.

For example, the Orientalist approach benefits the investigation by highlighting the sociological factors that explain how Muhammad's message and leadership could resonate so deeply with seventh-century Arabs, resulting in a global movement. Likewise, the critical approach reminds us that, no matter what one does with the traditional history, later political and military pressures affected the body of literature we have that attests to Muhammad, leaving significant impressions upon the contemporary practice of Islam. Both perspectives provide a healthy caution to those tempted to read the Islamic history from a posture of naive positivism.

Yet, as Christians engaged in conversation with Muslim neighbors, we do well to consider the confessional perspective at length. Whether or not the history recorded in Muhammad's biography or the traditions regarding Muhammad's teaching and practice can pass the test of historical reliability, we must acknowledge that they exert formative pressure on the worldview of the Muslims with whom we relate. Taking the time to understand the material that is shaping and informing our Muslim friends, we demonstrate neighborly love, dignifying our conversation partners by considering the world through their eyes. Such a posture encourages effective communication, loving challenge, and an opportunity to speak gospel hope into the places where the cracks in an Islamic worldview might appear.

Both faiths certainly do exhibit superficial similarities. However, Islam and Christianity operate on different understandings of who God is, the problem of sin, its solution, and the ultimate purpose for human life. As such, the deep theological differences ultimately outweigh the superficial similarities. The charitable posture encouraged by this book need not deny such differences. Rather, it aims to prepare Christians to anticipate deep theological differences while yet striving for meaningful interactions with their Muslim neighbors. Thus, Part 7 is dedicated to acknowledging the irreconcilable differences between Islam and Christianity while encouraging a loving approach to gospel communication.

With this tri-perspectival reality in mind, this book aims to highlight the pertinent issues that emerge from each approach. The first four parts will approach Islam from a confessional angle, treating Islamic history, theology, and practice from the perspective of its adherents. In the fifth section, comparison between biblical and qur'anic teaching will draw on Orientalist, critical, and evangelical perspectives. Following this, the sixth section will raise four significant questions that emerge from a critical approach. Finally, Part 7 considers six missiological questions that press upon an evangelical engaged in relationship with a Muslim friend.

Standing on the street outside of the curio shop, I found myself thinking about how one image of the celebrity in the poster, isolated from the rest, gave but a partial impression of his entire career. Likewise, taking any one approach to the study of Islam will distort the overall impression it produces. It is my hope that these three approaches will provide a broad, healthy, informed picture of our overall answer to the question posed by this book, "What is Islam?"

REFLECTION QUESTIONS

1. Why might it be important to consider each of the three approaches to Islam discussed in this first chapter?

2. From an Orientalist perspective, how do we explain the rise of Islam in seventh-century Arabia?

3. What makes the traditional narrative of Islam's advent doubtful from a critical perspective?

4. How does a confessional approach explain the success of Muhammad's prophetic career?

5. How might each perspective answer the question, "What is Islam?"

Who Was Muhammad and What Was His Message?

There is no god but The God,
and Muhammad is his Messenger.
~The Islamic Confession of Faith

As the world continues its rapid trend toward globalization and urbanization, it is likely that wherever you find yourself reading this book, someone bearing a name recalling the prophet of Islam lives nearby. For males, the name might take the form of Ahmed, Mustafa, Hamada, or Muhammad. Likewise, girls might bear the name of one of Muhammad's wives, such as Aisha, Khadija, Hafsa, or Zaynab. Regardless of the form, the ubiquity of Muhammad's name more than fourteen hundred years after his death makes inescapable the question, "Who was this man?"

While the previous chapter raised significant historical questions regarding what can be known of Muhammad's life, it is impossible to separate the practice of contemporary Islam from the idea of Muhammad. In other words, whether one views Muhammad as a hero of history or a fabricated fable, it is necessary to consider the influence this character has had on nearly two billion Muslims on earth today and upon world history in general. For those who want to understand Islam, the story surrounding the character named Muhammad cannot be ignored.

Further, Muhammad the prophet cannot be separated from the message that he proclaimed. The story of Muhammad's life is a chronicle of his religious message, without which his legacy would likely fade into obscurity. As evidence of this inseparability, the Islamic confession of faith requires the confessor to testify that "there is no god but God, and Muhammad is his messenger." This chapter, then, provides a brief sketch of Muhammad's life and teaching according to the traditional accounts found in the biography of Muhammad's life (the *Sira*) and from the perspective of the confessional community.

Humble Origins: Muhammad's Childhood

The traditional material that provides a window into Muhammad's early years does not paint an impressive picture of privilege or prowess for the young child. Instead, the first eight years of his life were marked by several significant deaths of family members.[1] His father, 'Abdullah of the Hashemite family, died before Muhammad was born. His mother, Aminah, lived only until he was about six years old.[2] Orphaned at such a young age, Muhammad was then taken into custody by his grandfather, Abd al-Muttalib. Tragically, Abd al-Muttalib died two years later, finally leaving the eight-year-old Muhammad in the care of his uncle, Abu Talib.

Despite these tragic deaths within his immediate family, Muhammad found in Abu Talib a loving guardian, and his formative years were spent in his uncle's household. While we lack a lot of detail regarding Muhammad's adolescence, two features stand out: his character, and the prophecies made about him. Regarding his character, one biographer asserts that "the Prophet Muhammad (SAWS) was, in his youth, a combination of the best social attributes. . . . He proved himself to be the ideal of manhood, and to possess a spotless character. . . . His fellow-citizens, by common consent, gave him the title of *al-Ameen* (the trustworthy)."[3] In addition to being known for his virtue, Islamic tradition reports that he was also known to have had great things prophesied about his future. Notably, at his birth, a Jew declared that the star of Ahmed had risen, and later a Christian monk recognized the mark of prophethood between his shoulders.[4] Marked by tragedy, Muhammad was also marked by expectation.

Mecca, Medina, and Back Again: Muhammad's Prophetic Career

As noted above, Islamic tradition contends that Muhammad was known to be pious and contemplative from his youth. He would often escape to the

---

1. A. Guillaume, trans., *The Life of Muhammad: A Translation of Ibn Ishaq's "Sirat Rasul Allah"* (London: Oxford University Press, 1982), 69–70.
2. Safiur-Rahman Al-Mubarakpuri, *The Sealed Nectar: Biography of the Noble Prophet*, rev. ed. (Riyadh, KSA: Darussalam, 2002), 56–59.
3. It is Islamic custom to pronounce a blessing or prayer after mentioning a prophet's name. The traditional blessing of Muhammad's name is "May Allah's prayers and peace be upon him." Transliterated, the Arabic is *sallallahu alayhi wa salaam*, producing the acronym, SAWS. Al-Mubarakpuri, *Sealed Nectar*, 64–65.
4. Guillaume, *Life of Muhammad*, 70, 79. Ahmed is a variant form of the name Muhammad.

Arabian wilderness for prayer, meditation, and fasting.[5] On one particular occasion, in the year 610 CE, Muhammad was praying in the cave of Hira when he had a life-changing encounter with an angel named Jibril.[6] There in the cave, Jibril appeared to Muhammad and commanded him to recite what would become the first of the verses of the Qur'an to be revealed.[7]

Though Muhammad himself was initially confused by the encounter, his wife Khadija interpreted the event as his prophetic initiation, exclaiming, "Rejoice, O son of my uncle, and be of good heart. Verily, by Him whose hand is Khadija's soul, I have hope that thou wilt be prophet of this people."[8] Shortly thereafter, Khadija's cousin Waraqa confirmed Khadija's hope, saying, "Holy! Holy! Verily by Him in whose hand is Waraqa's soul, if thou hast spoken to me the truth, O Khadija . . . he is the prophet of this people. Bid him to be of good heart."[9] Thus, with this dual affirmation of his prophetic office, Muhammad was thrust forward to become the focal point of what is today the world's second largest religion.

Though Muhammad's childhood was filled with loss, and despite receiving no formal education, he proved himself to be an exceptionally shrewd leader. As recorded in the traditional material, his ministry includes three distinct stages. The following brief sketch of the life and ministry of Islam's prophet provides context for later chapters that treat the theology and religious development of Islam in greater detail.

Stage One: Embryonic Call

After emerging from the cave of Hira and being encouraged by Khadija and Waraqa's confirmation of his prophethood, Muhammad began to privately call people to submission to the one true God. For the first three years of his ministry, Muhammad managed to gather only a handful of followers, mainly from among the lower classes.[10] In his fourth year of ministry, however, Muhammad's call became more public. As a result, he and his followers were persecuted by the Meccan polytheists who viewed monotheism as an affront to their way of life.

At this stage, Muhammad's message did not immediately result in the formation of the distinct and structured religion we know as Islam. In fact, Muhammad believed his monotheistic message to share similar contours with that of the Jews and Christians he had met during his work as a trader. Seeking relief from the persecution of the polytheists, and also hoping to find

---

5. Al-Mubarakpuri, *Sealed Nectar*, 64.
6. See Guillaume, *Life of Muhammad*, 106.
7. Qur'an 96:1–5 is traditionally taken to be the first section of the Qur'an to be revealed to Muhammad.
8. Guillaume, *Life of Muhammad*, 106–7.
9. Guillaume, *Life of Muhammad*, 107.
10. Bernard Lewis, *The Arabs in History* (New York: Oxford University Press, 1993), 36.

a welcome among the Jewish tribes to the north, Muhammad arranged for his followers to leave Mecca.[11] This transition leads to the second stage of Muhammad's ministry.

Stage Two: Formative Development
      In the year 622 CE, after about twelve years of preaching in Mecca, Muhammad and his followers received an invitation from a group of twelve converts who lived in the city of Medina (at the time known as Yathrib), located nearly three hundred miles north of Mecca. Seeking relief from the persecution of Mecca, envoys of his followers slowly began to migrate northward. Finally, late in the year, Muhammad himself arrived in Medina and was received by those who had gone ahead of him with a festive welcome.[12] This place proved so influential to Islam that the day of Muhammad's arrival in Medina, September 27, 622 CE, became the first day of the Islamic calendar.[13]

      In Medina, Muhammad quickly flourished as a statesman. Recognizing the bloody history between the tribes of Medina, Islamic tradition teaches that he brought peace and stability to the region by constructing a city constitution known as the Medina Charter. This charter created an association known as the Ummah, with Muhammad as its leader. It provided a common bond and rule of order for a region formerly marked by instability and vendetta. Historian Bernard Lewis notes that such influence over the affairs of the city granted Muhammad a role of significant de facto political leadership that he converted to religious authority.[14]

      Adding to his political leadership, Muhammad proved himself to be a skilled military strategist. Once the Medina Charter established the unity of the community, Muhammad led the Ummah to form strategic alliances in the region and to enter into a state of war with Mecca. He led successful raids on Meccan caravans and won important battles against the Meccans, thus proving his savvy to his constituents. Such political authority and military exploits provided Muhammad with sufficient social capital to continue his campaign of preaching Islam.

      Despite these successes, the Jews did not receive Muhammad as he had hoped. Courting their approval, Muhammad initially directed his prayers toward Jerusalem and observed Jewish fasts. When the Jews rejected him, however, his message took on its own distinct religious shape. As perhaps the most overt symbol of such distinction, Muhammad eventually commanded his followers to turn their prayers toward Mecca and to observe Ramadan

---

11. Lewis, *Arabs in History*, 37.
12. Al-Mubarakpuri, *Sealed Nectar*, 163–64.
13. Islamic dates are followed by AH, meaning *Anni Hegira*, which is Latin for "year of emigration."
14. Lewis, *Arabs in History*, 39; see also, Al-Mubarakpuri, *Sealed Nectar*, 174.

as their fast.[15] This shifting focus toward Mecca introduces the third stage of Muhammad's ministry.

Stage Three: Confident Dominance

Along with the direction of his prayers, Muhammad's vision turned to the city that had scorned him. Having amassed economic, military, and political power over eight years in Medina, Muhammad was poised to make a triumphant return to Mecca. In 630 CE, Muhammad marched successfully to Mecca and easily conquered the city with somewhere around ten thousand men in his army. His strength and confidence established, Muhammad viewed this as God's vindication of his message and ministry.

Following the victory in Mecca, Muhammad cleared the central temple (Ka'ba) of all of its idols. This action served as the pinnacle of Muhammad's ministry by clearing away the defilement of polytheism and returning this city to a place of worship of the one true God. To this day, faithful Muslims travel each year to Mecca in order to circumambulate the Ka'ba during the *hajj* pilgrimage. In conquering Mecca, Muhammad demonstrated for his followers and the surrounding peoples the veracity of the message he had long preached.

Though Muhammad lived only two years after this victory, dying in 632 CE (10 AH), these two years set the precedent for later Arab conquest as Muhammad sent delegations of his followers throughout all of Arabia, inviting submission to Islam.[16] After his death, and in the vacuum created by the waning power of the Byzantine and Persian empires, Arab armies would continue to go out from Mecca, seeing explosive growth and seemingly miraculous advance. As the Arab armies advanced, so too did Muhammad's message. The message Muhammad preached was no longer confined to a small corner in Arabia but was carried to nearly every corner of the known world.

The Oneness of God and Submission: Muhammad's Message

Perhaps the clearest way to summarize the central message of Muhammad is by considering the theology of the Islamic confession of faith (the Shahadah) cited at the beginning of this chapter: "There is no god but The God, and Muhammad is his messenger." Both phrases are important to Muhammad's message. The first teaches the singularity of God, while the second reinforces Muhammad's distinguished role as the seal of the true prophets.

In the first phrase of the confession, the original Arabic demonstrates the centrality of God's oneness. Some English translations obscure the fact that the Arabic word for "god" appears twice in the first phrase. The first

---

15. Guillaume, *Life of Muhammad*, 258–59; see also Lewis, *Arabs in History*, 39.
16. Al-Mubarakpuri, *Sealed Nectar*, 386–96, lists seventeen such delegations from the early years of the Medina stage through to the end of Muhammad's life.

occurrence is the indefinite, singular word (*ilaha*), which is always translated as "god." The second occurrence, however, adds the definite article (*al + ilaha*) and is often rendered as "Allah" in English, thus giving the impression that it is a proper name.[17] Yet, one could rigidly translate the phrase as, "There is no god but The God." Thus, the word "Allah" reinforces what is arguably the most important concept in Islam: the oneness of God (*tawhid*).[18]

In the second phrase of the Shahadah, then, Muhammad identifies himself as the messenger of God. While Muhammad believed himself to be one of those in the long line of biblical prophets, it is telling that the central confession of Islam names Allah and Muhammad as the two leading characters of the faith. Thus, while submission to the one true God is the thrust of the Islamic message (*islam* is the Arabic word for submission from which Islam is derived), such submission is unavoidably shaped by and connected to Muhammad as the final messenger.

Summary

Much more will be said about Muhammad's message, especially as we investigate the theology of Islam more deeply in the third section of this book. However, it is sufficient for our purposes here to note that, in the telling of Muhammad's life, Muhammad's biographers appear very willing to tie the message to the messenger, highlighting his noble and virtuous character and breathlessly singing his praises.

Likewise, Muhammad viewed himself as the final prophet whose message was in harmony with the message of the prophets who came before him. His was the God of Adam, Abraham, Moses, and Jesus, and it was his duty to call humanity back to the way preached by his predecessors. Since Muhammad believed himself to be continuing along the same trajectory, he expected to find willing converts and kinsmen in the other children of Abraham in Arabia.

Yet, those who also claimed to follow in the stead of Abraham were unconvinced of the consonance between the revelation of the God of the Bible and the message preached by the prophet of Arabia. Both the Jews and the Christians largely rejected Muhammad's message, causing him to turn his back on them and embrace his distinctive calling as the prophet of Islam.

---

17. Some scholars contend that the word *allah* in Arabic derives from the proper name for the moon god *'ilah*, worshipped in Arabia prior to Muhammad. See discussion in Timothy Tennent, *Theology in the Context of World Christianity* (Grand Rapids: Zondervan, 2007), 28–29. However, most Arabic speaking Muslims contend that this is not God's proper name, but rather a descriptor of his uniqueness as the only God.
18. Seyyed Hossein Nasr, *Ideals and Realities of Islam*, rev. and updated ed. (San Francisco: Aquarian, 1994), 29.

REFLECTION QUESTIONS

1. Why is it important to consider the confessional account of Muhammad's prophetic career?

2. What was Muhammad's early life like?

3. How was Muhammad's message originally received in Mecca?

4. What makes the year 622 CE so important to Islamic history?

5. What does the Islamic confession (the Shahadah) tell us about Muhammad's essential message?

Why Are Mecca, Medina, and Jerusalem So Important to Islam?

My People! Enter the Holy Land which God has
prescribed for you, and do not turn your backs, or
you will turn out (to be)[1] losers.
~Qur'an 5:21

In general, for those raised in Western countries, the concept of place does not enjoy the same sense of importance it does for those in the Middle East. In part this is due to the fact that nations such as the United States of America have a comparatively young history. Traveling the East Coast of the United States may allow for a stop-off at a site from the Revolutionary War, though even such a place tells a story that is a mere two hundred and fifty years old. Further, while important to US political history, such a site is not the hallowed ground of sacred writ.

On the other hand, North Africa and the Middle East boast of cities like Damascus, Alexandria, and Jerusalem, which have been inhabited for thousands of years. Furthermore, these sites and many others in the region appear in the religious texts of Judaism, Christianity, and Islam, giving them an additional measure of gravity. To this day, many such cities are home to faithful Jews, Christians, and Muslims who are intent on maintaining a connection to the ancient roots of their faith.

---

1. As a matter of translation convention, English renderings of qur'anic verse often utilize parenthetical additions to the text for the purpose of providing a smooth English reading. The parenthesis, however, indicates that the contents are implied in the Arabic original.

For the followers of Islam, three cities rise to the fore in consideration of such sacred geography: Mecca, Medina, and Jerusalem. These holy cities not only function as important components of the story of Islamic origins; they are also contemporary places of pilgrimage and reverence. A brief investigation of each of these cities will serve to show how and why they feature in Islamic history, theology, and practice.

Mecca

In the previous chapter, the city of Mecca featured primarily as the place of Muhammad's birth and initial ministry. One aspect of the city that the previous chapter did not cover is the importance that Islamic theology assigns Mecca through stories of prophets who preceded Muhammad. Before Muhammad's day, and even more important than the city itself, is the history of the temple around which Muhammad's contemporaries formed their society.

The temple, known as the Ka'ba, was filled with 360 pagan idols at the time that Muhammad marched on Mecca.[2] Ibn Hisham reports that on the day that Muhammad took over the city, he circled the Ka'ba seven times, entered into it, and began pointing a stick at the various idols housed inside.[3] One by one, they fell on their backs as Muhammad recited Qur'an 17:81, which commands, "And say: 'The truth has come and falsehood has passed away. Surely falsehood is (bound) to pass away.'" Thus, Muhammad liberated the city from pagan worship, and the Ka'ba became the geographic center of Islam.

As important as this day was, however, Islamic theology contends that the Ka'ba has yet a longer history and that this was not the first time it served as a place of worship for the one true God. In fact, according to Islamic teaching, Ibrahim and Ismail built the Ka'ba to serve as the house of God.[4] Though it fell into pagan hands over time, some of the original rituals associated with the worship of Allah were retained, including pilgrimage to the site, prayers, and circumambulation of the Ka'ba.[5] To this day, Muslims continue to make the pilgrimage to the Sacred Mosque (*al-Masjid al-Haram*) in Mecca, to walk

---

2. A. Guillaume, trans., *The Life of Muhammad: A Translation of Ibn Ishaq's "Sirat Rasul Allah"* (London: Oxford University Press, 1982), 552.
3. Guillaume, *Life of Muhammad*, 552.
4. Guillaume, *Life of Muhammad*, 35–36. Islamic tradition equates the Ka'ba with the *beyt Allah* or, "house of God." Qur'an 22:26 states, "(Remember) when We settled the place of the House for Abraham: 'Do not associate anything with Me, but purify My House for the ones who go around (it), and the ones who stand, and the ones who both (and) the ones who prostrate themselves.'" One might also note that conflicting traditions posit Adam as the first builder of the Ka'ba, though his temple was destroyed by Noah's flood. See F. E. Peters, *The Hajj: The Muslim Pilgrimage to Mecca and the Holy Places* (Princeton, NJ: Princeton University Press, 1994), 14.
5. Peters, *Hajj*, 21–27.

around the Kaʻba located at its center, and to rehearse the acts of faithful Muslims of old.

Not only is the Kaʻba the site of the annual pilgrimage, but it also indicates the direction (*qibla*) that the Qurʾan and *hadith* order Muslims to face while performing the five daily prayers.[6] Thus, two of the Five Pillars of Islamic practice relate directly to the city of Mecca.[7] Since Mecca plays such an important role in both the history and contemporary practice of Islam, it is no wonder that it is known as the holiest site on earth for Muslims.

Medina

Medina, the city that served as an incubator for the young Muslim community in 622 CE, is the second holiest city in Islam. Though it does not boast of the same theological import as Mecca, it does contain Muhammad's tomb. According to Ibn Hisham, when Muhammad fell sick and died in his home in Medina, his followers buried him directly beneath the bed in which he had been laying.[8] This home was adjacent to the mosque that Muhammad established upon his initial arrival in Medina. His tomb is now part of the Mosque of the Prophet (*Masjid an-Nabawi*).

While traditional Islamic teaching rejects the veneration of the dead, this site serves as a place of unofficial pilgrimage. Prayers offered at the prophet's tomb are often believed to be more effective, and visits to such hallowed ground are expected to bring blessing.[9] Medina may not have the same theological gravity as Mecca, yet its pull is strong.

Jerusalem

These first two cities derive their fame almost exclusively through their relationship to Islam. The historical record of the region prior to Islamic sources is scant and unimpressive. Furthermore, the Arabian Peninsula as a whole does not appear to be widely influential until the rise of Islam. Mecca and Medina, then, are largely uncontested features of Muslim reverence.

Jerusalem, on the other hand, played a critical role in world history long before Muhammad's birth. As a key city on a vital trade route between Africa, Asia, and Europe, it sits on a plot of land prized and fought over for centuries. Not only does its value derive from its strategic economic and military location, but it also features in the sacred history of Judaism, Christianity, and Islam.

---

6. Muhammad Khan, trans., *Summarized Sahih Al-Bukhari* (Riyadh, KSA: Darussalam, 1996), 170 (§260). Also, Qurʾan 2:144 states, "We do see you turning your face about in the sky, and We shall indeed turn you in a direction which you will be pleased with. Turn your face in the direction of the Sacred Mosque, and wherever you are, turn your faces in its direction."
7. See Question 13 for an explanation of the Five Pillars of Islam.
8. Guillaume, *Life of Muhammad*, 688.
9. See Peters, *Hajj*, 138–41.

For Jews, Jerusalem is the capital city of the land of divine promise and the place of the holy temple. For Christians, it is revered as the location of some of Jesus's ministry, his death, and his resurrection. And for Muslims, it is the destination Muhammad visited during his miraculous Night Journey.

The Night Journey is an important component of Islamic tradition regarding Muhammad, yet even within the traditions one finds discrepancy. Some renditions of the event record Muhammad physically riding on the back of a winged heavenly steed from Mecca to Jerusalem, while another account told by the prophet's wife, Aisha, claims that Muhammad journeyed to Jerusalem in spirit only.[10]

Regardless, the encounter that reportedly occurred in Jerusalem on this night supersedes the details of Muhammad's mode of transportation. Upon his arrival to the city, Muhammad was greeted by Abraham, Moses, and Jesus. Not only did he receive a welcome from these key religious figures, but he also led them in prayers at al-Aqsa mosque.[11] Thus for Muslims this event proves both Muhammad's continuity with and superiority to the prior biblical prophets.

In addition to this, some accounts of this night include a further journey into heaven itself. Tradition records a ladder being lowered to Muhammad, which he climbed and was given a tour of the heavens. In the seventh level of heaven, Muhammad received the divine command to observe the daily prayers (*salat*) that are mandatory for Muslims to this day.[12] Such monumental and formative events provide the adherents of Islam with a strong bond to the city of Jerusalem, and it serves as the third most important site to Muslims.

Summary

This brief account is sufficient to provide the rationale for each city's inclusion among the sacred spaces of Islam. As noted above, there is little controversy regarding Muslim control of Mecca and Medina. However, Jerusalem clearly provides a point of conflict in contemporary world politics. Jews and Muslims vehemently disagree over who has the right to control the Temple Mount area in Jerusalem, and such disagreement has often been cited as the reason for violent outbreaks and clashes.

The resolution of this fourteen-hundred-year-old disagreement is obviously far beyond the scope of this chapter. Yet, it behooves us to consider the difficulties presented to any Muslim leader sitting down at a negotiation table and discussing potential compromises. When a Muslim Palestinian leader is involved in peace negotiations, that person is not merely operating as a

---

10. Gabriel Said Reynolds, *The Emergence of Islam: Classical Traditions in Contemporary Perspective* (Minneapolis: Fortress, 2012), 25–26, 141–42.

11. Reynolds, *Emergence of Islam*, 25. This mosque is traditionally understood to be "the farthest mosque" referred to in Qur'an 17:1, the Arabic of which is *al-masjid al-aqsa*, from which it gets its English name.

12. Khan, *Sahih Al-Bukhari*, 158 (§228).

government representative. Any concession that would alter Islamic control over even a square inch of the sacred space of Jerusalem affects the entire Ummah (the global community of Muslims). No Palestinian leader holds the authority to make such a decision on their behalf.

The stalemate that has marked peace discussions between the Israeli government and Palestinian leadership for so long can be confounding to an outside audience, who view such discussions from a political angle. This is particularly true when the outsider hails from a context that does not prize the idea of place in the same way as those involved in the negotiations. It stretches the imagination of such a one to consider that no compromise has been reached, despite the horrific bloodshed that has occurred as a result of the stalemate.

However, when one considers the long history of the contested land from the perspective of two living faiths who lay claim to it, it becomes less confusing as to why an agreement has been so long in the making. Recently, I had the opportunity to lead a group of students on a trip to Israel, where we explored both the biblical history and the contemporary geopolitical situation. When we asked our guides and the program directors questions about the current state of peace discussions, the constant refrain we heard was, "It is complicated." Indeed, it is.

REFLECTION QUESTIONS

1. Why is Mecca considered the most important city to Muslims?

2. What did Medina provide for the Muslim community, and why is it so important?

3. How does Jerusalem fit in Islamic history, and what makes it important?

4. What is the Ka'ba, and why is it important?

5. Why is Jerusalem such a contested city, and why haven't the Israelis and Palestinians reached a settlement?

How Did the Religion of Islam Develop?

O men, if anyone worships Muhammad,
Muhammad is dead: if anyone worships God,
God is alive, immortal.
~Abu Bakr[1]

In many other contexts, Muhammad's death might have signaled the end of the message he preached. Muhammad viewed himself as a prophet of renewal rather than the leader of a new and distinct faith, so he did not bother to build the infrastructure required for Islam to continue as a well-defined religion. He left no system for appointing successors, the Qur'an had not yet been codified and collected, and little attention was given to how one might practice Islam in other cultural contexts. Thus, in 632 CE the community of his followers could have easily dissolved. Yet today a religion of nearly two billion adherents has emerged like a phoenix from the ashes of Muhammad's death. How did Islam succeed in becoming what it is today?

One key factor is that the middle of the seventh century proved itself to be a unique moment in history for a united community of Arabs to make their mark on the world's stage. For many years, the territory to the north of the Arabian Peninsula had been the bloody and contested battleground where the Byzantine and Persian empires collided. With the strength of both empires waning from long years spent fighting each other, the Arab armies seized the opportunity to expand northward, marching to victory after victory in the wake of Byzantine and Persian exhaustion. The success they enjoyed in their

---

1. A. Guillaume, trans., *The Life of Muhammad: A Translation of Ibn Ishaq's "Sirat Rasul Allah"* (Oxford: Oxford University Press, 1982), 683.

military exploits was credited to the favor of the God whose message they carried everywhere they went.

The Caliphate

In considering Islam's development, it behooves us to begin with the situation immediately following Muhammad's death. Prior even to the burial of Muhammad's body, a gathered group of believers called upon Abu Bakr and 'Umar to determine how the community was to function without Muhammad as its common bond.[2] Muhammad was seen as the final prophet and thus the final communication of God to humans. However, the fledgling community of his followers required someone to take on the organizational leadership that would determine the shape and trajectory of the faith as the believers continued their lives in new times and places.[3]

Eventually Abu Bakr emerged as the agreed-upon successor (caliph) to Muhammad.[4] Today, however, the diverging Sunni and Shia expressions of Islam trace their initial fissure to the issue of rightful succession.[5] Yet, whether Sunni or Shiite, one cannot avoid the influence that Abu Bakr and the three caliphs that followed him had on the religion of Islam as a whole.[6]

The first four caliphs to lead Muhammad's followers are Abu Bakr (632–634 CE), 'Umar (634–644 CE), 'Uthman (644–656 CE), and 'Ali (656–661 CE).[7] Sunni Muslims recognize these men as the Rightly Guided (Rashidun) Caliphs. Abu Bakr was one of Muhammad's early followers and the father of Muhammad's wife, Aisha. During his short time as caliph, Abu Bakr led the Muslim community to form an army that would ensure and consolidate power for the caliphate, expand Arab influence beyond the Arabian Peninsula, and spread the message of Islam to the surrounding lands.

After Abu Bakr died, 'Umar continued the expansion project. Historian Albert Hourani reports that, "by the end of the reign of the second caliph, 'Umar . . . , the whole of Arabia, part of the Sasanian Empire, and the Syrian and Egyptian provinces of the Byzantine Empire had been conquered; the

---

2. Guillaume, *Life of Muhammad*, 685–87.
3. Gabriel Said Reynolds, *The Emergence of Islam: Classical Traditions in Contemporary Perspective* (Minneapolis: Fortress, 2012), 60.
4. Reynolds, *Emergence of Islam*, 61.
5. The next chapter will investigate the distinction between Sunni and Shia Islam in more depth. However, it is important to note that the first point of departure between the two systems is the issue of succession. Sunnis contend that Abu Bakr was to be the first caliph, while Shia believe that 'Ali was to serve as the imam of the community following Muhammad's death.
6. The words Shia and Shiite can be used interchangeably. Both can function as nouns and adjectives.
7. Albert Hourani, *A History of the Arab Peoples* (Cambridge, MA: Belknap Press of Harvard University Press, 1991), 22–25.

rest of the Sasanian lands were occupied soon afterwards."[8] Muslims view this early expansion of the Arab empire, not primarily as a military initiative, but as the continuation of the precedent that Muhammad set by sending out emissaries to preach submission to God to the surrounding peoples.

As the Arab territories stretched further and further into North Africa and the Middle East, however, the unifying bond of Muhammad's message required more substantial definition, and Islam as a separate religion began to take a more distinctive shape. The third caliph, 'Uthman, provided the growing Muslim world with what would be its most binding tie: an officially endorsed, written compilation of the Qur'an.[9] Having decided on an official copy, 'Uthman ordered all competing versions of the Qur'an to be burned. This act ensured that the entire community of Muslims would have one standard and sacred document from which to read.[10] For this reason, 'Uthman's caliphate might be considered the most influential of the four Rightly Guided Caliphs.

However, 'Uthman was eventually murdered, and the fourth caliph, 'Ali, was appointed to lead the Ummah. 'Ali's caliphate was marked with controversy, and eventually he too was assassinated. Though the next leader of the Ummah, Mu'awiya, declared himself to be a caliph, this leadership transition marks a new epoch in Islamic history.[11]

The Umayyad and 'Abbasid Dynasties

With the close of the era of the Rightly Guided Caliphs, Mu'awiya (661–680 CE) provided initial leadership to the Ummah as Islamic history transitioned into a new phase of development under two successive dynasties. Not only did Mu'awiya begin what is known as the Umayyad dynasty (661–750 CE), he also moved the capital of the Arab empire to Damascus, Syria. This move provided a more strategic location than Mecca from which to govern the Arab empire, which now stretched all the way to Morocco.[12] In fact, the connection Mu'awiya made between his political governance and the religious leadership he assumed proved a formative development in how Islam and politics would coincide.

---

8. Hourani, *History of the Arab Peoples*, 23.
9. Reynolds, *Emergence of Islam*, 72.
10. Nabeel Qureshi, *No God but One: Allah or Jesus?* (Grand Rapids: Zondervan, 2016), 281. In a footnote, Qureshi cites al-Bukhari as one who records an authentic, Islamic report of 'Uthman's burning of variant copies of the Qur'an. To avoid the idea that the various copies presented different words, one might argue that these differences may be restricted to accents and pronunciation. Such a claim would fail to persuade, however, because at the time of 'Uthman, vocalization marks had not yet been added to the written language. Thus, only the consonantal text would have been able to admit of variants.
11. Hourani, *History of the Arab Peoples*, 25.
12. Hourani, *History of the Arab Peoples*, 26.

The Umayyad dynasty was relatively short, though the precedent Mu'awiya set in moving the capital and codifying the relationship between the faith and governance proved to be a staying change. Following the Umayyads, a much longer dynasty arose in the 'Abbasid dynasty (750–1258 CE). During this period of time, the capital of the Arab empire was again moved, this time to Baghdad, Iraq. This new location provided a place of incubation for Arab political, philosophical, and religious thought. In so doing, the 'Abbasid dynasty provided Islam with the space and time to find the definition it lacked during the short tenure of its early leaders.

During this time, Muslim scholars began intensively discussing and dissecting various claims about Muhammad's teaching. A biography of Muhammad was produced, a body of traditions known as the *Sunnah* was collected, and various schools of interpretation formed. These sources, produced during the 'Abbasid dynasty, are arguably the most influential components of Islamic development, proving more influential than even the Qur'an itself in the practice of Islam.

The *Sunnah* and Islamic Jurisprudence

While tradition teaches that a common Qur'an provided the expanding Muslim community with a unifying document, its interpretation and application in diverse contexts did not enjoy such uniformity. Various readings and explanations competed with one another, and the Ummah was in danger of splintering apart into endless factions. Two developments staved off such division and gave shape to the emerging faith now known as Islam: the compilation of traditions called the *Sunnah* and the formation of schools of Islamic jurisprudence.

The Biography of the Messenger of God (Sirat Rasul Allah)

According to tradition, in the middle of the eighth century CE, a man named Ibn Ishaq undertook to document the life of Muhammad. Seeking reliable stories about the prophet's life, Ibn Ishaq traveled the Arab empire seeking stories dating back to the prophet himself or one of his trusted contemporaries. Unfortunately, no copy of Ibn Ishaq's work remains extant today.

Ibn Ishaq's pupil, Ibn Hisham, however, purports to have included much of his teacher's original biography in his own record of Muhammad's life, *Sirat Rasul Allah* (usually referred to simply as the *Sira*). We don't know exactly when Ibn Hisham was born, nor when he wrote the *Sira*, but he died just over two hundred years after Muhammad's death in 833 CE.

This biography is the means by which Muslim scholars have determined when and where various portions of the Qur'an were revealed. The Qur'an itself does not internally disclose much information at all regarding the external circumstances occurring at the time of its recording. It is not a narrative-rich work, and therefore it requires some external account to provide the reader with a sense of when and why the various verses were revealed. As such, the chronology provided by the *Sira* has had an incredible influence on the interpretation of the Qur'an itself.[13]

The Traditions (Sunnah *and Hadith*)

In addition to Ibn Hisham's biography, thousands and thousands of individual claims about Muhammad's actions and sayings began to proliferate throughout the eighth and ninth centuries. It quickly became apparent to the Muslim community that many of these claims were being fabricated by those seeking Muhammad's endorsement of their preferences. To mitigate this abuse of their prophet's name, scholars like al-Bukhari investigated the chain of transmission of the reports and classified them according to the trustworthiness of their transmitters.

Today, for Sunni Muslims there are six collections of trusted *hadith* that exist. The two most famous are the *hadith* collections of al-Bukhari and Muslim. Al-Bukhari was one of the first who travelled broadly throughout the Arab empire to collect sayings about the life and teaching of Muhammad. He is said to have traversed the territory from Morocco to Iraq in search of any and all *hadith* reports he could amass. Having collected them all—reportedly more than six hundred thousand individual *hadith*—he went about the process of inspecting the chains of transmission.[14]

In the end, al-Bukhari rated less than eight thousand of these sayings as being true and reliable (*sahih*), and many of these were duplicates. Despite the relatively low percentage of reliable *hadith* reports, the compilations of these reports proved to be indispensable for the growing Muslim community in that they had concrete explanations of what were often debated and enigmatic sections of the Qur'an. Through the biography of Muhammad and the collection of his sayings, explanations, and way of life, the religion of Islam began to take a much more concrete form. By around 950 CE, the corpus of the *hadith* was collected and codified.[15] By collecting and disseminating such a collection, Islam retained essential unity across the span of its empire by returning to a focus on its founder.

Islamic Jurisprudence

Even though the corpus of *hadith* was relatively well formed and stable by the tenth century CE, issues of interpretation and application continued

---

13. Gabriel Said Reynolds, *The Qur'an and Its Biblical Subtext* (New York: Routledge, 2010), 1.
14. A. C. Jonathan Brown, *Hadith: Muhammad's Legacy in the Medieval and Modern World* (Oxford: OneWorld, 2009), 32. Muhammad Khan claims that al-Bukhari collected only three hundred thousand *hadith* (Muhammad Khan, trans., *Summarized Sahih al-Bukhari* [Riyadh, KSA: Darussalam, 1996], 18).
15. Abu Ameenah Bilal Philips, *The Evolution of Fiqh* (Riyadh, KSA: International Islamic Publishing House, 2005), 98.

to arise. Disagreements regarding how to apply Islamic law in new contexts abounded. Diverse approaches to the guiding documents of the faith gave birth to a variety of systems aimed at establishing authoritative Islamic teaching.

In light of this discord, various methods of interpretation consolidated themselves as schools of Islamic law (*fiqh*).[16] While many schools (*madhhab*) arose initially, four major Sunni schools emerged and survive to today.[17] Each of these schools is distinguished by what sources of information are allowed to affect the process of deriving Islamic teaching.[18] As one might assume, the prominent schools of the tenth century asserted formative pressure on the various expressions of Islam that each one produced.

Summary

In the three centuries following Muhammad's death, the religion of Islam took shape under the formative pressures of broad geographic expansion, multiple leadership changes, and the codification of its sacred texts. A superficial understanding of the importance of Muhammad's personal ministry can at times leave people thinking that the faith as it is practiced today is a replica of the instructions given to the Ummah by Muhammad himself. Furthermore, attributing the unique cultural elements of contemporary Islam to its supposed captivity to the seventh century exacerbates this misperception.[19]

In fact, the expressions of Islam that we see today bear the contours of later Arab developments that occurred during the post-Muhammad era traced throughout this chapter. As chapters 8 and 9 will demonstrate, without the *Sira* and the *Sunnah*, one would not know how to perform what are now known as the five central pillars of Islam. Furthermore, without systems of *fiqh* established, individual Muslims would be left to their own varied approaches to interpretation and application.

All of these later developments have left indelible impressions on the contemporary practice of Islam such that one cannot answer this chapter's question without considering these post-Muhammad political, theological, and ideological structures. From a Muslim perspective, this continued

---

16. Philips, *Evolution of Fiqh*, 19. *Fiqh* is here defined as "the science of deducing Islamic laws from evidence found in the sources of Islamic law."

17. Philips, *Evolution of Fiqh*, 148. Philips lists (1) Haneefa, (2) Malik, (3) Ash-Shafi'i, and (4) Hanbali as the remaining *madhhabs*.

18. Philips, *Evolution of Fiqh*, 94–96. Philips records six potential sources of knowledge: (1) the Qur'an, (2) the *Sunnah*, (3) opinions of the companions of Muhammad, (4) analogical deduction from accepted laws, (5) legal preference, and (6) local customs.

19. A Google search reveals that there is no shortage of claims that Islam is stuck in the seventh century. Such claims come from both outside and inside of Islam. See, for example, Meira Svirsky, "Women Rights in Saudi Arabia Stuck in the 7th Century," *Clarion Project*, October 13, 2016, https://clarionproject.org/women-rights-saudi-arabia-stuck-7th-century. See also Naser Khader, "Who Must Lead a Muslim Reformation," *Hudson Institute*, March 23, 2015, https://www.hudson.org/research/11153-who-must-lead-a-muslim-reformation.

evolution of the practice of Islam is not problematic. In fact, as *fiqh* expert Bilal Philips comments,

> Both *fiqh* (Islamic law) and the *Madh-habs* (schools of Islamic thought) were and are necessary additions complementing the divine revelations which define the basic principles governing man's rights and responsibilities in his relationships with Allah and his fellow man. It is through specific applications of the interpretations of the Qur'an and the Sunnah that Allah's divine will can be made manifest to man over time and through space.[20]

In other words, Muslims view the evolution of Islam during the first three centuries as a natural and appropriate way of bringing the instructions of God to bear on changing times and places. Contemporary Islam owes much of its development to the period following Muhammad's death.

REFLECTION QUESTIONS

1. What was it about the seventh century that made the Fertile Crescent region ripe for the Arab conquest?

2. Who are the four Rightly Guided Caliphs?

3. What is the *Sunnah*, and how does it shape Islamic theology and practice?

4. How many *hadith* did al-Bukhari collect, and how many did he deem authentic?

5. How does the process of Islamic jurisprudence contribute to the contemporary practice of Islam?

---

20. Philips, *Evolution of Fiqh*, 165.

What Is the Difference between Sunni and Shia Muslims?

So which of you will co-operate with me
in this matter, my brother, my executor,
and my successor being among you?
~Muhammad[1]

Intramural division is not a foreign concept to Christians. One oft-cited source records more than nine thousand different Christian denominations, and my hunch is that number may not have exhausted the truth.[2] To our shame, almost anything down to differing opinions over the color of the carpet can cause division among Christians. In other words, we are experienced in the ways of schism.

Initially, then, when looking at the Sunni and Shia sects of Islam, Christians might be tempted to view them as if they are Muslim versions of church denominations. While conceptual overlap does exist, we should allow Sunni and Shia Muslims to describe themselves on their own terms prior to assimilating them into the alien categories belonging to a different system. To begin, the very names Sunni and Shia are helpful in understanding at least the superficial distinctives between the two sects.

Sunni is a word derived from the word *Sunnah*, which we have already encountered and know to refer to the traditions about Muhammad. Shia, on the other hand, means "faction." Though Shia are equally committed to their

1. A. Guillaume, trans., *The Life of Muhammad: A Translation of Ibn Ishaq's "Sirat Rasul Allah"* (London: Oxford University Press, 1982), 118.
2. Todd M. Johnson and Gina A. Zurlo, eds., *World Christian Database* (Leiden/Boston: Brill, 2018), https://www.worldchristiandatabase.org.

own traditions about Muhammad, they exist as a faction formed shortly after Muhammad's death. With that in mind, it is helpful to consider the historical point of distinction before seeing how the various expressions divide in theology and practice.

'Ali versus Abu Bakr

The root source of the division between Shia and Sunni traces its way back to the original dissention regarding the appropriate line of succession. Following Muhammad's death, multiple opinions presented themselves as to who should step up and lead the Ummah in Muhammad's absence. According to tradition, most of the community favored appointing a representative chosen by the majority, while a small percentage believed that it would be best to appoint a successor from Muhammad's family.[3] Abu Bakr, the people's choice, won out, even though some believed the rightful successor should have been 'Ali, Muhammad's cousin and son-in-law (the husband of his daughter Fatima).

Despite the fact that 'Ali did eventually become the fourth caliph, his controversial leadership ended quickly when he was assassinated. Capitalizing on the power vacuum created by this assassination, 'Uthman's nephew Mu'awiya established himself as the first of the Umayyad caliphs.[4] In response to 'Ali's assassination, his second son, Hussein, went to battle against the Umayyads, only to be killed and mercilessly beheaded in 680 CE during the infamous Battle of Karbala in Iraq.[5]

Known by Shiites as the martyrdom of Hussein, the Battle of Karbala is often cited as the final breach between the Sunni and the Shia branches of Islam.[6] With the vast majority of the Arab world under Umayyad rule and centered in Damascus, the followers of 'Ali had established themselves in the east, in Iraq. Rather than submitting to the Umayyad caliphate, the Shia sought leadership and spiritual guidance from Muhammad's remaining descendants.[7]

Imam versus Caliph

Because of the obvious power associated with leading the Ummah, some scholars such as Bernard Lewis view the early Shia claim to 'Ali's right to succession as an attempt to grab political control of the growing Arab nation.[8] However, Shia purport to be more concerned with establishing spiritual

---

3. Irving Hexham, *Understanding World Religions* (Grand Rapids: Zondervan, 2011), 409.
4. Hexham, *Understanding World Religions*, 409.
5. Michael Molloy, *Experiencing the World's Religions*, 6th ed. (New York: McGraw Hill, 2013), 432.
6. Hexham, *Understanding World Religions*, 413. However, in a personal correspondence, Dr. Ayman Ibrahim pointed out that the religious division between Sunni and Shia does not occur until the rule of the sixth imam, Muhammad Baqr al-Sadr.
7. Hexham, *Understanding World Religions*, 414.
8. Bernard Lewis, *The Arabs in History* (Oxford: Oxford University Press, 1993), 73.

authority than governmental or political rule.[9] They contend that the proper line of succession should be connected to the family of Muhammad, not the volatile opinion of the majority. Demonstrating this distinction, Shia avoid using the name "caliph" for the successors of Muhammad, in part due to the political overtones of the word.

Instead, Shia Muslims refer to a line of successive descendants from Muhammad known as "imams." The term imam—a teacher of the ways of Islam—has a much clearer connection to religious authority.[10] As one begins to read about the Shia branch of Islam, however, one will quickly encounter references to "twelvers," "seveners," and "fivers." Such references indicate various subsets of Shia Islam and the number of authoritative imams they recognize.[11]

Dispute over the seventh and fifth imams is the key source of distinction within the Shia community, though most Shia are "twelvers," who trace the line of leaders (known as the imamate) to Muhammad al-Mahdi, who went into hiding around 900 CE. Many Shia expect the return of this twelfth imam to herald the end of the world.[12] Anticipation of the return of the Mahdi is one of several distinguishing features of Shiite theology.

Shiite Theological Distinctives

While the preceding treatment highlights the particularities of Shiite leadership and eschatological expectation, there are a few additional theological and practical distinctions between Sunni and Shia Muslims. For example, Sunni Muslims usually believe that Muhammad and the prophets that came before him were conduits of God's message. When Muhammad died, revelation ceased, and the revered companions of Muhammad and the caliphs were entrusted with the transmission, interpretation, and application of Islamic teaching.

The Light of Muhammad and the Imamate

Shia, however, believe that the "light of Muhammad" passed along as spiritual power to those of his family, beginning with his nephew 'Ali, whose name is added as a third component of the Shiite Shahadah.[13] Thus, as, Irving Hexham writes, "an imam is the final authority in all things and is believed to be guided by God in his decisions."[14] Shia, therefore, contend that legitimate imams continue to provide perfect guidance for the community. The rulings

9. Molloy, *Experiencing the World's Religions*, 430.
10. Hexham, *Understanding World Religions*, 414.
11. Molloy, *Experiencing the World's Religions*, 430–32.
12. Molloy, *Experiencing the World's Religions*, 432.
13. Molloy, *Experiencing the World's Religions*, 432. The Shia' add "wa 'Ali wali Allah" meaning, "and 'Ali is the *wali* of Allah," with the word *wali* meaning helper or friend, indicating investment with some kind of leadership.
14. Hexham, *Understanding World Religions*, 414.

of the later imams, then, carry the weight of divine revelation for Shia, allowing for their own corpus of Islamic law that expands upon the *Sunnah* recognized by the Sunni community.[15]

Celebrations and Festivals

In addition to this, traditional Sunni practice recognizes only two festivals: Eid al-Fitr and Eid al-Adha. Though some celebrate Muhammad's birthday, typically this is considered extra-Islamic. However, within Shiite practice, the birthday of 'Ali is a time of religious celebration. Likewise, as mentioned above, the martyrdom of Hussein is commemorated by pilgrimage to Karbala, where pilgrims demonstrate solidarity with Hussein's suffering through self-flagellation. Additional pilgrimages to the tombs of the imams are also common in Shiite practice.

Daily Prayer Distinctives

In Sunni Islam, the mandatory prayers of the faithful are to be practiced five times daily in keeping with the teaching of the *Sunnah*.[16] However, Shiite Muslims may pray only three occasions during the day, combining the two morning and two evening prayer times into single events.[17] Furthermore, Shia include a unique movement within their prayers that, to the keen observer, distinguishes them from Sunni. Whereas Sunni prayers cross their arms across their chests, Shia extend their hands along the sides of their body (the posture is called *sadl al-Yadayn*).[18] Neither of these distinctives indicate theological disparity, but, being more overt than other differences, observers often wonder about the meaning behind them.

Iran versus Saudi Arabia

Today, the issue of Sunni and Shia relationships is often couched in terms of geopolitical rivalries between countries such as Saudi Arabia and Iran. While Sunnis represent approximately 85 percent of the world's Muslims and are spread around the globe, the Shia population is most concentrated in Iran. Although one might assume that population concentration makes Iran the home of Shiite Islam, Iraq is often thought of as the heartland of Shia believers due to the memory of the martyrdom of Hussein.[19] As such, there is a

---

15. Gabriel Said Reynolds, *The Emergence of Islam: Classical Traditions in Contemporary Perspective* (Minneapolis: Fortress, 2012), 88.

16. Muhammad Khan, *Summarized Sahih Al-Bukhari* (Riyadh, KSA: Darussalam, 1996), 156–58 (§228).

17. "Shia Praying Differences," *Center for Islamic Shia Studies*, http://shiastudies.org/article/shi-a-prayer-rituals.

18. "Shia Praying Differences."

19. Molloy, *Experiencing the World's Religions*, 432. See also Albert Hourani, *A History of the Arab Peoples* (Cambridge, MA: Harvard University Press, 2010), 184.

high population of Shia living in Iraq, along with significant representation in Bahrain, India, Pakistan, and Azerbaijan.[20]

Listing the countries above may cause the reader to recall various head-lines from recent news stories about regional instability and sectarian vio-lence. With the appearance of the Islamic State in the last decade, stories of Sunni groups committing atrocities against Shia and other minority Muslim sects have proliferated. On one hand, tensions between the groups have ex-isted for centuries. On the other, however, we need not assume that violence and hatred are the inevitable result of Sunni and Shia Muslims sharing geo-graphical space.

Summary

Before making too sharp a division in our assessment of the divide be-tween Sunni and Shia, it is helpful to consider that in some places, Sunni and Shia exist side by side. In fact, an Iraqi family that my wife and I hosted for dinner a month ago laughed when we asked them if they were Sunni or Shia. Their response was that, until 2003 and George W. Bush's war in Iraq, they didn't pay attention to such things. As evidence of this, though they were cousins, they didn't know until their wedding whether the other was Sunni or Shia. It was a non-issue.

Likewise, less than an hour from my home in Springfield, Ohio, there is a mosque that intentionally invites Shiite and Sunni Muslims to pray side by side together. While there are certainly tensions between Sunni and Shia around the world, such exceptions should be noted to show that the differ-ences are not insurmountable.

REFLECTION QUESTIONS

1. What is often understood as the root cause of the Sunni and Shia division?

2. How do Sunnis trace the line of the caliphate?

3. What is the difference between the Sunni caliphate and the Shiite imamate?

4. How does the twelfth imam factor into Shiite eschatology?

5. What are the significant distinctives of Shia theology and practice?

---

20. "Muslims around the World," *Center for Islamic Shia Studies,* http://shiastudies.org/article/overview-of-shia-demographics.

What Other Expressions of Islam Exist?

> *Come, come, whoever you are.*
> *Wanderer, worshipper, lover of living,*
> *it doesn't matter. Ours is not a caravan of despair.*
> *~Rumi, thirteenth-century Sufi poet[1]*

According to Islamic studies professor Evelyne Reisacher, students of Islam must avoid what she calls the cookie-cutter approach, whereby Islam is treated as if it is a uniform and universal object of study. Instead, citing John Esposito and Dalia Mogahed, Reisacher argues that "religiously, culturally, economically, and politically there are multiple images and realities of Islam and of Muslims."[2] Lest the title of this book reinforce the misconception that Islam exists as a monolithic system of faith, it is important for us to briefly consider the breadth of diversity that occurs under its umbrella.

The previous chapter briefly covered some overarching differences between the two major divisions of Sunni and Shia Islam. Expanding beyond these two divisions, this chapter intends to highlight three additional trajectories of Islamic expression. Each of these three trajectories is but a broad category under which its own layers of diversity exist. However, this sample highlights the extremes by including treatment of the spirituality of Sufi

---

1. Fatih Citlak and Huseyn Bingul, *Rumi and His Sufi Path of Love* (Somerset, NJ: Tughra Books, 2007), 81.
2. John Esposito and Dalia Mogahed, *Who Speaks for Islam? What a Billion Muslims Really Think* (New York: Gallup, 2007), 2; cited in Evelyne Reisacher, ed., *Dynamics of Muslim Worlds: Regional, Theological, and Missiological Perspectives* (Downers Grove, IL: IVP Academic, 2017), 240.

Islam, the strict conservativism of Salafist Islam, and the blending of culture and theology of Western Islam.

Sufi

Despite being a minority branch of Islam, Sufism is somewhat well known as a revivalist-mystic phenomenon. Perhaps this is due to some of the spectacle that attends various expressions of Sufism, such as the hypnotic dances performed by the whirling dervishes of Turkey. Or perhaps it is due to the well-known and beloved writings of the Sufi poet Rumi, whose work is cited at the head of this chapter. Whatever the case, this minority expression of Islam bears some distinct features that deserve attention.

Knowing and Experiencing God

In traditional, orthodox Islamic belief, God's transcendence makes him personally unknowable. Despite the fact that the ninety-nine names of God are generally recognized in Islam and are memorized and recited by many faithful Muslims across all expressions, most contend that these are merely characteristics describing his will. For Sufis, however, knowing God intimately and experientially is at the core of their faith.[3]

Many scholars attribute this desire for personal communion with God to Islamic interactions with Christianity, and some of the language used by Sufis seems to reflect the same desires as Christian hermits and ascetics. At the same time, Buddhist and Zoroastrian tendencies also appear in the practice of self-denial and desire for union with the divine.[4] In some ways, Sufi Islam compares with Gnosticism in that it can assume characteristics from a variety of sources.

Philosophy and Meditation

Another distinctive of Sufism is a great appreciation for the power of meditation, philosophy, and personal acquisition of spiritual insight. The most famous advocate of this component of Sufi practice is the philosopher al-Ghazzali (1058–1111 CE). Al-Ghazzali is a unique figure within the Sufi movement in that while he adopted Sufism during part of his life, he also maintained orthodox Sunni law and practices.[5] As a systematic thinker and a respected scholar of Islam, al-Ghazzali proved influential in providing structure and credibility to Sufism.

Still, due to its blend of personal experience, apparent absorption of extra-Islamic practices, and connection with lower echelons of society, Sufism is

---

3. Michael Molloy, *Experiencing the World's Religions*, 6th ed. (New York: McGraw Hill, 2013), 436.

4. Abraham Kuyper, *On Islam*, trans. Jan van Vliet (Bellingham, WA: Lexham, 2017), 88.

5. Molloy, *Experiencing the World's Religions*, 440.

often considered to be mere folk religion by orthodox Muslims.[6] In fact, the following section will consider a strain of Islam that exists in part as a reaction against Sufism.

Salafi

On the other end of the spectrum from Sufism, one finds Salafist Islam refusing to admit of any innovation or alteration of the practice, faith, and law of the earliest Muslims. Westerners who have watched world news over the past twenty years are likely to recognize the word "Salafi" and to associate it with strict enforcement of Islamic law and the conflation of religion and politics. For example, Saudi Arabia is a country that has taken a version of Salafist Islam (Wahhabism) as the governing law of the land. Consideration of a few distinctives that mark Salafist thought will provide a basic understanding of how they differ from other expressions.

Rejection of Bid'a

Part of the reason that Salafists are known as conservative and strict is that they are wary of any innovation (*bid'a*) that might taint the pure expression of Islam.[7] In some respects, Salafists came into being as a contrast group, trying to steer away from the syncretistic practices that they observed in the Sufis. Particularly disturbing to Salafists are the Sufi and Shia practices that involve the veneration of Muslim saints, pilgrimages to tombs, and celebrating Muhammad's birthday.

However, perhaps the most offensive Sufi concept is the pursuit of direct experience with God.[8] All of these activities, from the perspective of a Salafist, threaten to erode the central Islamic doctrine of God's absolute unity (*tawhid*). In order to avoid compromising absolute monotheism, then, Salafists reject innovation of thought and practice. Their system is derived from only the earliest sources of authority in order to mitigate the infiltration of *bid'a*.

Salafi Sources of Authority

In a previous chapter we discussed some of the various schools of Islamic jurisprudence (*madhhabs*) and the manner in which they determine proper Islamic teaching on a given matter. All of these schools recognize the Qur'an and *Sunnah* as the primary guiding sources of authority, yet to varying degrees most of them also make use of philosophy, logic, tradition, and community consensus in the process of determining Islamic law.

---

6. Molloy, *Experiencing the World's Religions*, 442.
7. William Shepard, "Salafi Islam: The Study of Contemporary Religious-Political Movements," in *The Bloomsbury Companion to Islamic Studies*, ed. Clinton Bennett (New York: Bloomsbury, 2015), 163.
8. Molloy, *Experiencing the World's Religions*, 436.

Salafists, however, restrict their understanding of Islamic law to the interpretations given within the first three generations (*salaf*) after Muhammad.
This means that they adhere to the Qur'an, the *Sunnah*, and the rulings of
Muhammad's companions up until the death of Ibn Hanbal (855 CE).[9] Since
they are averse to using philosophy, contemporary reasoning, or tradition,
Salafists are technically not considered to be part of a *madhhab*, but are instead an expression of doctrinal discourse (*kalam*).[10]

Jihad and Radical Salafist Expressions
    While there are many different expressions of Salafist practice, not all of
which approve of violence, a tendency exists to conflate Salafism with terrorism and holy war (*jihad*). This association is particularly acute when considering that al-Qaida, Boko Haram, ISIS, and the Muslim Brotherhood are
expressions of Salafi Islam.
    Many of the statements made by radical Salafists regarding their posi-
tion on *jihad* further implicate them as those inclined to support violence in
the name of holy war. For instance, drawing from public records of Salafist
creeds, William Shepard includes the following statement as a representation
of radical Salafi thought:

> We believe that jihad will last until judgment day, between
> the just and unjust, in every time and place, with the pres-
> ence of a supreme leader or not. This jihad is accomplished
> by a single individual or by more, and will not be stopped
> by the tyranny of oppressors or the defeatist talk of the
> demoralizers.[11]

Statements like this, though not representative of all Salafis, reveal a willingness to subject all human judgment to a rigid interpretation of the Qur'an
and *Sunnah*.

Western
    Due to increased travel and globalization, Muslim communities have
been established throughout the world, including among Western nations.
Muslims living and educated in Western countries share some unique characteristics that warrant separate treatment. While some of the uniqueness will
remain on the cultural level—issues of dress and social habits—it is important

---

9. Shepard, "Salafi Islam," 164.
10. Shepard, "Salafi Islam," 164.
11. Shepard, "Salafi Islam," 178. Shepard cites Roel Meijer, *Global Salafism: Islam's New Religious
    Movements* (New York: Columbia University Press, 2009), 51–56, though Shepard here of-
    fers a condensed version of Meijer's statements.

to consider that Muslims raised in Western countries are adapting the practice of their faith to reflect the environments in which they reside. Specifically, for Christians engaged in conversation with their Muslim friends and neighbors, it will be helpful to recognize that a Muslim in Columbus, Ohio, may think differently about the world than a Muslim in Cairo, Egypt.

Linear Argumentation

In countries like Egypt, the public education system is shaped by the fact that the number of students far outpaces the availability of teachers. The classroom pressure this produces contributes to the adoption of pedagogies based on rote memorization. Likewise, such pedagogy is consonant with Islamic teaching in that the Qur'an itself derives its name from the root word meaning "to recite." As mentioned above, the Qur'an is the product of Muhammad's recitation of what Jibril (often understood as the biblical Gabriel) revealed to him. Furthermore, those who have memorized the entire Qur'an (*muhafiz*) are revered as some of the most pious Muslims.

Therefore, it is common in Islamic argumentation to find appeal to recitation and repetition of the conclusions of respected clerics. However, for Muslims raised under the tutelage of Western educational systems, producing an argument takes a much more Hellenistic approach, utilizing critical thinking, sequential argumentation, and scientific method. This linear, systematic approach to argumentation is exemplified in the writings of former-Muslim Nabeel Qureshi. His best-selling book *Seeking Allah, Finding Jesus* details his own intellectual journey of investigating the differences between Islam and Christianity.[12] Qureshi's work serves as an excellent example of how a Western-raised Muslim processes the claims of Islam.

Imbibing Western Liberalism

In recent years increasing numbers of civil liberties advocacy groups have emerged from within American Muslim communities. Some of these Muslim-led advocacy groups are surprising in their ardent support of social freedoms, including groups of Muslims who are practicing homosexuals.[13] Other groups of Muslims have made the news as they advocate for women's rights, including the right to lead prayers and serve as imams in American mosques.[14]

Support for these issues is uncommon throughout the global Ummah. In Saudi Arabia, by way of contrast, women just received the right to drive in

---

12. Nabeel Qureshi, *Seeking Allah, Finding Jesus*, 3rd ed. (Grand Rapids: Zondervan, 2018).
13. See, for example, Khakan Qureshi, "Coming Out as an LGBT Muslim," *Reaching Out*, Nov. 30, 2017, https://medium.com/reaching-out/coming-out-as-an-lgbt-muslim-b2b5704425bd.
14. See, for example, Andrea Elliot, "Woman Leads Muslim Prayer Service in New York," *New York Times*, Mar. 19, 2005, https://www.nytimes.com/2005/03/19/nyregion/woman-leads-muslim-prayer-service-in-new-york.html.

2018.[15] The idea of a woman leading a mosque in prayer, let alone serving as an imam, is unthinkable in most of the Arab world. Likewise, homosexuals in most Middle Eastern contexts are oppressed, persecuted, and often killed as prescribed by law.[16] Yet, the social environment of the West often allows Muslims to maintain their faith concurrently with practices that have been traditionally prohibited.

Cultural Distinctives Downplayed

Ever since 9/11, Muslim communities living in the United States have wrestled with how overtly to display their Islamic cultural markers. Some choose to avoid obvious markers of their faith in order to blend into the surrounding culture. Others are simply less inclined to adopt what seem to be Middle Eastern cultural forms while yet observing Islam faithfully.

For example, a Muslim woman raised in New York may not feel compelled to wear the head covering (*hijab*) and will have no problem drinking coffee in a café in mixed company. Likewise, a Muslim man raised in Chicago may have no desire to grow out his beard, though this is considered obligatory in certain expressions, such as in the Taliban, who formerly ruled Afghanistan.

While these personal choices distinguish some Western-raised Muslims from the stereotypical image, such differences provide great opportunities for conversation. One would be well served to ask why these individuals have chosen not to adopt such practices and to hear each person articulate their own beliefs for themselves. In the end, these unique features remind us that we are always having conversations about religious convictions with individuals rather than merely studying impersonal systems of belief.

Summary

This brief overview should suffice to cause the reader to pause before making universal claims about Islam or Muslim culture. In fact, drawing on what Dr. Reisacher noted at the beginning of this chapter, there is perhaps more legitimacy in speaking of Islamic family resemblance than there is in making overarching, universal claims about Islam. This provides a humbling reminder to know that, no matter how much one studies Islam and its theology, conversations occur with people who are not themselves the mere embodiment of theological propositions.

With that reminder, I hope you will read the rest of this book not as a manual to Islam, but as a means by which to familiarize yourself with some

---

15. Shannon van Saint, "Saudi Arabia Lifts Ban on Female Drivers," *NPR*, June 24, 2018, https://www.npr.org/2018/06/24/622990978/saudi-arabia-lifts-ban-on-women-drivers.

16. A. L., "How Homosexuality Became a Crime in the Middle East," *The Economist*, June 6, 2018, https://www.economist.com/open-future/2018/06/06/how-homosexuality-became-a-crime-in-the-middle-east.

basics that can provide fodder for conversation with your Muslim friends. Orienting oneself to the generally accepted core of Islamic belief and practice is helpful in guiding a person to have informed, meaningful questions to ask. From this posture, one demonstrates neighborly love by studying another's belief system, and at the same time grants dignity by asking questions and listening to the answers given.

REFLECTION QUESTIONS

1. What are some of the distinctive beliefs of Sufi Muslims?

2. What are some of the ways that Sufis arrive at religious truth?

3. What makes Salafi Muslims different than Sufis in terms of their view of religious truth and authority?

4. What is *bid'a* according to Salafis, and why is it rejected?

5. In what ways do some Western expressions of Islam shed some of the trappings of traditional Islam?

PART 2

The Sources of Authority for Islam

What Is the Qur'an?

Surely [the Qur'an] is indeed a sending down from
the Lord of the worlds. The trustworthy spirit has
brought it down on your heart, so that you may be
one of the warners, in a clear Arabic language.
~Qur'an 26:192–94

According to Islamic tradition, the world changed in the year 610 CE. It was in this year that a man named Muhammad entered a cave called Hira where he encountered an angel with a message: "Recite!"[1] The content of the subsequent recitation was recorded over a period of approximately twenty-two years of occasional revelation. We now know it as the Qur'an.

Today, if you enter the home, business, or even the car of a Muslim, it is likely that you will see a copy of the Qur'an prominently on display. It may rest on an ornate wooden book holder crafted for the expressed purpose of cradling the Islamic holy book. Or it may be a pocket-sized version resting on the dashboard. It is likely that you will see verses of the Qur'an in gold lettering, in artistic arrangement of the Arabic script, hanging on the wall. Regardless of form, these words are precious to Muslims from Cairo, Egypt, to Dayton, Ohio.

This reverence for the Qur'an derives from the fact that nearly two billion Muslims around the world maintain that this book contains the exact words of God as instruction on how to live. These words are read daily by pious individuals,

---

1. Roger Allen, "Qur'an," in *Islam: A Short Guide to the Faith*, eds. Roger Allen and Shawkat Toorawa (Grand Rapids: Eerdmans, 2011), 21.

by leaders of Mosques calling the faithful to prayer, and at major events such as births, weddings, and funerals. For the Muslim, the words and poetry of the Qur'an provide the rhythms and melodies to which their lives move.

Traditional Origins of the Qur'an

In an effort to clarify the difference between the Qur'an and the Bible, the well-known Muslim author Seyyed Hossein Nasr writes, "To fully understand the significance of the [Qur'an], a Westerner with a Christian background should realize that, although the [Qur'an] can in a sense be compared to the Old and New Testaments, a more profound comparison would be with Christ himself."[2] In other words, just as the Gospel of John contends that Jesus is the Word become flesh, Nasr contends that the eternal words of God have become book in the Qur'an. The difference, then, for the Christian is that God has most centrally revealed himself personally in the incarnation. The Qur'an, however, is the verbatim record of God's will committed to writing.

The Mother of the Book

Part of Nasr's contention comes from the Muslim concept of the "Mother of the Book." This phrase refers to the idea that there is an eternal, heavenly book from which the angel Jibril transmitted the material of the Qur'an to Muhammad. The Qur'an refers to this heavenly source in several places, one of which is Qur'an 13:39, which states, "God blots out whatever he pleases, and He confirms (whatever He pleases). With Him is the mother of the Book."[3] If the Qur'an is God's eternal message made accessible in writing, then the comparison with Jesus as the accessible version of God in flesh seems appropriate.

Some Muslims, however, reject the comparison of the incarnation and the Qur'an. They contend that the Qur'an is not the revelation of God *per se*; rather, it is merely the revelation of God's will.[4] Since God is transcendent, it is important that one maintains the distinction between God himself and God's will.

Revelation

As mentioned above, Muslim tradition records that Muhammad received parts of the Qur'an over a span of approximately twenty-two years, from 610–632 CE. Tradition teaches that the first verses he received are found in Qur'an

---

2. Seyyed Hossein Nasr, *The Heart of Islam: Enduring Values for Humanity* (New York: HarperOne, 2004), 23.
3. A. J. Droge, trans., *The Qur'an: A New Annotated Translation* (Bristol, CT: Equinox, 2015), 154n61. Commenting on Qur'an 13:39, Droge writes, "Mother of the book . . . is usually taken as a reference to the heavenly original or archetype of all revelation." Cf. Qur'an 43:2–4; 85:21–22.
4. Ziauddin Sardar, *What Do Muslims Believe? The Roots and Realities of Modern Islam* (New York: Walker, 2007), 48.

96:1–5, which instruct Muhammad to recite what he is told regarding God's role as creator and teacher. During the occasions of revelation, Muhammad recited what the angel Jibril revealed to him from the heavenly source. Such revelations often accompanied circumstances suited to the teaching that was revealed. Traditional Muslim accounts teach that his followers committed the verses and chapters to writing using a variety of materials available wherever they found themselves.[5]

Compilation

According to Sunni tradition, after Muhammad's death in 632 CE, his followers codified and formalized the Qur'an. Some of the Qur'an had been written down, though much of it was transmitted orally, having been committed to memory. The first caliph, Abu Bakr, began collecting and canonizing the recitations shortly after Muhammad's death. Though reticent to undertake a task that Muhammad himself did not sanction, Abu Bakr persisted for fear of losing access to the revelations, as the early Muslims who had memorized large portions of the Qur'an were killed in battle.

Abu Bakr's collection was passed down to successive caliphs until the time of 'Uthman (644–656 CE), when it became apparent that competing collections and readings existed within the Ummah. In response, 'Uthman commissioned Muhammad's secretary, Zayd ibn Thabit, and four other experts to refine and finalize the Qur'an in its original dialect as it had been revealed to Muhammad.[6] This authorized version, then, became the standard text of the Qur'an for the entire Ummah.

Transmission

Muslim tradition records that after 'Uthman's authorization of the final version, any competing copies and readings were destroyed.[7] One of the claims Muslims often make to support their confidence in the Qur'an as God's word to man is that from the time of 'Uthman, it has remained a single, standard text, referenced by Muslims all around the world. In the words of Badru Kateregga, "The Qur'an used today is the very same one as received by the Prophet, and authorized by Caliph 'Uthman and the companions (*sahaba*) of the Prophet in A.D. 651. No word, order, or punctuation mark has been changed, omitted, or added."[8] This claim has broadly convinced Muslims that their Qur'an is the record of the exact words given to Muhammad from the

---

5. Claude Gilliot, "Creation of a Fixed Text," in *CCQ*, ed. Jane Dammen McAuliffe (New York: Cambridge University Press, 2006), 44.
6. Gilliot, "Creation of a Fixed Text," 45.
7. Gordon Newby, *The Making of the Last Prophet* (Columbia: University of South Carolina Press, 1989), 25n7.
8. Badru Kateregga and David Shenk, *A Muslim and a Christian in Dialogue* (Scottdale, PA: Herald, 1997), 59.

Mother of the Book. Such confidence hinges upon the purportedly meticulous process of transmission, as well as the claim that God himself has miraculously preserved the Qur'an.[9]

The Miracle of the Qur'an

There are at least two claims that Muslims make about the Qur'an that intend to reveal its miraculous nature: (1) its textual integrity, and (2) its unlikely prophet. Islamic traditions accuse the Jews and Christians of allowing their scriptures to be corrupted. They claim that the Qur'an, however, has been protected through the centuries from a similar fate.[10] Likewise, whereas the Bible has many authors of various degrees of education who wrote over many centuries, the Qur'an's human agent was an unlikely candidate. Muhammad's lack of education lends credibility to the claim that what he received was not of his own devising, but rather came from a divine source.

Its Divine Protection

First, as the previous section indicated, Muslims believe that God has preserved the text of the Qur'an without corruption since the days of 'Uthman. The foundation for this claim comes from the Qur'an itself in Qur'an 85:21–22, which records, "Yes! It is a glorious Qur'an, in a guarded tablet." The guarded tablet here is taken to be a reference to the Mother of the Book, or the heavenly archetype of divine revelation.[11]

Thus, this heavenly book is not only from an eternal source, but its integrity is established and protected by the active providence of God. Furthermore, Qur'an 10:37 contends that the quality of the Qur'an and its continuity with previous revelation prove that it could only have a divine source, saying, "This Qur'an is not the kind (of Book) that it could have been forged apart from God. (It is) a confirmation of what was before it, and a distinct setting forth of the Book—there is no doubt about it—from the Lord of the worlds." Both the protection of the text and its content, then, derive from a divine source.

Its Unexpected Conduit

That the Qur'an comes from God is reinforced by the second miracle of the Qur'an, which relates to Muhammad as the conduit of qur'anic transmission.

---

9. This claim is made from the traditional Islamic account of history. Much of this traditional history will be revisited under the light of contemporary critical scholarship in Part 6. For an interesting article regarding the Qur'an's transmission history and the prevalence of apparently variant readings of the Qur'an, see Fred Leemhuis, "From Palm Leaves to the Internet," in *CCQ*, ed. Jane Dammen McAuliffe (New York: Cambridge University Press, 2006), 149–51.
10. For more discussion on this issue, see Question 28 and its investigation of the Islamic teaching that the Jews and Christians have allowed their books to be corrupted.
11. Droge, *Qur'an*, 429n11.

Islamic tradition claims that Muhammad was a common (*ummi*) man. This particular Arabic word can mean that he received no formal education, it can indicate that he was fully illiterate, or it can be understood to mean that he was merely a common member of the Arab tribes.[12] Regardless of which interpretation one takes, most Muslims understand that when revelation descended upon Muhammad, it was his followers who committed the recitations to writing on scraps of paper, leaves, bark, and other materials to record his precious words.

Traditional Muslims, following the interpretation that *ummi* refers to Muhammad's lack of education, contend that this circumstance further proves the miracle of the Qur'an. Its rhythmic beauty, according to Islam, is inimitable and could not be expected from one who had no formal training. In fact, when Muhammad's contemporaries doubted the divine origin of his proclamations, he challenged them to produce a proclamation like it as proof of his inspiration.[13]

Both the beauty and the content of the Qur'an are called into service when defending the claim that the Qur'an is Muhammad's prophetic miracle. Unfortunately for English-speakers, the rhyme and meter of the Qur'an cannot be appreciated apart from the original Arabic. However, the themes that arise can lend some insight into consideration of its message.

Reading the Qur'an

One complication that arises for a reader familiar with the Bible is that the Qur'an does not admit of much internal evidence suggesting a historical location or chronology for the events it records. Where the Bible has entire books such as Exodus and Kings to provide historical context, the Qur'an is a different kind of book. Instead of presenting a linear narrative, "the Qur'an uses metaphors, allegories and parables to delineate its themes and subjects, returning to the same topics again and again."[14] Its composition is elliptical and interdependent throughout.

Thus, the process of understanding the Qur'an requires reading it as a whole, then reflecting on the development of themes and concepts. While Part 3 will investigate six questions that unpack more of the teaching of the Qur'an, it is helpful to consider how three central themes that emerge from the first chapter help the reader hear the message of the Qur'an.

---

12. Droge, *Qur'an*, 102n157. Commenting on Qur'an 7:157, Droge states, "*Ummi* means something like 'gentile' in the sense of those who do not have a written scripture. . . . Traditional scholars interpret *ummi* as 'illiterate,' and claim that Muhammad could not read or write (further emphasizing the miraculous character of the Qur'an)."
13. Cf. Qur'an 2:23; 10:37; 11:13; 17:88; 52:33–34.
14. Sardar, *What Do Muslims Believe?*, 49.

Monotheism

Throughout the Qur'an one is confronted over and over with the idea that there is only one God who is responsible for creation. Countering the claims of native polytheists, tradition teaches that the Qur'an was revealed in Mecca in order to demonstrate the singularity of the one true God. In the first chapter of the Qur'an (*al-Fatiha*), the reader is confronted by repeated references to this God. Each reference is exclusive and singular, and the dominant theme of Islamic monotheism is established from the very first phrase, "In the Name of God (*Bismillah*)."

The word used for God here in Arabic is absolute, singular, and unequivocal. It might rigidly be translated as "The God" in English, demonstrating that there is no other contender to this title. While God is known by many characteristics in Islam, his essential unity binds all of his characteristics together in singularity. Thus, the first phrase of the Qur'an establishes one of the themes that will predominate the message of the Qur'an: there is only one God.

Guidance

Likewise, the Qur'an repeatedly presents itself as a book of guidance (*hidayah*) to the faithful. This function of the Qur'an is on display in Qur'an 1:6, which petitions God to guide the believer to the straight path (*as-sirat al-mustiaqim*). That the Qur'an has been revealed as a means of guidance can be established from this first verse, containing the first account of human transgression of divine decree.

In Qur'an 2:34–39, a story resembling the biblical account of the fall appears. In the Qur'an, however, the story takes place in heavenly gardens, is caused directly by the activity of the serpent-like antagonist (Iblis), and results in humanity being sent down to earth. In response to human slipping from felicity, however, God provides Adam with certain words that brought about forgiveness and are later referred to as guidance. Qur'an 2:38 warns subsequent believers, "If any guidance comes to you from Me, whoever follows My guidance—(there will be) no fear on them, nor will they sorrow." As such, the Qur'an repeatedly presents itself as divine guidance to humanity.

Judgment

The third theme that emerges from the opening chapter of the Qur'an is that of impending judgment. In Qur'an 1:4, God is referred to as "Master of the Day of Judgment." Furthermore, Qur'an 1:7 goes on to warn that those who do not follow God's guidance are those upon whom the anger of God falls. God's justice and willingness to punish those who wander from the straight path is not eclipsed by his mercy or compassion. Thus, the reader is provided the Qur'an not only as guidance, but also as a clear warning of impending judgment.

Throughout the Qur'an, God is presented as the sole creator of all things, the guide of humanity, and the master to whom obedience and service are due. Life is presented as a test of one's willingness to follow God's instructions. Those who fail to heed his guidance and walk the straight path are subjected to his righteous judgment in this life and in the next. Though God is often referred to as the Merciful and the Compassionate one, the Qur'an everywhere reminds the reader that he will also punish those who fail to follow his guidance.

Summary

Reading the Qur'an for a Christian requires patience and a commitment to hear the book on its own terms. It does not follow the familiar organization of the Bible, nor does it care to spend much time recounting stories and narratives. Instead, the Qur'an is focused on establishing God's oneness, providing guidance for the faithful, and warning those who wander.

As such, the day of judgment looms large in the warnings of the Qur'an, reinforcing the idea that each person lives under the authority of the one true God and will be held responsible for the life one lives. Yet, before determining that the God of Islam is merely wrathful, the reader must recognize that the Qur'an also repeatedly affirms, "God is the Merciful, the Compassionate." As the compassionate one, he has extended guidance to humanity in the Qur'an so that they might remember who they are and follow God's will.

Describing the role of the Qur'an in Islam, Seyyed Hossein Nasr contends that the Qur'an permeates the entirety of the Muslim life, writing, "In a way, the soul of the traditional Muslim is like a mosaic made up of phrases of the [Qur'an], which are repeated throughout life."[15] For every major event, decision, and moment in life, there is a corresponding reference to be made to the Qur'an's instruction. Since the Qur'an provides access to the guidance of God for humanity, then, it is not surprising that the Qur'an has so permeated the Muslim experience as to be inseparable from the Muslim individual.

REFLECTION QUESTIONS

1. What is the Mother of the Book, and how does that affect our understanding of the Qur'an?

2. What are three possible meanings of the word *ummi* as it is used to describe Muhammad?

---

15. Seyyed Hossein Nasr, *Ideals and Realities of Islam* (San Francisco: Aquarian, 1994), 22.

3. What are the various reasons that the Qur'an is understood to be a miracle?

4. What role did 'Uthman play in how the Qur'an was transmitted?

5. What is the primary teaching of the Qur'an?

What Is the *Sunnah?*

Next to the Holy Qur'an the [hadith] is the
second source of the Islamic Law of social and
personal behavior, because the commandments
of the Holy Prophet are as binding on the
believers as the commands of Allah.
~Introduction to Sahih Muslim[1]

The Qur'an is a book written in seventh-century Arabic, following the con-ventions of the poetry and literature of its day. As the previous question discussed, its poetic features are considered part of the proof of its divine origin. As such, however, it does not lend itself to a systematic account of how one might apply its principles to the daily activities of life. Also, since its mes-sage is bound to the Arabic of its day, the clarity that it purports to have is no longer clearly apprehended by those speaking the living, evolving dialects of modern Arabic.

These two difficulties, however, are not recent recognitions. Within two centuries of the traditional date of the Qur'an's compilation, Muslims found themselves living in very different cultures, climates, and conditions. In such environments, the Qur'an did not provide uniform instruction as to how one was to participate in the shared practice of the Ummah while being geograph-ically and culturally far removed from its origins.

---

1. As quoted in Edward Hoskins, *A Muslim's Mind: What Every Christian Needs to Know about the Islamic Traditions* (Colorado Springs: Dawson, 2011), 23.

In an effort to establish the uniform practice of Islam, during the ninth century CE Muslim scholars began to compile accounts of Muhammad's life and interpretation of the Qur'an. A biography of Muhammad's life was compiled and recorded along with volumes upon volumes of accounts of Muhammad's various teachings and activities that were not included in the Qur'an. The result of this effort is the body of literature known as the *Sunnah.*

Trustworthy Transmission

In the *Sunnah* one encounters a systematized record of Muhammad's sayings and behaviors pertaining to all spheres of life. These accounts cover everything from how to brush one's teeth to how a Muslim should pray each day. While Muslims contend that the Qur'an is the verbatim word of God, the *Sunnah* depicts Muhammad as the exemplar of qur'anic application.

Each report or account of Muhammad's life and teaching is referred to as a *hadith.* Due to the authority that inheres from attributing a *hadith* to Muhammad, certain unscrupulous Muslims found it expedient to their political and economic desires to produce false accounts in support of personal agendas. Thus, it quickly became apparent that not all *hadith* are trustworthy.

Sahih al-Bukhari

In his introduction to the most trusted Sunni collection of *hadith, Sahih al-Bukhari,* Muhammad Khan confirms the presence of dubious *hadith,* writing, "[Al-Bukhari] was born at a time when *hadith* was being forged either to please rulers . . . or to corrupt the religion of Islam."[2] Al-Bukhari, traditionally understood to be a committed Muslim known for his exceptional integrity and honesty, was burdened to compile a trustworthy collection that excised false material while highlighting that which was reliable.

Providing the impetus for this great undertaking, Khan recounts that al-Bukhari had a dream that was interpreted to mean "that he will drive away the falsehood asserted against the Prophet."[3] Following this dream, al-Bukhari set himself to the task of analyzing between three hundred thousand and six hundred thousand reports of *hadith* in order to determine their authenticity.[4] When he concluded his task, al-Bukhari had a mere 2,230 unique and unrepeated *hadith* that he classified as true and reliable (*sahih*).[5]

---

2. Muhammad Khan, trans., *Summarized Sahih al-Bukhari* (Riyadh, KSA: Darussalam, 1996), 18.
3. Khan, *Sahih al-Bukhari,* 19.
4. The six hundred thousand number is reported by A. C. Jonathan Brown, *Hadith: Muhammad's Legacy in the Medieval and Modern World* (Oxford: OneWorld, 2009), 32. Khan, *Sahih al-Bukhari,* 18, however, states that al-Bukhari collected only three hundred thousand *hadith.*
5. Khan, *Sahih al-Bukhari,* 19.

Isnad Inspection

The first criteria for authenticating a *hadith* was that it needed to be traced back to either Muhammad himself or one of his trusted companions (*Sahabah*; Muhammad's disciples who knew him personally).[6] Both the lapse of time between Muhammad's life and the collection of the *hadith* materials and the broad geographical expanse of the Islamic empire made the task of thorough *hadith* collection difficult in and of itself. However, analyzing each *hadith*'s authenticity required significantly more work.

In order to determine whether or not the account was believable, the entire chain of transmission (*isnad*) must be inspected all the way back to Muhammad or his companions. Since nearly every *hadith* was passed along orally, the inspection focuses not only on the report itself, but also on the reputation of those who transmitted it. The trusted collectors were known to hold would-be transmitters to rigid standards of personal integrity.

Illustrating these strict criteria, tradition teaches that al-Bukhari once traveled a long distance in order to meet with a man who claimed to have a single *hadith*. Upon arrival, al-Bukhari found the man attempting to entice his horse to follow him with an empty bag of feed. Without bothering to hear the man's report, al-Bukhari turned around and made the journey back home empty-handed. Al-Bukhari rationalized this decision by asking, "How could he be trusted . . . to convey a [*hadith*] if he was deceitful to his horse?"[7]

Once the *isnad* is proven trustworthy, the text itself needs to be analyzed critically to verify its fit with the corpus of Muhammad's life and teaching. Analysis of each *hadith* assesses grammar, thought, and corroborating accounts from other sources in order to establish authenticity.[8] Thus Islamic jurists have produced an entire "science" of *hadith* criticism.

The Six Reliable Sunni Collections

Following the process for inspecting the chain of transmission detailed above, six collections emerged within Sunni Islam as the semiofficial, authoritative canon of the *Sunnah*.[9] Though al-Bukhari's *Sahih al-Bukhari* is the most widely accepted collection of *hadith*, the revered Imam Muslim also collected more than nine thousand reports included in his work *Sahih Muslim*, which is likewise considered impeccable.[10]

---

6. Ziauddin Sardar, *What Do Muslims Believe?* (New York: Walker, 2007), 51.
7. Sardar, *What Do Muslims Believe?*, 52.
8. Jonathan Brown, *Hadith: Muhammad's Legacy in the Medieval and Modern World* (Oxford: OneWorld, 2011), 92.
9. Shiite Muslims follow similar procedures in the process of doing *hadith* criticism, though the Shiite preference for the family of 'Ali and subsequent imams as transmitters shapes their *hadith* collections differently than the Sunni collections. Both Shiites and Sunnis, however, draw on many shared traditions within the *Sunnah*. See Brown, *Hadith*, 123–49.
10. Sardar, *What Do Muslims Believe?*, 53.

The fame of these two compilations of *hadith* material casts a shadow of relative obscurity over subsequent collections. However, four other volumes of *hadith* are considered authoritative throughout the Sunni world. These collections are titled as follows: (1) *Sunan al-Nasa'i*, (2) *Sunan Abu Dawud*, (3) *Sunan al-Tirmidhi*, (4) and *Sunan ibn Majah*.

In total, these six collectors are believed to have combed through millions of reports of *hadith* in order to compile their final volumes. Ziauddin Sardar contends that, despite the millions of collected *hadith*, "The [*hadith*] that really matter are the authentic ones."[11] Throughout the six canonical volumes, slightly more than 34,500 records of *hadith* appear, though many of these reports are repeated throughout the collections.

Following al-Bukhari's estimation, approximately 2,350 unique *hadith* are authentic and reliable (*sahih*). Those *hadith* that are not completely trustworthy are not dismissed out of hand, but are assigned a different designation. In descending order of reliability, such designations are: (1) good (*hasan*), (2) shaky (*mudtarib*), (3) weak (*da'if*), (4) fabricated (*mawdua'*).[12] Islamic jurisprudence considers a *hadith*'s authenticity before including its teaching in Islamic law.

The Biography of Muhammad (*Sirat Rasul Allah*)

One final component of the corpus of early influential Islamic writing is the biography of Muhammad attributed to a man named Ibn Ishaq. Ibn Ishaq was a controversial figure in the collection of *hadith* due to his indiscriminate inclusion of dubious reports. However, the biography (often referred to as the *Sira*) that tradition attributes to him provides the most widely relied-upon account of the life of Muhammad.[13] It should be noted here, however, that what we have today is not the *Sira* itself, but an edited and censored recollection of Ibn Ishaq's *Sira* written by a man named Ibn Hisham who died two hundred years after Muhammad's death.

The influence of the *Sira* is not restricted merely to the effect it has on corroborating the *Sunnah*, nor even as it contributes to a historical portrait of the central prophetic figure within Islam. Instead, the greatest impact that the *Sira* has had on Islam is that it directly shapes the way that most Muslims—and many Orientalists—read and order the chapters of the Qur'an. Due to the fact that the Qur'an itself provides very little internal evidence of its own chronological ordering, the biography has come to provide a means of organizing the chapters of the Qur'an as they fit within the story told by the *Sira*.

11. Sardar, *What Do Muslims Believe?*, 53.
12. An excellent free resource for reading and searching *hadith* literature can be found at www.sunnah.com.
13. Brown, *Hadith*, 86.

Thus, most editions of the Qur'an will identify each chapter as being received in the early or late Meccan periods or during the Medinan period.

Corroborating this biographically structured reading of the Qur'an, Islamic scholar Gabriel Said Reynolds states, "The idea that each [chapter of the Qur'an], as a unity, can be placed in a certain moment of the Prophet's life is a tenet of Islamic religious tradition." However, Reynolds goes on to contend that this idea is not native to the Qur'an because "the text itself nowhere demands to be arranged according to the life experiences of an individual."[14] Part 6 of this book will address the emerging scholarly discussion regarding these issues, but it is sufficient to note at present that the *Sira* has widely shaped and influenced the reading of the Qur'an since it appeared in writing approximately two hundred years after Muhammad's death.

Summary

As the last two questions have shown, the Qur'an and the *Sunnah* provide the Muslim community with sacred writings by which to order their lives. As one scholar puts it, the Qur'an and the *Sunnah* form a "textual umbrella" under which the rulings of Islamic law are formed.[15] However, most Muslims contend that there is still a distinction between the Qur'an and the *Sunnah.*

The Qur'an is the verbatim word of God, while the *Sunnah* is the record of human efforts to record the interpretation and application of the Qur'an as seen in the exemplary life of Muhammad. While the two bodies of literature function together, it remains important to ask which body of literature proves more influential in the life of an average Muslim.

REFLECTION QUESTIONS

1. What makes it difficult for contemporary readers to understand and apply the Qur'an?

2. What kinds of literature make up the *Sunnah*, and how does that affect the way one reads the Qur'an?

3. When did the Muslim community commit the *Sunnah* to writing?

4. How did the community decide if a *hadith* was authentic?

5. What role does the *Sira* play in shaping Islam?

---

14. Gabriel Said Reynolds, *The Qur'an and Its Biblical Subtext* (New York: Routledge, 2011), 4.
15. Ahmad Ahmad, *Islamic Law: Cases, Authorities, and Worldview* (New York: Bloomsbury, 2017), 27.

Which Is More Influential: The Qur'an or the *Sunnah*?

Whenever the Prophet got up for Tahajjud prayer he
used to clean his mouth (and teeth) with Siwak.
~Sahih al-Bukhari[1]

As you begin to further explore the religion of Islam, one reality that confronts you is that there is a *hadith* for just about everything. One such example is listed above. Muhammad was known to select a particular root (*siwak*) for the purposes of cleaning his teeth and eradicating halitosis. This habit was recorded by the companions and made its way into the collection of *hadith* as a prescription for the future dental hygiene practices of Muslims.

To this day, in Islamic grocery stores and markets, one can readily find *siwak* root prepackaged and ready for use. Likewise, some Western companies (Crest and Colgate are examples I have seen) have found ways to satisfy this Islamic practice without drastically altering their product by offering *siwak*-infused versions of their toothpaste. Thus, even in contemporary settings, Muslims seek to maintain the seventh-century lifestyle of Muhammad by applying the *hadith* to their daily routines.

While the *hadith* guide everyday interactions, the most revered and respected Muslims are those who are able to commit the entire Qur'an to memory. This reverence derives from the Islamic belief that the Qur'an is the verbatim word of God. To commit it to memory reflects one's allegiance to

---

1. Al-Bukhari, *Sahih al-Bukhari*, https://sunnah.com/bukhari/19, book 19 (§17).

God's revealed will. The question then remains, Which of these bodies of literature is more influential in the Muslim's life?

The Influence of the Qur'an

If one were to force the average Muslim to decide whether the Qur'an or the *Sunnah* wields the greatest authority in Islam, most would reluctantly conclude that the Qur'an is more authoritative.[2] That conclusion derives from the belief that the Qur'an is the verbatim transmission of the eternal message of God and has been preserved by divine power. The *Sunnah*, however, as the record of Muhammad's interpretation and application of the Qur'an, has been sorted and preserved by extensive human effort.

Furthermore, the revelation and message of the Qur'an provides the basis for Muhammad's life and ministry. It would therefore seem illogical to claim that actions that derived from the Qur'an—even as exhibited by the exemplar of Muslim living—could function more authoritatively than the Qur'an itself. Therefore, if pressed, most Muslims would likely concede that the Qur'an is the ultimate source of authority within Islam.

Yet, before concluding that the Qur'an is therefore more important, one must recognize that the question of priority between these two sources of authority introduces a false dilemma for most Muslims. In the words of Ziauddin Sardar, "Prophet Muhammad is not just the Messenger of God who conveyed His message to humanity. He is also the person who concretized and realized the Divine message in a particular situation."[3] Therefore, both collections serve as sources of authority in Islam, and Muslims contend that, when properly understood, no final contradiction exists between them.[4] Therefore, one need not choose to elevate the Qur'an above the *Sunnah* in practice.

While the issue of authority may ultimately tip the scales in favor of the Qur'an over the *Sunnah*, if one compares the two corpuses as to their level of influence in Islamic life, the balance shifts dramatically. The Qur'an functions in Islamic life as a heaven-sent record of God's will and as a sign confirming Muhammad's prophetic role. However, as a heavenly book, it is inherently difficult to understand.

As Edward Hoskins contends, "Muslims agree that because the Qur'an is heavenly, it is also mysterious and does not completely address every minute aspect of life. The Qur'an is fully understood only by Allah himself."[5] Since the Qur'an is mysterious, understanding its teaching is best done through

---

2. Edward Hoskins, *A Muslim's Mind: What Every Christian Needs to Know about the Islamic Traditions* (Colorado Springs: Dawson, 2011), 24. Hoskins here includes a quote from the introduction to the *Sahih Muslim* collection in which the Qur'an is seen as a primary source of Muslim law and guidance while the *Sunnah* is next to it.
3. Ziauddin Sardar, *What Do Muslims Believe?* (New York: Walker, 2007), 50.
4. Sardar, *What Do Muslims Believe?*, 52.
5. Hoskins, *A Muslim's Mind*, 24.

investigation of Muhammad's life. Thus, Sardar contends that the life of Muhammad, as the perfect exemplar of Islam, "provides us with the best means of understanding the purpose and intentions of the sacred text."[6] If, then, the Ummah understands the Qur'an most clearly as it is explained and applied by Muhammad, the *Sunnah* exhibits a greater influence on the daily life of a Muslim.

The Influence of the *Sunnah*

The introduction to this chapter highlights the fact that the *Sunnah* contains instructions for some of the minutest details of life. Though this is true, one must also consider that some of the most central components of Islamic practice are also shaped and informed by this body of traditional literature. In fact, if one were to excise the teaching of the *Sunnah* from Muslim practice, several of the five central pillars of Islam would be affected.

First, the Islamic confession of faith (Shahadah) does not appear in the Qur'an as such. Though the two phrases—*There is no god but The God* and *Muhammad is his messenger*—are derived from qur'anic teaching, one must consult the *Sunnah* in order to find them connected as the Shahadah by which one commits to Islam.

Second, the daily prayers (*salat*) that make up a second pillar of Islam and impose themselves on the daily rhythms of Muslim life derive their shape not from the Qur'an, but from a story recounted in *Sahih al-Bukhari*.[7] In *Sahih al-Bukhari*, Muhammad is said to have ascended into heaven where he received the command from God that believers must pray fifty times per day. Moses, however, encourages Muhammad to request a reduction in the number of prayers because the people would not be able to bear fifty daily prayers. Muhammad requested such a reduction, and, subsequently, *salat* is only required five times per day.[8]

Third, while the Qur'an calls believers to give of their resources through acts of charity (*zakat*), it gives no explicit instructions as to how much one must give in order to fulfill this requirement. In the *hadith* of *Sunan Abu Dawud*, however, one finds Muhammad instructing his followers to pay *zakat* equal to one-fortieth of their property. This amount—2.5 percent—provides clarity regarding the expectation for completing this pillar of Islam.[9]

Finally, both the Ramadan fast (*sawm*) and the pilgrimage to Mecca (*hajj*) are required by qur'anic mandate, yet both are dependent upon the

---

6. Sardar, *What Do Muslims Believe?*, 50.
7. Hoskins, *A Muslim's Mind*, 24. Hoskins recounts a Muslim friend's statement, "The Qur'an tells us to pray, but it doesn't tell us how. The hadith gives us the details of how to do it."
8. Muhammad Khan, *Summarized Sahih al-Bukhari* (Riyadh, KSA: Darussalam, 1996), 156–58 (§228).
9. Abu Dawud, *Sunan Abu Dawud*, https://sunnah.com/abudawud/9, book 9 (§17).

Sunnah for detail.[10] If one asks whether the Qur'an or the *Sunnah* is more authoritative, the Qur'an presents itself as the answer by virtue of its divine origin. However, the practice of Islam would be ill-defined and unrecognizable without the *Sunnah*. Therefore, the *Sunnah* is the most influential body of literature in Islamic practice.

Summary

In the foreword to Edward Hoskins's book *A Muslim's Mind*, Don McCurry quotes long-time pioneer missionary to Islam Samuel Zwemer as saying, "If you want to know Islam, study the hadith."[11] While there are a few emerging scholars and even practicing Muslims who argue that Islam should be disconnected from the *Sunnah*, the vast majority of the world's Muslims are bound to the *Sunnah* to guide them as they engage in the regular practice of their faith.

According to Seyyed Hossein Nasr, the Qur'an itself anticipates the collection of the *Sunnah* as seen in Qur'an 33:21, which instructs, "Certainly the messenger of God has been a good example for you—for the one who hopes in God and the Last Day, and remembers God often."[12] Therefore, though the Qur'an presents itself as a clear sign, as guidance to humanity, and as a book of remembrance of the ways of God, it also expects that believers will seek to imitate the exemplar of their faith, Muhammad.

Following the varied qur'anic references to Islam's prophet as a model, contemporary Muslims such as Badru Kateregga contend that Muhammad "told the Muslims to follow his instructions in regard to all he received as revelation from Allah. . . . [Muhammad's] life was sanctioned as a model life for all humankind. His explanation of the Qur'an was Divinely sanctioned.[13] Thus, while the Qur'an is viewed as a sign of God's final revelation to humanity, its message requires the *Sunnah*'s interpretation in order for most contemporary Muslims to practice its commands.

---

10. As Qur'an 22:27 states, "And proclaim the pilgrimage among the people. Let them come to you on foot and on every lean animal. They will come from every remote mountain pass." The context suggests that the place of pilgrimage is the Sacred House of Abraham (Ka'ba), though the reader is left wanting for any other details. Cf. Qur'an 2:196–203 and 3:97. A. J. Droge, trans., *The Qur'an: A New Annotated Translation* (Bristol, CT: Equinox, 2015), 216. In footnote 41, Droge states, "The detailed regulations pertaining to the Hajj are not recorded in the Qur'an."

11. Don McCurry, foreword to Hoskins, *A Muslim's Mind*, 11.

12. Seyyed Hossein Nasr, *The Heart of Islam: Enduring Values for Humanity* (New York: HarperOne, 2004), 28. Nasr cites this verse incorrectly, however, so the reader will note that Nasr's volume references Qur'an 32:21.

13. Badru Kateregga and David Shenk, *A Muslim and a Christian in Dialogue* (Scottdale, PA: Herald, 1997), 87.

REFLECTION QUESTIONS

1. Which is believed to be the verbatim record of God's revealed will: the Qur'an or the *Sunnah?*

2. What makes the Qur'an authoritative?

3. What makes the *Sunnah* authoritative?

4. How does the *Sunnah* affect the understanding and practice of the daily prayers (*salat*)?

5. Which one exhibits more influence upon the contemporary practice of Islam: the Qur'an or the *Sunnah?*

What Is Sharia Law?

*Then We placed you on a pathway [Sharia] of the
matter. So follow it, and do not follow the (vain)
desires of those who do not know.*
~Qur'an 45:18

Since the Iranian Revolution of 1979, Islamic law has provided the foundations for civil law in Iran. Likewise, in 1980, under pressure from Islamist
groups such as the Muslim Brotherhood, Egypt adopted a constitutional
amendment that made the principles of Islamic law the basis of legal legislation.[1] In the 1990s, Afghanistan, Pakistan, and Iraq were the focus of Western
news stories as various groups, such as the Taliban, instituted governments
and law based upon Islamic principles.

As a result of these major news stories, the Arabic word used for Islamic
law—Sharia—made its way into Western vocabulary. Due to the fact that
Western exposure to Sharia is often connected to insurgencies and revolutions, however, one might be inclined to connect it disproportionately with
politics and government. In fact, for the average Muslim, the word "Sharia" is
more intimately connected to personal practice of Islam.

According to Islamic law expert Bilal Philips, the word "Sharia" means,
literally, "a waterhole where animals gather daily to drink."[2] In its qur'anic
usage, however, it is used to refer to the straight path upon which God guides

---

1. Geneive Abdo, *No God but God: Egypt and the Triumph of Islam* (New York: Oxford,
2000), 12.
2. Abu Ameenah Bilal Philips, *The Evolution of Fiqh*, 3rd ed. (Riyadh, KSA: International
Islamic Publishing House, 2005), 19.

believers. Thus, before it affects constitutions and public law, Sharia is the means by which one individually lives out the Islamic faith.

Determining Islamic Law

The previous three questions have engaged the two most prominent sources of Islamic law: the Qur'an and the *Sunnah*. However, while one might consider the *Sunnah* to be a commentary or interpretation of the Qur'an, the process of determining Islamic law goes beyond merely consulting the *Sunnah*. Though the *Sunnah* displays Muhammad's exemplary application of the Qur'an's teaching, his example is inextricably bound to his seventh-century life.

Since the *Sunnah* is bound to the times and places in which Muhammad is believed to have lived, modern society has introduced many new conventions that neither the Qur'an nor the *Sunnah* address. Recognizing the difficulties that would be presented by attempting to apply the *Sunnah* directly in changing times and places, early Muslims formed schools of Islamic law and jurisprudence.

Such schools sought to rigorously and consistently apply Sharia in changing environments by developing a science of producing Islamic law, known as *fiqh*. Four major schools of *fiqh* continue to produce Islamic law to this day. However, in order to better understand these schools and the process of determining Islamic law, it is important to first define the terms "Sharia" and *fiqh*.

Sharia

In its strictest sense, the word "Sharia" describes the timeless teaching of the Qur'an and the *Sunnah*. It is a reference to the revealed laws of God that can be derived directly from these two sources of authority. As such, Sharia is fixed and unchanging. It also tends toward general regulation of Islamic life, rather than providing specific and detailed instruction.[3]

Fiqh

Though the material in the Sharia provides the skeleton for Islamic law, the process of *fiqh* clothes the skeleton in flesh. In other words, a ruling produced by the process of *fiqh* will not contradict the Sharia. However, where the Sharia lacks specificity, the process of *fiqh* is designed to bring detailed instruction and clear rulings on how a Muslim might apply Sharia to their own changing environment.

In many ways, the process of *fiqh* could be compared to the Christian concept of contextualization. While Christians maintain that the Bible is the key to understanding the gospel and how one lives in the light of the gospel,

---

3. Philips, *Evolution of Fiqh*, 20.

the process of applying the gospel's teaching to new situations requires contextually appropriate forms. Though the forms may change over time and in
different cultural environs, the message of the gospel remains consistent.

Tools of *Fiqh*

The previous section noted that there are four major Sunni approaches to
the process of *fiqh* that are most influential in contemporary Islamic life. In
addition, two Shiite schools have been recognized within the Ummah. These
six schools were endorsed by the 2005 *Amman Message* that was issued following a summit of Muslims gathered by King Abdullah of Jordan.[4]

While many others have existed and continue to exist within Islamic life,
these six represent the most broadly influential schools in the Islamic world.
Across all schools of Islamic thought, the process of *fiqh* is understood to be
a human endeavor to understand and apply divine guidance. The major disagreement between the schools, then, arises at the point of considering what
tools are appropriate for the task of discerning Islamic law.

Qur'an and Sunnah

As noted above, the Qur'an and the *Sunnah* provide the textual basis for discerning Sharia. However, as Ahmad Atif Ahmad recognizes, "Of its more than
six thousand verses, the Qur'an's legal content is limited to a few hundred verses."[5]
Thus, the Qur'an is rarely the decisive factor in coming to a specific ruling.

As was seen in Questions 8 and 9, the *Sunnah* provides significant material regarding the life and sayings of Muhammad that serve to interpret and
apply the teaching of the Qur'an. Ahmad describes the role of the *Sunnah* in
the process of *fiqh*, saying,

> [The *Sunnah* is] either a source subsequent in power, or, as
> Shafi'ai argues, equal in power to the Qur'an, given that the
> Qur'an is in need of the [*Sunnah*] more than the [*Sunnah*]
> is in need of the Qur'an (in the sense that the [*Sunnah*] pro-
> vides details without which the Qur'an would not convey its
> full meaning).[6]

Together, the Qur'an and *Sunnah* form the universally accepted foundation of
Islamic law for both Sunni and Shiite jurists. Despite this common foundation, Ahmad notes that both are "often silent about situations that demand

---

4. *The Amman Message*, "The Three Points of the Amman Message, V.1," http://ammanmes-
   sage.com/the-three-points-of-the-amman-message-v-1, §1. The *Amman Message* also includes two lesser-known schools associated with *Ibadi* and *Thahiri fiqh*.
5. Ahmad Atif Ahmad, *Islamic Law: Cases, Authorities, and Worldview* (New York:
   Bloomsbury, 2017), 53.
6. Ahmad, *Islamic Law*, 54.

rulings."[7] In response to this silence, then, Islamic jurists offer diverse recommendations for issuing definitive rulings.

Consensus (Ijma')

When the Qur'an and *Sunnah* are silent regarding an issue, the first step for most schools of *fiqh* is to discern whether or not a precedent exists within the consensus (*ijma'*) of the early Islamic community.[8] If the companions of Muhammad (*Sahabah*) provide a conclusion on the matter, it is taken as binding upon the contemporary community. If not, however, further steps are required.

Reasoning (Ijtihad) of the Sahabah and Caliphs

If the companions of Muhammad did not produce consensus on a given issue, the individual opinions of Muhammad's companions (*Sahabah*) are often consulted. Such opinions are viewed as the result of Muhammad training the *Sahabah* in proper reasoning (*ijtihad*).[9]

Analogies (Istihsan) from Prior Rulings

Another tool employed by some schools of *fiqh* is that of analogy (*istihsan*) from prior cases. For example, since the Qur'an prohibits drinking wine, it provides a precedent by analogy for prohibiting other intoxicants.[10] Likewise, some schools use a process of linking (*istishab*) similar cases one to another to establish a precedent in an unprecedented situation.[11]

Reasoning (Qiyas) of Jurists

An additional step in establishing Islamic law is that of deductive reasoning (*qiyas*). Such reasoning is usually reserved for established jurists rather than individual Muslims. Some schools embrace *qiyas*, others reject it for fear of introducing a precedent of innovation.[12]

Welfare (Istislah) of the Community

Another tool employed by some schools of *fiqh* is the determination of a ruling's effect on the general welfare (*istislah*) of the community. While this process is related to reason, its focus is on the contemporary needs of the local community. Philips summarizes one approach to *istislah* when he writes, "Imam Malik also applied the principle of *Istislah* to deduce laws more

---

7. Ahmad, *Islamic Law*, 38.
8. Philips, *Evolution of Fiqh*, 68.
9. Philips, *Evolution of Fiqh*, 63.
10. Philips, *Evolution of Fiqh*, 54–55.
11. Philips, *Evolution of Fiqh*, 124.
12. Ahmad, *Islamic Law*, 55.

in keeping with the needs which arose from current situations than those deduced by *Qiyas*."[13]

Schools (*Madhhab*) of *Fiqh*

Over time, and throughout the Sunni world, four distinct schools (*madhhab*) of *fiqh* emerged. While they agree upon the essentials, the specific tools with which they produce rulings vary. Likewise, Shiite *fiqh* is divided into two main schools that similarly agree upon the essentials while differing in what components of the *Sunnah* and sources of later jurisprudence are acceptable and authoritative. Without delving deeply into the details, the following section will inspect the differences between the four major *madhhabs* of the Sunnis.

Hanifite Madhhab

The first *madhhab* that formed is named for its founder, Abu Hanifa (c. 699–767 CE).[14] Abu Hanifa began his career in academics as a student of philosophy and dialectics, but eventually transitioned into the study of *fiqh*.[15] In a fashion that is distinct from other *madhhabs*, the school of Abu Hanifa holds analogical deduction to be a valuable tool in establishing binding rule.

While other schools appeal to the consensus and reasoning of the *Sahabah*, Hanifa and his followers produce their own reasoning and hold it to be equally as binding as that of the *Sahabah*.[16] Students in his school regularly participate in group discussions of real and hypothetical situations. As Philips contends, "Because of this interactive approach to making legal rulings, we could say that the Hanafi [*madhhab*] was as much a product of [Abu Hanifa's] students' efforts as it was a product of his own efforts."[17] As such, Hanifites tend to be more flexible than others.

Malkite Madhhab

Perhaps the most dominant of Sunni *madhhabs*, the Malkite school derives its name from Malik ibn Anas (c. 710–796 CE).[18] This *madhhab* distinguishes its approach from others by its willingness to include appeal to the known customs (*istislah*) of the people of seventh-century Medina and to social customs prevalent throughout the Muslim world.[19]

---

13. Philips, *Evolution of Fiqh*, 111.
14. Bernard Lewis, *Islam* (Upper Saddle River, NJ: Wharton School Publishing, 2009), 30.
15. Philips, *Evolution of Fiqh*, 101.
16. Philips, *Evolution of Fiqh*, 104.
17. Philips, *Evolution of Fiqh*, 102.
18. Lewis, *Islam*, 30.
19. Philips, *Evolution of Fiqh*, 110–11.

For the Malkite *madhhab*, individual rulings are inherently more contextual than universal.[20] As such, Malkites exhibit flexibility in the formation and application of Islamic law. However, Malkites are less optimistic than Hanafis about the ability of contemporary *ijtihad* to produce accurate and authoritative rulings.

Shafi'ite Madhhab

The Shafi'ite *madhhab* emerges from the teaching of Abu Abdallah Muhammad ash-Shafi'i (c. 767–820 CE).[21] Shafi'ite thought also exerts significant influence over the Ummah, having taken root in southern Arabia, Egypt, and stretching into central and southeastern Asia.

The distinguishing feature of the Shafi'ite approach is the rejection of the Malkite and Hanafite use of reasoning by analogy or deductive reasoning. Ash-Shafi'i saw these tools as being predicated upon inherently weak human logic and intuition, and therefore inadmissible in the process of *fiqh*.

Confronting the problem of applying seventh-century teaching in changing environments, however, Shafi'ites follow a pattern of linking contemporary circumstances with earlier ones. As Philips summarizes, "*Fiqh* laws [are] applicable to certain conditions [and] remain valid so long as it is not certain that these conditions have altered."[22] In other words, if nothing is known to have changed fundamentally, then former rulings remain in force, and one should not utilize contemporary circumstances to alter prior law.

Hanbalite Madhhab

Finally, Ahmad ibn Hanbal (c. 780–855 CE) is credited with being the founder of the fourth Sunni *madhhab*.[23] This school is known for rejecting the use of the more dynamic tools of *fiqh* such as independent reasoning. In an attempt to remove human imposition on the process of issuing Islamic law, Hanbal went so far as to prohibit his followers from committing his rulings to writing if they were formed by appealing to his own *qiyas*.[24]

As noted by William Montgomery Watt, "[the Hanbali *madhhab*] had a distinctive anti-rationalist position in theology."[25] This *madhhab* has proved especially influential in Saudi Arabia, as the revivalist movement known as Wahhabism emerged from a student of the Hanbali *madhhab*.[26] Hanbalis typically espouse the most conservative and literal theology and practice.

---

20. Philips, *Evolution of Fiqh*, 108–9.
21. Lewis, *Islam*, 31.
22. Philips, *Evolution of Fiqh*, 124.
23. Lewis, *Islam*, 31.
24. Philips, *Evolution of Fiqh*, 126.
25. William Montgomery Watt, *Islam: A Short History* (London: Oneworld, 2015), 89.
26. Philips, *Evolution of Fiqh*, 128–29.

Summary

The process of discerning and contextualizing Sharia requires much more involved discussion than can be treated here. However, this question has sought to highlight some of the key differences in how Islamic jurists go about the task of determining and applying historical Islamic teaching and precedent to contemporary situations. The task of *fiqh* is shaped by one's *madhhab* and the tools that are considered appropriate for use in forming Islamic law.

While the word "Sharia" has come into Western parlance through coups, revolutions, and insurrections, it should not be understood to attach to violence. Rather, Sharia is simply the rule of law that is derived from Islamic sources. Since Islam is an all-encompassing system of faith, the application of Islamic law transcends personal piety and imposes itself upon the expectations of government, commerce, and society at large. Thus, when a country bases its laws upon Sharia, the whole of the society feels the impact.

REFLECTION QUESTIONS

1. What does the word "Sharia" mean?

2. What makes the *Sunnah* insufficient to determine contemporary Islamic law on its own?

3. What are the sources used in determining Islamic law?

4. What are the four major Sunni *madhhabs*?

5. What sources of authority are universal to all Sunni *madhhabs*?

What Is the Role of the Clerics?

Does the man who lifts his head before
the Imam not fear that Allah may change
his face into that of an ass?
~Sahih Muslim[1]

Having lived for several years in both Jordan and Egypt, I have had countless discussions with Muslims regarding issues of faith. Many of these conversations concluded with my Muslim friends appealing to the fact that they are untrained in Islamic theology. Often, upon reaching a theological impasse, my friends would conclude, "I'm not an expert. We would need to speak with an imam to know how to answer that question."

Such a response demonstrates the fact that a local mosque leader (imam) provides expertise and guidance to a community that goes beyond that of a typical layperson. In addition to expertise, the *hadith* quoted at the beginning of this chapter shows that the imam is to be respected as a leader within the local community. As a respected expert, then, a local imam often exerts significant influence within his community.

However, influence is not to be confused with authority. Technically and theologically, there is no authoritative hierarchy within Islam.[2] Yet, as the previous question demonstrates, scholars, judges, and modern governments do produce official rulings regarding specific cases and issues. This chapter will briefly address the relationship between the authority and

---

1. Muslim, *Sahih Muslim*, https://sunnah.com/muslim/4/126, book 4 (§126).
2. Seyyed Hossein Nasr, *The Heart of Islam: Enduring Values for Humanity* (New York: HarperOne, 2004), 85.

influence of the Islamic scholars ('ulama), the judges (qadi), the imams, and the local mosques.

The Authority of the Islamic Scholars ('Ulama)

In attempting to trace the line of authority from Allah and his Sharia to the average Muslim, it is important to consider the role of the scholars of Islam ('ulama) prior to addressing a particular mosque or imam. While there is no theological hierarchy within the Islamic faith and practice, those who have memorized the Qur'an, trained in Islamic law, and been credentialed as judges wield an added measure of influence over the rulings on particular cases and questions in a given community. The most influential source for such training and credentialing for Sunni Muslims is Al-Azhar University in Cairo, Egypt.

For Sunnis, Al-Azhar provides expertise on matters of Islamic law, practice, and faith. The university extends its influence throughout the Ummah by training and sending imams around the world. Additionally, Al-Azhar has commissioned many branch schools throughout Egypt and the region in which children are trained by the university's graduates and scholars. Al-Azhar's impact on the Ummah has increased dramatically over the last century, though it has been operating since 975 CE.[3] Under Al-Azhar's broad umbrella, scholars from each of the four major Sunni *madhhabs* train imams, future scholars, and judges in Islamic law and theology.

In her book *Islamic Reform and Conservatism*, Indira Gesink argues that the increased access to Islamic literature, along with the modernist reforms of the nineteenth century, have allowed Al-Azhar to play a significant role in shifting the Sunni world toward independent, individual interpretation of the Qur'an for purposes of personal piety.[4] Yet the task of Islamic jurisprudence and religious ruling remains the responsibility of trained scholars. Such scholars exert influence through the imams and *qadis* they train.

The Authority of the Imam and the *Qadi*

The twentieth-century reforms of Al-Azhar mentioned above have been referred to as the "Protestantization of [Sunni] Islam."[5] As the Reformation dismantled the priestly hierarchy for Protestant Christians, so too the reforms at Al-Azhar have encouraged lay Muslims to look to the sources of their faith for themselves. Yet in the same way as a Protestant pastor is usually viewed as a more highly educated and discerning interpreter of the Bible and Christian theology than a layperson, so too are imams expected to speak with greater

---

3. Indira Gesink, *Islamic Reform and Conservatism: Al-Azhar and the Evolution of Modern Sunni Islam* (New York: I. B. Tauris, 2014), 2.
4. Gesink, *Islamic Reform and Conservatism*, 233.
5. Gesink, *Islamic Reform and Conservatism*, 228.

precision on matters of theology and practice. Thus, the imam holds a position of honor, prestige, and influence within the mosque.

The Imam

Technically, the word "imam" in Arabic simply means "one who stands in front." Throughout the *Sunnah*, this word is used to refer to the person who stands in front of the gathered believers and leads the daily prayers. However, in common Sunni parlance it has come to mean the recognized leader of a mosque.[6] Usually, one who assumes the title "imam" has been educated in Islamic theology and has received an endorsement from the recognized faculty of the *'ulama* (the body of recognized Islamic scholars) commissioning the person to serve as a teacher of Islam.

The Imam and the Friday Sermon

Once an imam has been endorsed and has taken a position in a mosque, that person is then typically responsible for the job of leading prayers and teaching the Friday sermon (*khutba*). While imams influence members of the community throughout the week by providing counsel and religious teaching, the *khutba* offers a significant platform from which to impact the community. The *khutba* provides the weekly medium for an individual imam's theology and teaching to reach the community.

The Imam as Officiate

Though the *khutba* is the most theological and interpretive of the tasks that are performed by the imam, the influence that an imam has in the lives of the people of the community is not limited to teaching. In Islamic practice, the imam is also expected to officiate and preside over various moments in people's lives. He is often responsible for reciting blessings over newly born children, presiding over the signing of marriage contracts, and overseeing Muslim funerals. Furthermore, the imam is often called upon to give counseling and advice or to answer religious and theological inquiries. Having such a role in these important moments in the community's life allows the imam to have a significant impact on the community at large.

The Qadi

If a lay Muslim has a question about a specific point of Islamic theology or practice, the imam is often the first person to be consulted. In most scenarios,

---

6. For Shiite Muslims, the word "imam" is reserved for 'Ali and his direct, male descendants. See Alexander Knysh, "Multiple Areas of Influence," in *CCQ*, ed. Jane Dammen McAuliffe (New York: Cambridge University Press, 2006), 221. Knysh writes that Shiites view their imams as "the only authentic interpreters of the qur'anic message by virtue of a divinely inspired and infallible knowledge granted to them by God."

the imam's word is sufficient to guide the individual to an answer. However, when more complicated issues arise—or when a dispute between Muslims requires legal intervention—the imam may refer the case to a judge (*qadi*) in an Islamic court who serves as an expert in Islamic law.

The Qadi *and the* Mufti *in Consultation*

The *qadi* will often work in consultation with another scholar of Islamic law called a *mufti* to determine how to rule in a particular case.[7] Though similar in many ways, the main difference between these two offices is that the *qadi* is a position that is to remain independent of the state, while the *mufti* is often an employee and consult of the state. In a process that is similar to secular jurisprudence, the *qadi* and the *mufti* sift through Islamic legal history to determine whether or not precedent exists for the case at hand. Having determined applicable precedent, the *qadi* interprets the contemporary case and issues a ruling that is to be enforced as Sharia.[8]

The Qadi *and the State*

Throughout much of Islamic history, the *qadi* and *mufti* have functioned independently from the national government. In other words, to protect their integrity as unbiased rulers, the *qadi* and the *mufti* traditionally refused to take posts within the state legal system. While distance from state governments provides harbor from accusations of complicity with national interests, it also causes difficulty in enforcing the rulings produced in the Islamic courts.

In light of this difficulty, Bernard Lewis and Buntzie Churchill recognize, "the *qadi*, in order to make his judgments enforceable, had to have the state authority behind him, and in due course, he and his court of law became part of the state apparatus."[9] In countries that have incorporated Islamic law into their very constitutions—such as Saudi Arabia, Iran, Pakistan, Malaysia, and Egypt—such a conflation of Islamic law and the legal arm of the state has become prevalent.

In such countries, then, state authority has come to provide legal enforcement of the *fiqh* of the *'ulama* through the specific decisions reached by the *qadi* and the *mufti*. By training under the *'ulama*, and through access to referral of cases to the *qadi* and *mufti*, some of this authority extends to the imam and the local mosque. Theoretically, the Ummah remains a theologically egalitarian community. Yet, in practice, the influence of experts and the incursion of state powers give the impression of an authoritative hierarchy. It remains to consider what influence a local mosque bears on a Muslim's life.

---

7. Bernard Lewis and Buntzie Churchill, *Islam: The Religion and the People* (Upper Saddle River, NJ: Wharton, 2009), 45.
8. Lewis and Churchill, *Islam*, 45.
9. Lewis and Churchill, *Islam*, 45.

The Authority of the Mosque

For a Christian learning about Islam, it is easy to assume that the mosque is the Islamic equivalent to the church. Since a mosque is a place in which Muslims gather to worship and pray, Christians accustomed to equating the church building with the church itself are quick to make such a comparison. In the sense that the mosque is a gathering place for prayer and worship, then, it can be equated to a church building.

However, Christian churches usually recognize the importance of some form of formal membership within a local church that allows one to speak of the church as something more than merely the building, but as a covenanted community that exists both in a gathered and a scattered state.[10] Muslims, on the other hand, are more inclined to view themselves simply as members of the universal Ummah over and against being members of a particular place of prayer.[11] The mosque, then, is a place of worship, but it is not a way to refer to the people who worship there.

The Mosque

The word "mosque" itself is an Anglicized form of the Arabic word *masjid*, which simply means a place of prostration for prayer. As the etymology suggests, theologically speaking, a local mosque is merely a practical reality that expresses a localized part of the global Ummah. As such, most mosques do not keep records of members.

Lacking a concept of mosque membership, an individual Muslim is free to pray at any mosque for any of the daily prayers. Likewise, a Muslim may attend the Friday *khutba* at any mosque in order to hear a particular imam who teaches from a particular *madhhab*, political persuasion, or some other preferred feature.

Since an individual Muslim may attend any mosque at any time, the local mosque does not exercise significant authority over its attendees. If multiple mosques exist in an area, a believer can simply attend a different mosque without any penalty or ill will. Thus, apart from formal legal cases referred to the courts by an imam, the mosque commands little authority.

The Center of the Community

Where the mosque does exhibit its influence, however, is through its role as an informal community center. In rural areas, a local mosque can serve as a de

---

10. For more discussion on the idea of the church gathered as an institution and the church scattered as an organism, see the work of Abraham Kuyper, *Rooted and Grounded* (Grand Rapids: Christian Library, 2013).

11. This is not the place for a treatment of the Christian doctrine of the church. However, it will suffice to say that biblical teaching on the local church does not have much to say about the location at which the church gathers. Rather, the Bible is far more concerned with the commitment of believers to be the church in covenant with one another.

facto city hall where the imam and the local government will confer in the process of determining justice and local laws. Likewise, the pulpit of the mosque often provides a platform for civic and political announcements and news.[12]

In more urban settings, mosques can function as political and ideological centers. For example, in Alexandria, Egypt, during the tumultuous years after Hosni Mubarak was ousted from power, one downtown mosque was known for endorsing the Muslim Brotherhood and their ideals. In contrast, a mosque that supported the state was located near the military hospital. On Fridays, after hearing respectively partisan *khutbas*, large groups would rally outside of these two mosques and march toward one another in protest of the opposition.

Summary

Neither the imams nor the learned scholars of the *'ulama* are supposed to have any ultimate theological authority over the individual Muslim. Yet both play formative roles in Islamic theology and practice. Such formation is exhibited most clearly through the imam's teaching in the local mosque, which is itself an extension of the *'ulama* by whom he was trained.

However, when it comes to legal affairs, the Islamic courts—particularly those embedded within the judicial system of the state—do produce binding rulings based upon their interpretation of Sharia. Thus, practically speaking, the *qadi* and the *mufti* serve within the Ummah as the closest version of authoritative clerics who determine and enforce Sharia.[13]

REFLECTION QUESTIONS

1. What is an imam, and how does the imam function in the mosque?

2. What is a *qadi*, and what role do they play in establishing Islamic law rulings?

3. What is the process for determining Islamic ruling on contemporary issues?

4. What does it mean to say that the twentieth-century Al-Azhar reforms contributed to the "Protestantization of Islam"?

5. What are the functions of a mosque in the religious and social life of a Muslim community?

---

12. Lewis and Churchill, *Islam*, 43.
13. Lewis and Churchill, *Islam*, 46. Using Iran as a Shiite example of such clerical authority, Lewis and Churchill loosely compare the Ayatollahs to the Catholic College of Cardinals, and the Supreme Guide to the Pope.

What Is the Role of the Family?

> *Men are supervisors of women because God has*
> *favored some of them over others, and because they*
> *have contributed from the wealth. Righteous women*
> *are obedient, watching over (affairs) in the absence (of*
> *their husbands) because God has watched over (them).*
> *(As for) those women whom you fear may be rebel-*
> *lious: admonish them, avoid them in bed, and (finally)*
> *strike them. If they obey you, do not seek (any further)*
> *way against them. Surely God is most high, great.*
> *~Qur'an 4:34*

The previous five questions have focused on various sources of authority within Islam. From sacred writ to the authorized interpreters thereof, this section has focused on how authority works practically in Islamic society. Thus, it behooves us to conclude this section by addressing the most practical and immediate ramifications of Islamic law: the family unit.

As Maria Curtis writes, "Because Islam is a religion that places so much emphasis on community, the family is often at the center of Islamic law."[1] Not only does Islamic law provide specific instructions as to how one's family is to function, but it endows certain members with immediate authority within the family. As with other questions, however, it will prove helpful to consider both authority and influence as we investigate the Islamic family structure.

---

1. Maria Curtis, "*Fiqh*, the Science of Islamic Jurisprudence," in *The Bloomsbury Companion to Islamic Studies*, ed. Clinton Bennett (New York: Bloomsbury, 2015), 218.

A Plea for Charity

As a disclaimer at the beginning of this chapter, I want to admit my reticence to include the verse quoted above. Uncharitable uses of this verse by non-Muslims have at times maligned the Muslim family, painting every Muslim husband as an abusive authoritarian and every Muslim wife as his helpless servant.[2] While one might find heart-wrenching examples that reinforce such a picture, it is certainly not the case that all Muslim husbands avail themselves of this qur'anic injunction to employ corporal punishment.[3]

At the same time, the Qur'an unequivocally invests husbands with such authority within their household.[4] Such authority indelibly shapes the Muslim home. Therefore, if we are intent on considering the authority structures within Islam, we must attend to the injunctions that reinforce patriarchal authority. As we proceed, however, a charitable posture requires us to recognize that the details of how a particular Muslim husband exercises this authority are likely as varied as the number of Muslim families in the world. Painting the details of individual Muslim households with a broad brush is unfair, so we proceed with caution.

The Authority of Husbands

The verse cited above provides the reader with the most basic understanding of male authority in the Islamic household. The Muslim husband is to be the head of the family, and as such he is invested with the authority to lead, direct, and enforce his directives—even to the extent of physical punishment. Early Muslim commentators along with many contemporary Muslim writers living in Western countries contend that such authority is an irrevocable qur'anic injunction.

As an example, the early sixteenth-century commentary *Tafsir al-Jalalayn* records the following regarding the understanding of Qur'an 4:34–35:

> Men are in charge of [and] they have authority over women
> disciplining them and keeping them in check because of that

---

2. Nabeel Qureshi is an example of a former Muslim who maintained a laudably loving attitude toward his family and upbringing. I highly recommend his autobiographical narrative of his conversion from Islam to Christ. Nabeel Qureshi, *Seeking Allah, Finding Jesus*, 2nd ed. (Grand Rapids: Zondervan, 2018).
3. The desire to be fair and charitable as an outsider has driven me to paint as positive a picture of these relationships as possible. At the same time, I recognize that many Muslim women have undergone abuse—physical and otherwise—by their Muslim husbands who cite this verse as permission. The charitable posture I seek to take should not be understood to downplay the real and pervasive trauma that many Muslim women do face as a result.
4. Nicholas Awde, ed. and trans., *Women in Islam: An Anthology from the Qur'an and Hadiths* (New York: Hippocrene, 2005), 204. In reference to Qur'an 4:34–35, Awde comments, "Despite the existence of hadiths contrary to this, since there is no counter provided in the Qur'an, there is a strong argument that one is bound [to] take the beating of one's wife under these conditions as law."

with which God has preferred the one over the other that is because God has given them the advantage over women in knowledge, reason, authority, and otherwise and because of what they expend on them the women of their property.[5]

Seeking rationale for the investment of authority in husbands, early writers such as these often appeal to what was prevailing opinion in the Arab world: that men have intellectual and physical advantages over women.

In contemporary Western society, however, Muslims often find themselves fighting against the current of popular, egalitarian opinion. Daniel Haqiqatjou addresses the difference between Islamic hierarchy and contemporary society in Canada, writing,

> The authority aspect . . . has been de-emphasized or outright erased in modernist discourse because it contravenes feminist standards of "equality." How can one sex be in authority over another? Male authority does not align with gender egalitarianism, so, some surmise, it must be a relic of more barbaric times. But this is the clear meaning of the Divine Address, the Final Message to humanity meant to apply to all humanity at all times until the Last Day.[6]

Haqiqatjou goes on to say, "Based on the clear message of the [Qur'an] and [Sunnah], all exegetes and all jurists without exception have recognized and continue to recognize that one of the central rights of the husband is obedience."[7] In other words, while contemporary Muslim writers are less inclined to appeal to male intellectual superiority as rationale for such authority, the teaching of the Qur'an remains binding.

Positively, the authority that a husband wields in the home is connected to his role as the figurehead and protector of the family's honor. Edward Hoskins helpfully explains this role in terms of how Muslim collectivism differs from typical Western individualism, writing,

> Muslims tend to see people, and women in particular, not as separate individuals but as members of a larger group. As a rule, societal rights of the larger group are not voluntarily sacrificed in favor of a single member. Additionally, one of

---

5. Feras Hamza, trans., *Tafsir al-Jalalayn* (Qur'an 4:34), https://www.altafsir.com/Tafasir.asp?tMadhNo=0&tTafsirNo=74&tSoraNo=4&tAyahNo=34&tDisplay=yes&UserProfile=0&LanguageId=2.
6. Daniel Haqiqatjou, "The Authority of Man in the Muslim Family," in *Muslims in Calgary*, July 19, 2018, http://muslimsincalgary.ca/the-authority-of-man-in-the-muslim-family.
7. Haqiqatjou, "Authority of Man."

the most important commodities in this culture is honor. Anything that adds honor to a family is highly valued. Female modesty and morality also rank near the top of the list.[8]

Thus, the husband's leadership is not necessarily intended to institute him as an authoritarian, but to establish him as the one who will guard the reputation of the family. Since he is responsible for the family name, he is also invested with authority to ensure its protection.[9]

The Rights of Wives

While men are given the authority in the Muslim home, women are not left without rights in Islam. Ibn Majah records Muhammad instructing his followers to be good to their wives because they are helpers to their husbands. He includes a *hadith* that quotes Muhammad as saying, "I command you to be good to women because they are your helpers. You have a right over your women and they have rights from you."[10]

These rights appear more explicitly in *Sunan Abu Dawud*, where Muhammad is asked to list the rights that wives can demand from their husbands. Abu Dawud records Muhammad responding, "Feed her when you eat and clothe her when you are clothed and don't hit her in the face. Don't disgrace her or separate yourself from her except in your house."[11] Therefore, while the husband is the protector of family honor, he is also to uphold his wife's individual honor and to keep her from disgrace. Thus, it would be an unfair caricature of Islamic society to claim that women have no rights at all. Women are to be viewed as honorable, and it is a husband's duty to guard his wife's reputation and provide for her needs.

Furthermore, many Muslim women enjoy significantly more rights today than were available to their forebears. Cathy Hine notes that "increased literacy, greater access to education, more opportunities to participate in employment, and access to technology and information have all contributed to creating change for women."[12] While it is true that women are enjoying higher rates of education and employment in Arab countries, much of this is occurring prior to marriage. When a Muslim woman gets married, her husband has the right to end her schooling or working outside of the home if he deems it inappropriate.

---

8. Edward Hoskins, *A Muslim's Mind: What Every Christian Needs to Know about the Islamic Traditions* (Colorado Springs: Dawson, 2011), 73.

9. Bill Musk, *Touching the Soul of Islam* (Crowborough, UK: MARC, 1995), 29.

10. *Sunan ibn Majah*, vol. 3 (§1851). As cited in Hoskins, *A Muslim's Mind*, 83–84.

11. *Sunan Abu Dawud*, vol. 2, book 11 (§2137). As cited in Hoskins, *A Muslim's Mind*, 84.

12. Cathy Hine, "Negotiating from the Margins: Women's Voices (Re)Imagining Islam," in *Dynamics of Muslim Worlds: Regional Theological, and Missiological Perspectives*, ed. Evelyn Reisacher (Downers Grove, IL: IVP Academic, 2017), 114.

In Muslim-majority countries like Jordan and Egypt, a high percentage of the women living in major cities complete their college education and find meaningful jobs where their contributions are appreciated by their employers. However, in rural communities, education and literacy among women drops off drastically. While the nature of rural work and a lessened emphasis upon education in rural communities contribute to this trend, such disparity often revolves around the age at which women are married. For many women living in rural settings, marriage interrupts their school years and their husbands decide that their time is best spent in the home rather than completing their education.

Influence in the Muslim Family

Having sketched a basic picture of the authority structures in the Muslim home, it is helpful to conclude our discussion by considering the influence that husbands and wives have on their family in daily matters. Husbands are invested with authority, and often make the big decisions pertaining to employment, education, and marriage. Wives, however, are often much more influential in shaping the atmosphere in the household.

This influence can be particularly acute in regard to the children's religious exposure. The husband fulfills the role of the representative of the family in the community and the mosque. Thus, the husband's public piety determines the religious reputation of the family. However, women are often much more directly involved in the development of their young children's faith.

In Islamic societies, most often a husband is occupied outside of the home, while his wife is responsible for maintaining the home and rearing the children.[13] As such, mothers usually have much more consistent, direct contact with their children during the early years. Naturally, then, a mother's daily example of personal piety and her informal instruction in matters of faith influence the development of her children.

In a book on raising Muslim children, Tahera Kassamali confirms the parental role in religious instruction, writing, "Providing the right type of training is the primary duty of the parents. Every child needs to be taught the right things, for he is not born with that awareness."[14] Thus, it is the duty of Muslim parents to instruct their children directly on matters of faith.

Kassamali goes on to say that, despite later exposure to the mosque, the most influential religious training comes through the home. As such, observing the faith of his or her mother provides a lens through which a child views the world. Kassamali summarizes this point, writing, "The mother plays an important part in introducing him to the world. . . . His attitude, his views—religious

---

13. See Musk, *Touching the Soul of Islam*, 24.
14. Tahera Kassamali, *Raising Children* (Richmond, BC: Tayyiba, 1998), https://www.al-islam.org/print/book/export/html/40470.

or otherwise—his perspective on life and its goals, will all be gained from her."[15] Since mothers are responsible for the home and child rearing, then, the influence that they have on the upbringing, faith, and environment in which their children grow can be greater than that of a Muslim father.

Summary

Much more remains to be said about the relationship between men and women in Islam. In an effort to expand on these issues, Question 34 will ask whether or not Islam is inherently misogynistic. However, the preceding treatment is sufficient for investigating layers of authority and influence in the Muslim family.

As seen above, Muslim husbands bear the responsibility of providing for their family, representing them in the community, and protecting the honor of the family.[16] In light of these responsibilities, the Qur'an grants a husband total authority—including corporal punishment—within the family. Most often, this patriarchal authority is exhibited through making the decisions that shape the direction of the family and its members—decisions regarding education, work, and marriage.

Muslim wives are not afforded such authority. However, they are tasked with rearing children and maintaining the home. Thus, wives often determine the shape and environment of the household. In doing so, despite a lack of authority, women exert significant influence in the Muslim family.

REFLECTION QUESTIONS

1. Why does Islam focus so much on the family?

2. What rights and responsibilities do the Qur'an and *Sunnah* assign to husbands regarding their family?

3. What rights and responsibilities do the Qur'an and *Sunnah* assign to wives regarding their family?

4. What are some potential reasons for endowing husbands with the right to expect their wives to obey them?

5. What are some of the tensions between traditional Islamic family structure and contemporary Western egalitarian expectations?

---

15. Kassamali, *Raising Children*.
16. Musk, *Touching the Soul of Islam*, 25.

PART 3

The Theology of Islam

What Are the Five Pillars of Islam?

Islam is based upon five (pillars/principles).
~Muhammad (Hadith of al-Bukhari)[1]

At times scholars of religion have described Christianity as a faith that is focused on orthodoxy, while Islam is concerned with orthopraxy.[2] While it is true that following Islam requires a believer to perform a set of five perfunctory practices, saying that Islam is merely concerned with orthopraxy is painting with too broad a brush. While this current question focuses on Islamic practice, it should be considered in tandem with the following question that investigates the essentials of Islamic belief.

Despite the fact that this book has labored to demonstrate the impropriety of discussing Islam as if it were monolithic, this chapter and the next comprise what is considered to be the most universal description of Islamic faith and practice. As indicated by the *hadith* cited above, Islam is based upon Five Pillars of practice. In addition to these five practices, however, Muslims are committed to the Six Articles of Faith that will be the subject of the following chapter.

The Five Pillars serve to remind Muslims throughout the rhythms of their daily lives that they are to live in submission to God. These pillars are not found listed in the Qur'an as such. However, the *Sunnah* provides the details and description that the Qur'an lacks in order to guide the faithful toward the proper fulfillment of each pillar.

---

1. Muhammad Khan, trans., *Summarized Sahih al-Bukhari* (Riyadh, KSA: Darussalam, 1996), 59 (§8).
2. John Esposito, *Islam: The Straight Path*, 4th ed. (New York: Oxford University Press, 2011), 85.

Islamic Confession (Shahadah)

The first pillar of Islam is the confession of faith (Shahadah), which every Muslim must recite. This confession consists of two distinct claims, both of which are essential components in the process of becoming a Muslim. The first part pertains to the God of Islam, while the second identifies his final messenger.

In Arabic, the confession is "*La ilaha illa Allah, wa Muhammad ar-rasul Allah.*" Translated into English, the confessor testifies, "There is no god but The God, and Muhammad is his messenger." This phrase is ubiquitous throughout the Muslim world. It is part of the public announcement heard five times per day as an announcer (*muezzin*) calls the faithful to prayer. In modern majority-Muslim societies, this call is amplified by loudspeakers, and can be heard for miles around. It is a phrase that binds the community together in their shared confession while also summoning them to put their faith into practice.

On an individual level, the Shahadah also plays an important role as part of the initiation rite into the community of believers. In places like Egypt, it is tradition for the patriarch of the family to recite the Shahadah into the ear of every baby born into the family. This practice seeks to ensure that the first statement the child hears outside of the womb is the testimony of Islamic faith.

Likewise, personal confession of the Shahadah is the rite by which a new Muslim officially enters the Ummah. In most cases, even when a new Muslim speaks another language, the confession is made in Arabic in order to adhere directly to the traditional version recorded in the *hadith*.[3] Beyond this initiation, Muslims will often display the Shahadah in their homes, places of business, or on their cars in decorative Arabic calligraphy. It is a defining statement.

Five Daily Prayers (*Salat*)

The second pillar of Islam is the observation of five daily prayers (*salat*). As noted above, five times per day the Shahadah is recited as part of the public call to gather for prayer (*adhan*). Shortly after the *adhan*, a second announcement (*iqama*) signals the beginning of the prayers.[4] Muslims are to perform the compulsory prayers, preferably in the mosque, sometime before the next call to prayer. In the Middle East this often results in shops closing for fifteen minutes to an hour in the middle of the workday. Some regularly gather in a local mosque while others will find a corner or a back office in which to perform their prayers.

The exact timing of each of the prayers depends upon the position of the sun, thus they change throughout the year and according to where one resides

---

3. The traditional source of the Five Pillars comes from al-Bukhari's volume of *hadith*. It is cited at the beginning of this chapter.
4. Khan, *Sahih al-Bukhari*, 215–16 (§371).

on the globe. However, the general times of day that these prayers occur are just before sunrise (*fajr*), noon (*dhuhr*), afternoon (*'asr*), at sunset (*maghrib*), and at night (*isha'a*).[5]

Prior to performing the prayers, faithful Muslims perform a ritual washing (*wudu*). Water is provided at the mosque, usually in a separate room with multiple spigots so as to accommodate many worshipers at once. The ritual involves pouring water over the hands and forearms, feet and ankles, in the mouth and nose, and over the head.[6] Symbolically, this cleanses the Muslim prior to voicing prayers to God.

These prayers are different than what Christians think of when hearing the word "prayer." The prayers are not petitions or supplications. Rather, each prayer consists of a certain number of ritualized motions (*rakat*) and a scripted prayer including citations from the Qur'an.[7]

Instead of viewing these prayers as cold, lifeless habits, Seyyed Hossein Nasr highlights the spiritual rejuvenation they provide for those who view them correctly:

> The life of the practicing Muslim is punctuated ever anew by the daily prayers, which break the hold of profane time upon the soul and bring men and women back to a sacred time. . . . The prayers are a rejuvenation for the soul, protection against evil acts, and a shelter for believers amid the storm of the life of this world.[8]

Seen in this light, these ritualized prayers serve an admirable and noble purpose through this regular interruption of the mundane with a reminder of the divine.

Ramadan Fasting (*Sawm*)

The third pillar of Islam is keeping the fast of Ramadan. Annually, for a period of thirty days, Muslims disrupt their daily rhythms by fasting from sunrise to sunset during a month called Ramadan. This fast consists of abstaining from food, drink, tobacco, and sexual relations for thirty days each year. Families will wake and gather before the sunrise to feast for the day. Then, each night, families, neighborhoods, and communities gather together to celebrate the breaking of the fast (*iftar*) at sunset. In the places I have lived,

---

5. Clinton Bennett, ed., *The Bloomsbury Companion to Islamic Studies* (New York: Bloomsbury Academic, 2015), 363.
6. Khan, *Sahih al-Bukhari*, 116 (§128).
7. This is not to say that Muslims do not pray in spontaneous, unscripted fashion. The word for this type of petition to God in Islam is *du'a*, but it is unrelated to the *salat*.
8. Seyyed Hossein Nasr, *The Heart of Islam: Enduring Values for Humanity* (New York: HarperCollins, 2004), 131–32.

the atmosphere during the *iftar* is festive, welcoming, and hospitable for Muslims and non-Muslims alike.

The reason this month is remembered is that Ramadan is the month during which Muhammad began receiving the Qur'an. In addition to the heightened spirituality of the month as a whole, the last ten days of Ramadan are intensely spiritual as many Muslims remain in the mosque for extended prayers throughout the night. These ten days are believed to include one night known as the Night of Power (*Laylat al-Qadr*) on which God pours out additional blessings, forgives sins in abundance, and is extraordinarily inclined to answer one's prayers.[9]

Almsgiving (*Zakat*)

Usually practiced in abundance during the month of Ramadan, the fourth pillar of Islam involves acts of charity (*zakat*). In Islam it is customary that one should give two and a half percent of one's wages throughout the year.[10] This money can be given to the mosque, to Islamic charities, or directly to the poor.

The *zakat* is viewed as an opportunity for Muslims to recognize that their wealth ultimately belongs to God. Furthermore, *zakat* reminds believers of their duty to care for the less fortunate within the Ummah.[11] The Qur'an reminds believers of this duty to steward what God has given them in Qur'an 2:267, which states, "You who believe! Contribute from the good things you have earned, and from what We have provided for you from the earth."

During Ramadan especially, increased numbers of beggars tend to congregate in Muslim cities so as to avail themselves of people's charity. Begging is often considered a reciprocal act whereby the needy are cared for and the faithful are able to fulfill their duties during a month of additional merit.[12] Qur'an 2:271 speaks of the rewards of giving, promising, "If you make freewill offerings publicly, that is excellent, but if you hide it and give it to the poor, that is better for you, and will absolve you of some of your evil deeds. God is aware of what you do."

Another common time for increased almsgiving is approximately seventy days after the end of Ramadan, during the Feast of the Sacrifice (Eid al-Adha). This festival will be the subject of Question 29, "Who is Abraham in the Qur'an?" However, it is pertinent to mention at this point that the meat of the sacrificial animals is divided into quarters and distributed to family members, neighbors, and the poor as an act of charity.

---

9. Carole Hillenbrand, *Introduction to Islam: Beliefs and Practices in Historical Perspective* (New York: Thames & Hudson, 2015), 103.

10. Bennett, *Bloomsbury Companion to Islamic Studies*, 373–74.

11. Hillenbrand, *Introduction to Islam*, 99.

12. Hillenbrand, *Introduction to Islam*, 101.

Pilgrimage to Mecca (*Hajj*)

The celebration of Eid al-Adha is connected to the final pillar of Islam: the pilgrimage to Mecca (*hajj*). While the previous four pillars are daily and annual features of Islamic practice, the pilgrimage is obligatory only once in a person's life, and then only if the individual is able to afford it.[13] Those who do not have the resources to make the journey are excused from the obligation, though it is usually the dream of observant Muslims to visit the birthplace of Islam.

The centerpiece of the *hajj* journey is the circumambulation of the black granite temple known as the Ka'ba, which is located in the middle of the Sacred Mosque in Mecca. Qur'an 22:26–27 instructs believers to walk around the Ka'ba, while later tradition records various other elements of the ritual connected to Ibrahim's precedent.[14] Following in Ibrahim's footsteps effects purification and blessing for Muslims during the *hajj*.

The traditional *hajj* journey is taken approximately seventy days after the end of Ramadan, during the month known in the Islamic calendar as Dhu al-Hajja, from the eighth day through the thirteenth. Observation of Eid al-Adha occurs on the tenth day of Dhu al-Hajja. Sacrificial animals are ritually slaughtered at daybreak all around the world on this day.

This feature of the *hajj* celebration serves as a rehearsal of Ibrahim's sacrifice as recorded in Qur'an 37:107 and the surrounding verses. This passage in the Qur'an is understood to draw on Genesis 22, where Abraham ascends Mount Moriah with his son. Contemporary Islamic scholarship nearly unanimously contends that the son was Ismail. This allows Muslims to maintain ethnic connection between Muhammad and the Arab peoples who trace their lineage through the son of Ibrahim and Hagar.

Summary

While there are many additional practices shared by most of those throughout the Ummah, these five are recognized nearly universally as irrevocable components of what it means to practice Islam. It might be noted that some expressions of Islam—especially Twelver Shia Muslims—make the practice of *jihad* obligatory such that it has at times been referred to as a sixth pillar.[15]

Post-September eleventh, the word *jihad* will likely trigger alarm bells in Western ears, yet it is not always understood to refer to physical violence. Many Muslims wage a form of internal holy war when they seek to eradicate sin within themselves. In other words, the call to *jihad* can be added to the necessary duties of a Muslim who is intent on struggling to follow the straight

---

13. Bennett, *Bloomsbury Companion to Islamic Studies*, 338.
14. F. E. Peters, *The Hajj: The Muslim Pilgrimage to Mecca and the Holy Places* (Princeton, NJ: Princeton University Press, 1994), 7–9.
15. William Montgomery Watt, *Islam: A Short History* (Oxford: Oneworld, 1996), 85–86; cf. John Esposito and Dalia Mogahed, *Who Speaks for Islam?* (New York: Gallup, 2007), 17, who argue that it is improper to speak of *jihad* as a sixth pillar.

path of divine guidance despite sinful inclinations and the human tendency to forget the ways of God.

In many ways, the practice of Islam can be summed up by this final pillar of *jihad* as it is understood in its spiritual sense: struggling to remember Allah. From the daily prayers to the annual fast, Islam is a system of reminders to walk on the straight path. In fact, as Question 16 will discuss, the great problem that Islam recognizes is not an issue of a sinful nature. Instead, it is a problem of weakness of memory.

REFLECTION QUESTIONS

1. Why is it misleading to contend that Islam is a faith that is most concerned with orthopraxy?

2. What role do the Five Pillars of Islam play in the formation of the Muslim community?

3. How does the Shahadah feature in the ongoing life of the Muslim community?

4. How does the *Sunnah* influence the understanding of the Five Pillars?

5. What is the relationship between Eid al-Adha and Genesis 22?

What Are the Six Articles of Faith for Islam?

Iman [faith] means having faith in Allah,
angels, heavenly Scriptures, Messengers of Allah, life
after death, and good and bad destiny.
~Muhammad (Hadith of Muslim)[1]

While there are many visible components of Islam that relate to its practice, Islam is not merely concerned with external expression. Often caricaturized as being a religion consisting solely of works, Islamic practice is inextricably connected to a Muslim's inner faith. In order to be a Muslim, one must not only practice the Five Pillars of Islam, but must also believe in six central concepts known as the Six Articles of Faith.

Corroborating this claim, early Muslim commentator Ibn Taimiyah writes, "Unless one has faith in these six things in accordance with the Qur'an and the *Sunnah*, his faith will not acquire perfection."[2] Thus, in the attempt to investigate the central teaching of Islam, one must attend to both the Five Pillars of practice and the Six Articles of Faith. Therefore, this chapter will briefly explore these Six Articles of Faith and how they affect the lives of faithful Muslims.

---

1. Ibn Taimiyah, *Sharh Al-Aqeedat-il-Wasitiyah*, trans. Muhammad Khan (Riyadh: Darussalam, 1996), 28.
2. Taimiyah, *Sharh Al-Aqeedat-il-Wasitiyah*, 28.

Article 1: Oneness of God (*Tawhid*)

As the previous chapter indicates, the first of the pillars of Islam is the Shahadah, which states, "There is no god but The God, and Muhammad is his messenger." Connected to this, the first article of faith in Islam is to believe in the oneness of God. The first phrase of the Shahadah distinguishes between the array of competing ideas concerning the gods of other religions and the Islamic contention that only one true God exists.

Arguably, there is no more central concept in Islam than the oneness of God. Islamic scholar Seyyed Hossein Nasr views this attribute of God's nature as essential to the entire faith, writing, "Islam is based from beginning to end on the idea of Unity (*tawhid*)."[3] Islam defines God's absolute oneness in terms that make a Trinitarian understanding of God untenable. In Islamic thought, God is a monad, undivided in person and absolutely other than his creation.

Providing a corollary to this central belief, the greatest sin in Islam is *shirk*, which means associating partners with God or belief in polytheism.[4] The Qur'an refers to those who commit such a sin as the *musharikun* (those who assign partners to God; infidels) and much of the content of Islam's holy book intends to counter and defy such blasphemy. While the Christian doctrine of the Trinity, precisely articulated in its Nicene form, does not qualify as *shirk*, the accusation is often made that praying to Jesus and viewing him as the Son of God does in fact number Trinitarians among the *musharikun*.[5]

Article 2: Angels (*Al-Malaika*)

Belief in angels is another requirement for Muslims as one of the Six Articles of Islamic faith. Popular expressions of Islam often include extensive stories and teachings regarding angels and angelic activity. However, the Qur'an itself is less forthcoming regarding the details of the nature and explicit activities of the angelic host. Most of the Qur'an's teaching about angels identifies them as messengers, and anything further is speculation.[6]

Ibn Taimiyah highlights the relative paucity of qur'anic detail concerning angels while warning believers to avoid excessive speculation regarding such issues: "It is enjoined upon us to have faith in all the Attributes and actions of the angels described in the Qur'an and the *Hadith*, and keep quiet about such as have not been mentioned, for these constitute the affairs of the Unseen

3. Seyyed Hossein Nasr, *Ideals and Realities of Islam*, rev. and updated ed. (New York: Aquarian, 1994), 28.

4. Gabriel Said Reynolds, *The Emergence of Islam: Classical Traditions in Contemporary Perspective* (Minneapolis: Fortress, 2012), 212.

5. Manfred Kropp, "Tripartite, but Anti-Trinitarian Formulas in the Qur'anic Corpus, Possibly Pre-Qur'anic," in *New Perspectives on the Qur'an: The Qur'an in Its Historical Context*, vol. 2, ed. Gabriel Said Reynolds (New York: Routledge, 2011), 261.

6. John Kaltner and Younus Mirza, *The Bible and the Qur'an: Biblical Figures in the Islamic Tradition* (New York: Bloomsbury, 2018), 21–22.

which are known to us only to the extent Allah and His Messenger have told us."[7] Though it is human tendency to wonder about the supernatural realm, Ibn Taimiyah here reminds Muslims that the Qur'an and *Sunnah* are sufficient for what God intends them to know.

The Qur'an and *Sunnah* do, however, specifically discuss the role that the angel Jibril played in communicating the message of the Qur'an to Muhammad. As noted in Question 2, when Muhammad entered the cave of Hira in 610 CE, he encountered the angel Jibril. There in the cave, Jibril commanded Muhammad to recite what he revealed, serving as an intermediary between the heavenly copy of the Qur'an and Muhammad.[8] The Qur'an also names the angel Mikal alongside of Jibril in Qur'an 2:98 and Malik, the keeper of hell, in Qur'an 43:7–8.

Beyond these named angels, most others are known by their tasks. For example, the angel of death is mentioned in Qur'an 32:11. Also, Qur'an 69:17 speaks of eight angels known as the *hamalat al-'arsh* who bear up the throne of God.[9] Furthermore, Qur'an 50:16–18 teaches that everyone has two angels watching over them known as the *kiram al-katibin*. These two angels are responsible for recording the good and bad deeds of each individual.

Finally, there is some question about the nature of Iblis. Iblis, also referred to as Shaytan, is the Satan figure in the Qur'an.[10] While Iblis in some places appears to be an angel, other verses refer to him as a *jinn* (a supernatural, nonhuman creature with free will).[11] Regardless of whether or not Iblis is included among the angels, belief in angels is mandatory for Muslims.

Article 3: Holy Books (*Al-Kutub*)

Muslims are also required to believe in a number of revealed books. The Qur'an teaches that God has revealed his will through various dispensations of written revelation throughout history, each intended for a different audience. The Qur'an specifically mentions the Psalms of David (Zabur), the Torah of Moses (Tawrah), and the Gospel of Jesus (Injil).[12] While the Bible read by Christians and Jews today is believed to be corrupted, it remains the case that

---

7. Khan, *Sharh Al-Aqeedat-il-Wasitiyah*, 29.
8. Mark Robert Anderson, *The Qur'an in Context: A Christian Exploration* (Downers Grove, IL: IVP Academic, 2016), 16.
9. Qur'an 13:39 and 43:4 refer to a heavenly source for the Qur'an referred to as *um al-kitab* (lit. Mother of the Book). Many Muslims believe that the Qur'an has existed eternally, and Jibril transmitted it to Muhammad.
10. Qur'an 7:11–18. Cf. 2:34–39; 15:28–48; 18:50. The Qur'an refers to Iblis as one of the *jinn*, though some Muslims believe that he became an angel. See Kaltner and Mirza, *Bible and the Qur'an*, 62–65.
11. See Qur'an 15:26–27 and 18:50; Clinton Bennett, ed., *The Bloomsbury Companion to Islamic Studies* (New York: Bloomsbury Academic, 2015), 346.
12. There is debate as to whether the reference to the Gospel of Jesus is a nonextant book that Jesus received in the same fashion as Muhammad received the Qur'an or a reference to the four canonical Gospels. Most Muslims will grant that this appears to be a reference to the

the Qur'an presents itself as a continuation of the singular message believed to be contained in and carried by these previous books of revelation.[13]

Of course, for Muslims, prior revelation is of less importance than that which Jibril delivered to Muhammad in the Qur'an. Most Muslims hold to the idea that the Qur'an is the verbatim record of a book that eternally exists in heaven, called *'um al-kitab*, or Mother of the Book. Jibril's communication of the Qur'an also marked the final dispensation of revelation, thus sealing divine communication and establishing Islam as the final religion. In Qur'an 5:3, one reads this definitive statement regarding the advent of Islam as God's final dispensation of religion: "Today I have perfected your religion for you, and I have completed My blessing on you, and I have approved Islam for you as a religion."

Thus, the Qur'an admits willingly that previous books of revelation have been given, yet it claims to be the final and perfected form of revelation. In other words, the Qur'an presents itself as a continuation or a sequel to the biblical testimony. Since revelation is contained in the books of Christians and Jews, Muslims contend that there is no final conflict between what has been revealed to prior prophets and the Qur'an. Yet in contemporary Islamic practice, there is little appeal to previous scriptures for guidance.

Article 4: Prophets (*An-Nabi*) and Messengers (*Ar-Rasul*)

Supporting the belief in the revealed books, Muslims must also believe in all of the prophets and messengers of Islam. A distinction that is sometimes made between these two roles is that a messenger (*rasul*) is sent with a book, while a prophet (*nabi*) orally proclaims God's message. Thus, all the messengers are prophets, though not all prophets are messengers. However, others argue that the Qur'an seems to use the words more interchangeably than such a clean distinction would suggest.[14]

The number of prophets recorded in the traditions significantly outnumbers those recorded in the biblical account, but the Qur'an specifically mentions twenty-five prophets, many of whom appear to be references to biblical characters.[15] As described by Badru Kateregga, "[Prophets] all brought es-

---

synoptic Gospels, though they will also contend that they have been corrupted, as later chapters will indicate.

13. Qur'an 5:41–50 indicates that the Jews and the Christians have revelation from God. Though, as Question 28 will discuss, most Muslims believe that the biblical texts have undergone corruption (*tahrif*).

14. Qur'an 31:1 refers to the angels as messengers. Likewise, Qur'an 2:285 calls believers to recognize God, angels, books, and messengers, while Qur'an 2:177 recognizes God, the last day, the Book, and prophets. These and other verses seem to suggest a less strict distinction between the terms. For further treatment, see Arthur Jeffrey, *The Qur'an as Scripture* (New York: Russel Moore, 1952).

15. Badru Kateregga and David Shenk, *A Muslim and a Christian in Dialogue* (Waterloo, ON: Herald, 1997), 64. Kateregga here claims that Islamic traditions number the prophets at 124,000, with only twenty-five appearing in the Qur'an itself.

sentially the same message—Islam. God gave them greater knowledge about His will, His religion, the human heart, and good and evil. They guided humankind, taught them to live happily in this world and to be prepared for life after death."[16] From a Muslim point of view, then, all prophets proclaim the same, singular message of submission to God.

Throughout the Qur'an, one encounters prophets that resemble biblical characters. This can cause confusion because the Qur'an is keen to find the message of Islam in the lives and on the lips of these biblical characters. It is not always concerned, however, to record the same details of their lives in the narrative. For instance, the Qur'an records a story in which *Talut/* Saul leads his army to water in order to test them based upon how they would drink prior to going into battle with *Jalut*/Goliath. The Qur'an here features "Saul," though the Bible records Gideon as the leader whose army was reduced at the river, and it was David who faced Goliath.[17] The fifth section of this book will treat these issues in greater detail than is possible or necessary here.

Article 5: The Day of Resurrection and Judgment (*Yom aq-Quiyamah wa ad-Din*)

It may surprise some readers to discover that the resurrection of the dead is part of the Islamic system of belief. Not only is it a belief, but it is one of the six mandatory articles of faith. Jane Smith and Yvonne Haddad see the issue of resurrection as ubiquitous within Islamic teaching, as they write, "The promise, the guarantee, of the day at which all bodies will be resurrected and all persons called to account for their deeds and the measure of their faith is the dominant message of the Qur'an."[18] Smith and Haddad claim that virtually every page of the Qur'an testifies to this impending reality that one day all will face the judgment of God.

Four stages of resurrection and judgment can be distilled from within the corpus of Islamic teaching. First, there will be signs of the end of the world, or signs of the hour (*isharat as-saʾa*). These signs will consist of interruptions of the natural order and a disastrous reversal of the process of creation.[19] Second, after this calamity, a trumpet will blow, the dead will be raised to life, and all will be gathered to God.[20]

---

16. Kateregga and Shenk, *Muslim and a Christian*, 63.
17. Qur'an 2:246–251. To avoid this confusion and conflation, the reader will notice that this book has chosen to transliterate the qur'anic names of characters in an attempt to distinguish them in their qur'anic setting from the characters they resemble in the Bible.
18. Jane Smith and Yvonne Haddad, *The Islamic Understanding of Death and Resurrection* (Albany: State University of New York Press, 1981), 63.
19. Smith and Haddad, *Islamic Understanding of Death*, 66.
20. Smith and Haddad, *Islamic Understanding of Death*, 70.

Once all are gathered before God, the third stage of reckoning will begin whereby all humankind is judged for the lives they lived on earth.[21] As recorded in Qur'an 9:19–31 and 17:71, each individual will be presented with an account that details his or her good and bad deeds. Finally, tradition records that each person will cross a bridge (*siraat*) over hell's fire. Those who successfully cross the bridge will be admitted to paradise, while others will be dragged off of the bridge into hell. Hell is described as a place of fire and torture, while paradise is described in terms of pleasures and reward.[22]

Article 6: Predestination/Fate (*Qadar*)

This final article of faith is probably the most contentious of the six, both within Islam and for those looking at it from the outside. This article requires the Muslim to willingly accept that which has been fated to occur—both the good and the bad. Intramural division has existed between Muslims who hold this view and those who believe that God knows the future but has not determined it (*qadariyya*). Most of the latter group follow in the footsteps of the Mu'atazilites and wed philosophy with traditional Islamic teachings.[23]

On the other hand, those who follow what is called the 'Ashariyyah understanding of *qadar* are willing to deny human free choice in order to maintain the doctrine of divine predestination. Such Muslims believe that all of history—past, present, and future—is recorded on a tablet in heaven. Written by God from eternity past, human agents perform actions that appear to be freely willed, but which cannot be other than that which God predetermined for them. As stated by Mashhad Al-Allaf, "Human beings can will, but they cannot will other than what God willed."[24] Or, in the words of Ziauddin Sardar, "Muslims believe that their destiny is firmly in the hands of God. The outcome of every effort, every good intention and action is subject to the will of God."[25]

This conception of destiny or fate can be seen in the everyday life of many of the Muslims I have lived among. My Muslim friends regularly received bad news by saying, "Praise God (*Hamdillah*)." When I asked them why this was their first response, invariably they would respond by saying that God had written their destiny before it happened. Thus, if they received it with anything less than praise, it would be as if they were criticizing God's wisdom in determining it. Thus, I became accustomed to hearing the phrase, "This was written beforehand."

---

21. Smith and Haddad, *Islamic Understanding of Death*, 76.
22. Ziauddin Sardar, *What Do Muslims Believe? The Roots and Realities of Modern Islam* (New York: Walker, 2007), 45.
23. Mashhad Al-Allaf, "Islamic Theology," in *The Bloomsbury Companion to Islamic Studies*, ed. Clinton Bennett (New York: Bloomsbury Academic, 2015), 130.
24. Al-Allaf, "Islamic Theology," 130.
25. Sardar, *What Do Muslims Believe?*, 46.

Summary

These Six Articles of Faith are but a few of the dearly held beliefs of the world's Muslims. However, they provide a basic set of commitments that unify the Ummah's faith and offer the outsider a glimpse of what it takes to follow Islam in one's heart. The more overt practices are easier to analyze and discern; however, without these faith commitments, one cannot be a true Muslim.

The following four chapters continue to explore Muslim belief regarding creation, sin, salvation, and eschatology. One will find greater diversity of belief throughout the Ummah regarding the details of these four areas of belief than regarding the more uniform conceptions of the Six Articles of Faith. However, these four areas remain central to the Islamic system of belief. Likewise, exploration of these four components of Islam allows more direct comparison with Christian answers to the same questions.

REFLECTION QUESTIONS

1. How do the Six Articles of Faith connect the Muslim community with Judaism and Christianity, and where do they part ways?

2. What is the most central commitment for Islamic belief?

3. What are the holy books in which a Muslim is supposed to believe?

4. What does belief in the day of resurrection entail?

5. What are the competing views on fate within Islam?

What Is the Islamic View of Creation?

*Surely your Lord is God, who created the heavens
and the earth in six days. Then He mounted the
throne. The night covers the day, which it pursues
urgently, and the sun, and the moon, and the stars
are subjected, (all) by His command. Is it not (a fact)
that to Him (belong) the creation and the command?
Blessed (be) God, Lord of the worlds!*
~Qur'an 7:54

It seems inevitable that at some point everyone wrestles with the question, "Where are we and how did we get here?" Since no thoughtful worldview or religious system is able to avoid this obvious question, various answers present themselves for consideration. While this question can often lead into esoteric territory, the Qur'an provides Muslims with concrete material for proposing an Islamic answer.

As a faith that traces its roots back to biblical narrative, it is unsurprising that the Islamic teaching on creation exhibits many parallels with Christian and Jewish understandings. However, while the Qur'an echoes Genesis at many points, this chapter will highlight several features that are unique to Islam. In particular, this chapter considers the Qur'an's teaching on the physical world, the creation of supernatural beings, and the creation and nature of the first human couple.

Creation of the Material World

As indicated by the verse quoted at the beginning of this chapter, the Qur'an, like the Bible, contends that God is the sole creator of the material universe. The Qur'an cites God's role as creator in multiple places as the ground for his claim to receive the worship and subordination of humanity.[1] Furthermore, the Qur'an coincides with the biblical account of creation taking place over six days or periods of time.

Modern Islamic scholarship has attempted to reconcile the apparent tension between the six "days" of creation and the prevailing scientific opinion that the earth is extremely old. Many contemporary scholars of Islam contend that the Arabic word for day (*yom*) can refer to a literal twenty-four-hour period or a much larger time more aptly translated as "age."[2] Furthermore, Qur'an 71:13–17 indicates that God's created world has undergone a gradual process of development, which is perhaps compatible with evolutionary theory. Such attempts at reconciling scientific theory with holy writ find parallels in some contemporary Christian writings, though consensus regarding the issue of evolution remains elusive in both faiths.

Possibly the greatest distinction between biblical and qur'anic understanding of the material world arises when considering its original condition and purpose. In the biblical account, Genesis 1:31 records God's endorsement of his creation as "very good." The first two chapters detail God's intentional, ordered design of the world and the garden in which he would place humanity.

The Qur'an, on the other hand, includes no such description of such a careful process of earth's creation. To the contrary, the accounts of the first sin of humanity depict earth as a place of banishment. Qur'an 2:36 records an account of humanity's first failure, after which God states, "Go down, some of you an enemy to others! The earth is a dwelling place for you, and enjoyment (of life) for a time." In Islam, then, humans first inhabited a heavenly garden from which they and their adversary were cast down.[3] Elsewhere, the Qur'an describes the earth as the place of human testing rather than a place designed for them and deemed to be "very good."[4]

Creation of Creatures

In addition to creating the universe, the Qur'an also speaks of God's creation of multiple kinds of nonhuman creatures. Animals are mentioned as helpers to the human population, while angels are regularly viewed as messengers of God. Perhaps less familiar to those outside of the Muslim faith,

---

1. Cf. Qur'an 7:21, 30–33; 50:38.
2. Qur'an 22:47; 70:4.
3. A. J. Droge, trans., *The Qur'an: A New Annotated Translation* (Bristol, CT: Equinox, 2015), 5n48.
4. Cf. Qur'an 6:165.

however, are the *jinn* of the Qur'an and Islamic traditions. Each of these categories of creatures deserves attention in sketching the Islamic understanding of creation.

Animals

The Qur'an establishes the idea that God created cattle for humans. Qur'an 16:5 states, "And the cattle—He created them for you. (There is) warmth in them and (other) benefits, and from them you eat." The passage goes on to include horses and beasts of burden for transportation as the provision of God for humankind. The Islamic texts teach that whatever evolutionary process may have occurred, God has purposed to fill the earth with creatures that are to serve humanity in their labors.

One distinction between the Qur'an's account of the animal kingdom and the biblical record comes at the point of the naming of the animals. In Genesis 2:19–20, God parades the whole host of the animal kingdom before Adam in order to see what he would call them. Tasked with naming the animals, Adam both demonstrates his authority over creation and develops the linguistic capacity to describe his world.

The Qur'an, however, teaches that God taught Adam the names of the animals, then brought him before the angelic host. There, Adam and the angels are challenged to recall the names of all of the animals. Adam's ability to do so, contrasted with the angelic failure, confirms his status as being higher than the angels.

Angels

Angels play a significant role in Islam. As discussed in Question 14, the belief in angels is counted as one of the six essential faith commitments required of a Muslim. Multiple reasons for this exist. According to the *Sira*, Muhammad's reception of the Qur'an was mediated by the angel Jibril. On an individual level, angels record a person's deeds, and an angel is responsible for leading each soul away at the time of their death. On a corporate level, at the end of time there will be an angel to blow the final trumpet, signaling the resurrection and judgment day.[5] Angels are involved in nearly every major event in history past, present, and future.

The Qur'an only mentions a few angels by name (Jibril and Mikal, and possibly Harut and Marut).[6] However, an innumerable angelic host is

---

5. The Qur'an does not name the angel of death nor the angel who will blow the final trumpet. However, later Islamic traditions name the angel of death Azrael, and Israfil is the angel who will blow the final trumpet.

6. Qur'an 2:30–34; 7:11; 15:29–30; 89:21–23. See John Kaltner and Younus Mirza, *The Bible and the Qur'an: Biblical Figures in Islamic Tradition* (London: T&T Clark, 2018), 20–22. It should be noted that some commentators do not believe Harut and Marut are angels, but rather wicked kings. The concept of fallen angels in Islam is contended.

mentioned in several key places in the Qur'an pertaining both to creation and to the end of time. Some specific angels are known not by name but by function. For example, eight angels are responsible for holding up God's throne (Qur'an 69:17) and nineteen others guard the gate to Gehenna—a fiery place of torment similar to hell (Qur'an 74:30–31).

The function of the angels in Islam varies, yet they are everywhere depicted as created servants of God. Overall, the primary task of angels is to be messengers, as described in Qur'an 35:1: "Praise (be) to God, Creator of the heavens and the earth, (who) makes the angels messengers having two, and three, and four wings."[7] Regardless of their activities and responsibilities, angels in Islamic thought are viewed as created, supernatural beings who exist to serve God and to carry out his will in heaven and on earth.

Jinn

While Muslims believe that God created Adam and his wife along with the animal kingdom and the angels, they also include another category of creatures. This other category consists of intelligent spiritual beings called *jinn* that are regularly involved in the affairs of the material world while not material creatures themselves.[8] The *jinn* are not mentioned in detail in the Qur'an, though the *Sunnah* and popular Islamic folklore is filled with stories and details that fill in the gaps.

What the Qur'an does teach about the *jinn* is that they are created from fire (Qur'an 7:12) and that the Satan character of the Qur'an (Iblis) was one of them (Qur'an 18:50). Despite the association with Iblis, the character of the *jinn* in Islamic thought is not always wicked. For example, Qur'an 72 is a chapter of the Qur'an almost entirely written from the perspective of the *jinn* in which they declare, "Some of us are righteous, and some of us are other than that—we are on different roads."[9] Thus, just like humans, *jinn* are divided into the righteous and unrighteous.

The *jinn* often feature in popular stories and fables. Usually they are viewed as capricious and fickle creatures. Yet, as Islamic scholar Gabriel Said Reynolds comments, "in Islamic literature, the *jinn* indeed have a special place as magical creatures who are often up to mischief but who can also be compelled to grant favors to humans."[10] As such, folk tales and superstitions regarding how to appease the *jinn* proliferate throughout the Islamic world, even if not endorsed by orthodox Islamic theology.

---

7. Kaltner and Mirza, *Bible and the Qur'an*, 21.
8. Gabriel Said Reynolds, *The Emergence of Islam: Classical Traditions in Contemporary Perspective* (Minneapolis: Fortress, 2012), 138. The English word "genie" and its popular expression in children's stories derive from caricaturized versions of this Islamic concept.
9. Qur'an 72:11.
10. Reynolds, *Emergence of Islam*, 138.

Humanity

The previous section noted that some contemporary Muslim perspectives synthesize qur'anic and scientific theories of the development of the world. However, such synthesis disintegrates when considering the creation of humans. The Qur'an repeatedly speaks of God's special, direct, and immediate creation of humans out of a variety of substances (dust, water, molded clay, a drop of semen).[11] What the primary substance of human creation is, however, pales in importance when compared to the purpose the Qur'an gives to humanity.

Humanity in Islam serves the honorable purpose of being God's vicegerent (*khalifa*) on earth.[12] This includes holding a status that is higher than the angels and receiving the breath of God as an animating force.[13] Despite this elevated status, however, according to Islam, humans do not bear the image of God in the same way as recorded in Genesis 1:26–27. Neither are humans designed in or for direct, personal relationship with God.[14] As discussed in chapter 14, the doctrine of *tawhid* (oneness of God) precludes the comingling of God's transcendent essence with his creation. Thus, most Muslims reject the idea of a direct, intimate, and interpersonal relationship between the creation and the creator.

Islam's distinct anthropology naturally affects the expectations and responsibilities placed upon humanity. Though humans are created as God's vicegerents and are responsible for living according to his laws, they are not expected to be perfect because direct human relationship with a holy God is not the goal. Islamic theology contends that life is a test of one's ability to remember God's laws. The reward for those who pass the test is a garden of delights, though it is debated as to whether believers will even see God in the garden, let alone dwell with him.[15]

Distinctive Beginnings Lead to Distinctive Trajectories

Christianity and Islam both contend that God is the source of all that exists in the created world. Both contend that humans were the special creation of God and that humanity plays a significant role in the greater creation. However, this chapter has also sought to highlight perspectives on creation that are unique to Islam. In the following chapters, two of these unique perspectives will prove to be especially formative in Islamic teaching regarding other doctrines.

---

11. Cf. Qur'an 3:59 (dust); 21:30 (water); 15:26–34 (clay/mud); 16:3 (semen).
12. Qur'an 2:30.
13. Qur'an 15:28–34.
14. One exception might be some of the Sufi expressions of Islam, which speak more positively about experiencing or knowing God directly.
15. John Renard, ed., *Islamic Theological Themes: A Primary Source Reader* (Oakland: University of California Press, 2014), 209–11.

Purpose of the Material Universe

First, Islam and Christianity exhibit differences in their understanding of the purpose of the material world. Muslim teaching calls believers to respect creation and care for the flora and fauna around them. In an oft-cited *hadith*, Muhammad warns his followers not to recklessly cut down trees, or they will face the penalty of being cast into hellfire.[16] Yet, despite warnings and instruction pertaining to ethical treatment of the material world, the Qur'an itself teaches that earth is merely a temporary habitation for humans. As such, the created world is never endorsed as "very good," nor does Islamic teaching anticipate its restoration in the eschaton.

In the Qur'an, the earth is a temporary place of testing. Once the test is completed, humanity will reside in the fires of hell or in the pleasures of the heavenly garden. As stated in Qur'an 29:57–59, "Every person will taste death, then to Us you will be returned. Those who have believed and done righteous deeds—We shall indeed settle them in exalted rooms of the Garden, through which rivers flow, there to remain. Excellent is the reward of the doers, who are patient and trust in their Lord." Islam, then, views the material world as somewhat incidental to the true meaning of life. The material world will dissolve into the eternal reality of torment in hell or pleasure in the gardens of paradise.

Theological Anthropology

Second, Islam and Christianity diverge significantly at the point of each faith's anthropology. Christianity teaches that humans were made in God's image and for intimate relationship with God. This intimacy is indicated by the portrayal of God as Father. Perfection is required for satisfaction of human purpose because imperfection cannot exist in the holy presence of God. Sin is thus construed as an unrighteous pollution, and it poses a danger to any human who would approach God's presence.[17]

To the contrary, with the exception of some of the more mystical Sufi expressions, most Islamic understandings of *tawhid* contend that God is wholly and eternally transcendent. God cannot and would not condescend to dwell with humanity—and he certainly would not take on flesh—thus, humanity cannot entertain the idea of having an intimate relationship with this God whereby they would call him "father."[18]

Since intimate relationship is downplayed if not outright rejected in Islam, human perfection is not required. Humanity, as described by Seyyed Hossein Nasr, "is by nature negligent and forgetful; [humanity] is by nature

---

16. Sunan Abu Dawud, *Kitab Al-Adab*, book 43 (§467), https://sunnah.com/abudawud/43/467.
17. Jay Sklar, *Sin, Impurity, Sacrifice, Atonement: The Priestly Conceptions* (Sheffield, UK: Sheffield Phoenix, 2015), 182.
18. Seyyed Hossein Nasr, *Ideals and Realities of Islam*, rev. and updated ed. (San Francisco: Aquarian, 1994), 18–22.

imperfect."[19] While Islam requires adherence to a high moral code, this code merely provides the ethical standard for the test of human willingness to walk the straight path of God's guidance.

Summary

Islam, like all other faiths, offers an answer to the existential question, "Where did everything come from?" In so doing, it tells a story that displays several common characteristics about an all-powerful creator who freely willed the material world into existence. However, as Islam omits key details regarding the creator's orderly preparation of the earth along with his special creation of humans as his image-bearers, the story Islam tells begins on a different trajectory than that which is told by the Bible.

Tracing the implications of this alternative account of the beginning, the following three chapters will further describe the Islamic understanding of sin, salvation, and the end times. In so doing, it will become clear that the differences between the Islamic and Christian understandings of creation affect how one responds to questions about the nature of sin, salvation, and eschatology. Thus, as Islam answers some of the most foundational worldview questions about cosmic origins, the problem of sin, its solution, and the end toward which all things are heading, it tells a different story than the one narrated by the Bible.

REFLECTION QUESTIONS

1. What are some of the similarities and differences between the qur'anic and biblical accounts of creation?

2. Where does the Qur'an appear to place the creation of Adam and his wife?

3. What is the purpose of humanity as indicated by the Qur'an?

4. How does this perspective on human purpose affect the role of ethical living?

5. If this chapter is an accurate depiction of the Qur'an's teaching regarding the beginning, how do you anticipate the narrative arc of the Qur'an's teaching to continue?

---

19. Nasr, *Ideals and Realities of Islam*, 22.

What Is the Islamic View of Sin?

Then Satan [Shaytan] caused them both to slip from there, and to go out from where they were. And We said, "Go down, some of you an enemy to the others! The earth is a dwelling place for you, and enjoyment (of life) for a time."
~Qur'an 2:36

It takes very little time on this earth before one recognizes the fact that something is wrong. Humanity is universally faced with the reality of pain, suffering, death, and destruction. Naturally, the question arises, "What is wrong?" This question often determines the shape of a religion. By identifying that something is wrong, one implies that there is some standard from which creation has deviated. A worldview that includes such a recognition of sin or deviation from a standard often also suggests a way forward in how to correct our course.

Islam is no exception. If humans are the creation of a good, just, and powerful God, why is it that we fail to live consistently with God's law? In answer to this question, the Qur'an narrates a story about the original fall of humanity that bears similar contours to the biblical account of Adam and Eve's first sin. In the Qur'an, Adam and his wife encounter a deceiver named Shaytan who sets himself up as their enemy, causes them to doubt God's commands, and persuades them to grasp and eat forbidden fruit.

However, upon closer inspection, the Qur'an's teaching regarding the nature and effects of sin—including the first sin—proves to be radically different than that which is found in the Bible. This chapter will look at the idea of sin and the fall in the Qur'an and *Sunnah* in order to define sin from a qur'anic perspective. The doctrine of sin provides a clear vantage point from which to catch a glimpse of one of the most irreconcilable differences between Islamic and Christian theology.

The Story of the Fall

As the previous chapter indicated, some questions regarding the location of humanity's original habitation remain unclear within the Qur'an. What is clear, however, is the fact that the first human couple was deceived by Shaytan and made to transgress the command that they had been given.[1] Qur'an 7:10–25 provides a narrative of this event, describing Shaytan's deception.

In Qur'an 7:19, God instructs Adam, saying, "Adam! Inhabit the Garden, you and your wife, and eat freely of it wherever you please, but do not go near this tree, or you will both be among the evildoers." Immediately following this command, however, Shaytan whispers to the couple, "Your Lord has only forbidden you both from this tree to keep you both from becoming two angels, or from becoming two of the immortals." Completing the deception, Shaytan swears to the couple in Qur'an 7:21, saying, "Surely I am indeed one of your trusty advisers." Both humans eat some of the fruit and immediately recognize that their "shameful parts" are exposed.

As the chapter continues, God responds to Adam and his wife's transgression in Qur'an 7:22, saying, "Did I not forbid you both from that tree, and say to you both, 'Surely [Shaytan] is an enemy to you?'" The verses that follow show Adam's repentance and plea for God's forgiveness. In Qur'an 7:24, God responds by telling Adam, his wife, and Shaytan, "Go down, some of you an enemy to others! The earth is a dwelling place for you, and enjoyment (of life) for a time."

In the Qur'an, this story serves as a warning to the offspring of Adam to reject Shaytan and remember God's guidance. It does not teach that Adam's offspring inherit his sin, nor that original sin distorts the human will.[2] Instead, the Qur'an sees sin as the result of an individual's natural human forgetfulness, wandering from the straight path, or succumbing to deception.[3]

The Expressions of Sin

In Islamic teaching, humans are essentially imperfect by virtue of their finiteness, not sinful by accident of their Adamic lineage. Adam and each of his offspring are all individually responsible for heeding God's guidance, yet

---

1. Qur'an 2:36 and 7:22 blame Shaytan explicitly for the sin of humanity.
2. Seyyed Hossein Nasr, *Ideals and Realities of Islam*, rev. and updated ed. (San Francisco: Aquarian, 1994), 24.
3. Badru Kateregga and David Shenk, *A Muslim and a Christian in Dialogue* (Scottdale, PA: Herald, 1997), 43. Kateregga writes, "[Man] is good but imperfect. Being imperfect, he needs constant reminding."

weak in their ability to remember God's ways.[4] Though humanity is naturally weak and fallible, no one has experienced corruption due to the actions of another. In the words of Badru Kateregga,

> No single act has warped the human will. Any concept of original sin is contrary to the true teachings of Islam. It is not a sin for man to be fallible. As a finite creature, he is bound to be imperfect. However, it becomes a sin if man has the means of perfection and decides not to avail himself of them.[5]

Any act of straying from the straight path of obedient submission to God is a sin in Islam. Sins manifest in at least three broad ways: disbelief, *shirk*, and disobedience. Each of these three types of sin can be traced back to a weakness of memory.

Disbelief

Throughout the Qur'an, one finds verses addressing those who are called believers and those who are called unbelievers. In fact, disbelief is one of the sins or misdeeds most often cited throughout the Qur'an. Anyone guilty of disbelief is known as a *kafir*. The Qur'an itself purports to be a litmus test by which true believers will return and submit to its message. However, it likewise contends that those who are wicked will reject it and maintain their disbelief.

The result of such persistent disbelief is illustrated in verses such as Qur'an 8:36: "Surely those who disbelieve spend their wealth to keep (people) from the way of God—and they will (continue to) spend it. Then it will be a (cause of) regret for them, (and) then they will be overcome. Those who disbelieve will be gathered into Gehenna." Gehenna is a fiery place of torment and purgation, similar to hell in Christianity.

Furthermore, the Qur'an implicates those who encounter God's signs and choose to reject them. For example, Qur'an 14:28–30 states,

> Do you not see those who have exchanged the blessing of God for disbelief, and caused their people to descend to the home of ruin—Gehenna—where they will burn? It is an evil dwelling place! They have set up rivals for God in order to lead (people) astray from His way. Say: "Enjoy (yourselves)! Surely your destination is to the Fire!"

Thus, the Qur'an is not shy regarding the punishment that awaits those who fail to heed God's command and to follow his guidance into right belief.

---

4. Qur'an 35:18.
5. Kateregga and Shenk, *Muslim and a Christian*, 45.

Likewise, God's guidance is viewed as a sufficient reminder of that which humans in their innermost parts know to be true.

Shirk

The grave sin of *shirk* is condemned throughout Islamic theology in the strongest of terms. This sin is different than disbelief in that it involves actively associating partners or equals with God. Essentially, *shirk* is any polytheistic expression of worship or belief.[6] As such, it is an affront to the essential Islamic conception of God's absolute oneness (*tawhid*).

Since *shirk* is the active denial of the central tenet of Islamic monotheism, it is known as the greatest sin and at times understood to be an unforgivable transgression.[7] Since Muhammad won converts from among the polytheists of Mecca, however, it must be possible to be forgiven of *shirk* in this life. On the other hand, one who persists in *shirk* to the end may not be released from Gehenna's fire.

Disobedience

Alternatively, there are multiple reminders to Muslim believers that they are bound by duty to obey God's commands and remain on the straight path. Believing Muslims may still choose to violate God's law, and this is considered to be an act of sin that requires repentance and God's forgiveness. For example, Qur'an 5:90–92 states,

> You who believe! Wine, games of chance, stones, and divination arrows are an abomination, part of the work of Satan [Shaytan]. So avoid it in order that you may prosper. Satan only wishes to cause our enmity and hatred among you with wine and games of chance, and to keep you from the remembrance of God and from the prayer. Will you refrain? Obey God, and obey the messenger, and beware! If you do turn away, know that only (dependent) on Our messenger is the clear delivery (of the message).

Ultimately, Islam exists as a reminder to humanity to return and submit to God. The Qur'an reinforces this idea, as it refers to itself as a book of remembrance (*dhikr*).[8] In so doing, it reveals the Islamic understanding of the essential nature of sin.

---

6. Gabriel Said Reynolds, *The Emergence of Islam: Classic Traditions in Contemporary Perspective* (Minneapolis: Fortress, 2012), 212. Reynolds defines *shirk* as "a term based in the frequent qur'anic condemnation of those who attribute power or authority to anything or anyone other than God."

7. Reynolds, *Emergence of Islam*, 111.

8. Cf. Qur'an 3:58; 38:1, 8.

The Nature of Sin

Though Islam speaks of sin manifesting itself in various ways, in its essence the Qur'an teaches that sin is forgetfulness of the ways of God. Corroborating this from a Muslim perspective, Seyyed Hossein Nasr writes,

> [Humanity] has a theomorphic being and is always in the process of forgetting it. He has in himself the possibility of being God-like but he is always in the state of neglecting this possibility. That is why the cardinal sin in Islam is forgetfulness. It is negligence of what we really are. It is a going to sleep and creating a dream world around us which makes us forget who we really are and what we should be doing in this world.[9]

At the core of the Islamic answer to the question "What is wrong?" is the recognition of human weakness and the persistent failure to remember and submit to the ways of God.

Furthermore, this concept of human forgetfulness is inherent to human nature, not the result of Adam's sin. As Nasr summarizes,

> [In Islam] there is no original sin. There is no single act which has warped and distorted the human will. Rather, man by being man is imperfect, only God being perfection as such. Being imperfect, man has the tendency to forget and so is in constant need of being reminded through revelation of his real nature.[10]

In Islamic thought, then, life is an extended test of one's ability to heed divine guidance, remember the ways of God, and walk on the straight way. There are many ways to fail to submit to God's laws that are described as sins. However, the nature of sin itself is forgetfulness of God.

Summary

Throughout the Qur'an, one finds life described as a test. Qur'an 29:2–3 asks, rhetorically, "Do the people think that they will be left (in such a position) that they (can) say, 'We believe,' but (that) they will not be tested? Certainly, we tested those who were before them, and God will indeed know those who are truthful, and He will indeed know the liars." As this chapter has indicated, passing this test in Islam is a matter of overcoming forgetfulness, not the restoration of a sin-warped will.

---

9. Nasr, *Ideals and Realities in Islam*, 23.
10. Nasr, *Ideals and Realities in Islam*, 24.

In light of the Qur'an's teaching on human forgetfulness, the following chapter will address the Islamic answer to this problem. It is clear at this point that the conception of the problem in Islam requires a solution that is different than that which is offered in the Bible. If the problem is forgetfulness, the solution will be a reminder, not a savior.

REFLECTION QUESTIONS

1. What role did Shaytan play in the first account of sin?

2. What effect did the first account of sin have on subsequent humanity?

3. How do the various sins help us to understand the ethical priorities in Islam?

4. Why is *shirk* considered to be such a grave sin?

5. According to Seyyed Hossein Nasr, what is "the cardinal sin" in Islam, and how does this differ from Christian teaching?

What Is the Islamic View of Salvation?

Then Adam received certain words from his Lord,
and He turned to him (in forgiveness).
Surely He—He is the One who turns
(in forgiveness), the Compassionate.
~Qur'an 2:37

The previous chapter discussed the Islamic view of the nature of sin and its expression in human experience. As was seen, Islam teaches that sin arises from a different source than it does in Christianity. Christianity grounds the human sin problem in the doctrine of original sin, which holds that sin bends the human will and worship away from God. Sin is essentially understood as misdirected worship, and it results in separation from a holy and righteous God.

Islam, on the other hand, teaches that sin is a manifestation of natural human forgetfulness. As Seyyed Hossein Nasr explains, "Being imperfect[,] man has the tendency to forget and so is in constant need of being reminded through revelation of his real nature."[1] Since forgetfulness is the problem, Islam offers a solution different than that of Christianity.

Christians are conditioned to discuss sin in its relationship to our Savior Jesus the Messiah. However, for the Muslim, the remedy for human forgetfulness is not a savior, but rather a reminder. Thus, it is more appropriate to compare Jesus in Christianity with the Qur'an in Islam than it would be to compare

---

1. Seyyed Hossein Nasr, *Ideals and Realities of Islam*, rev. and updated ed. (San Francisco: Aquarian, 1994), 24.

Jesus with Muhammad.[2] In Islam, the Qur'an provides the solution to our for-getfulness, as it is a book of guidance and reminder of the ways of God.

The Qur'an as Guidance

One concept that is often used to describe the Qur'an's role in the Muslim's life is that of divine guidance. For example, Qur'an 7:52 recounts, "Certainly We have brought them a Book—We have made it distinct on (the basis of) knowledge—as a guidance and mercy for a people who believe." Later in the same chapter, Qur'an 7:174 concludes, "In this way We make the signs dis-tinct, so that they will return [or repent]." The signs provided by God, chiefly through the Qur'an, are intended to guide people to remember and return to the straight path of submission and obedience.

The *Sunnah* corroborates the idea that the Qur'an has been delivered to Muhammad as guidance for humanity. One example from the *hadith* col-lection *Sahih Muslim* states, "The Book of Allah contains right guidance, the light, and whoever adheres to it and holds it fast, he is upon right guid-ance and whosoever deviates from it goes astray."[3] Thus, one's response to the Qur'an serves as the determining factor of one's path. Those who follow the guidance are on the right path, and deviation from the path results in wandering.

Additionally, the *Sunnah* expands on the Qur'an's understanding of di-vine guidance by including Muhammad himself as a source of guidance. In the most trusted collection of *hadith*, *Sahih al-Bukhari*, one finds a section entitled "The righteous way or guidance." In this section is a *hadith* that states, "The best talk is Allah's Book (Qur'an), and the best guidance is the guidance of Muhammad."[4] Therefore, for Muslims seeking the straight path for their lives, two sources present themselves as means of guidance: the Qur'an and the collection of stories relating the life and teaching of Muhammad.

The Qur'an as Reminder

The idea that humans are inherently forgetful of the ways of God is per-vasive in Islam. Some Muslims find etymological proof of this idea in the fact that the Arabic word for human (*insan*) shares a root with the word for forgetfulness (*nisyan*).[5] It is unsurprising, then, to find places throughout the

---

2. Seyyed Hossein Nasr, *The Heart of Islam* (New York: HarperOne, 2004), 23. Nasr writes, "Although the Qur'an can in a sense be compared to the [Bible], a more profound com-parison would be with Christ himself." Though, even this comparison breaks down be-cause Muslims contend that the Qur'an reveals only God's will, not His character, while the incarnate Son of God reveals God himself.

3. Al-Muslim, *Sahih Muslim*, book 44 (§57), https://sunnah.com/muslim/44/57.

4. Al-Bukhari, *Sahih al-Bukhari*, book 78 (§125), https://sunnah.com/bukhari/78/125.

5. Rabab Jeffery, "Forgetfulness," *Islamic Insights*, http://www.islamicinsights.com/religion/forgetfulness.html.

Qur'an that refer to God's revelation and Muhammad's example as a reminder (*dhikr*) for the people who have forgotten the ways of God.

One such place is Qur'an 3:58 which states, "We recite it to you from the signs and the wise Reminder." This verse references the Qur'an itself as a divine reminder of the ways of God. Furthermore, Qur'an 16:43 and 21:10 identify those who have received divine revelation as People of the Reminder.

Likewise, in a footnote expounding upon Qur'an 3:58, A. J. Droge explains what the Qur'an means by remembrance, writing,

> The meaning is not simply the remembering of something forgotten, but rather the keeping something before the mind by repeatedly calling it to attention. . . . Thus at [Qur'an 50:45] he is instructed to "admonish" (lit. "remind") by the Qur'an. . . . Once the Prophet himself is referred to as the "reminder."[6]

In other words, the Qur'an and Muhammad himself function within Islam as a mechanism for reminding and admonishing people to live their lives conscious of the law of God.

It is fitting, then, that much of the practice of Islam is built around repetition. The five daily prayers remind Muslims of their duty before God. Fasting during the month of Ramadan provides an annual reminder of dependence upon God as creator and sustainer. Even the Qur'an itself derives its name from the word "recite," implying repetition. In Islam, the rhythms of life help resolve the problem of fallible memory by reminding of the ways of God.

The Qur'an and Redemption

Though the solution to the problem has been stated as guidance and remembrance, the Islamic traditions do not leave these concepts vague and undefined. Instead, one finds throughout the Qur'an, and especially the *Sunnah*, very specific ways that one might live favorably before God. Not only do the traditions provide Muslims with laws for right living, but one also finds in them instructions as to how to obtain forgiveness and purification for missteps and wicked deeds.

Forgiveness

The Qur'an speaks of forgiveness in manifold ways. Believers are called to repent of their sins and to seek forgiveness from God. An example of this instruction can be found in Qur'an 40:3 in which God is depicted as "Forgiver of sin and Accepter of repentance, harsh in retribution, full of forbearance.

---

6. A. J. Droge, trans., *The Qur'an: A New Annotated Translation* (Bristol, CT: Equinox, 2015), 36n85.

(There is) no god but Him." The opportunity for repentance extends even to idolaters, as seen in Qur'an 9:5 which says,

> Then, when the sacred months have passed, kill the idola-
> ters wherever you find them, and seize them, and besiege
> them, and sit (in wait) for them at every place of ambush.
> If they turn (in repentance), and observe the prayer and
> give the alms, let them go their way. Surely God is forgiving,
> compassionate.

While this verse will be discussed further in Question 23, it is important for the purposes of investigating the Islamic understanding of repentance to note that even the idolaters can find forgiveness from God if they repent and perform the required duties of a Muslim.

Likewise, Islamic tradition depicts God as being quick to forgive those who repent, as described in the following passage, "Each night, during the third watch, God descends to the lowest heaven and asks, 'Is there anyone who calls me that I might answer? Who makes a request of me that I might grant it? Who seeks my forgiveness that I might forgive?'"[7]

Purification

Another problem that the Qur'an addresses is that of impurity. Humans defile themselves through contact with various impure things throughout their lives and must be reminded of the fact that they speak to God while in a state of impurity. Thus, one of the first steps in offering the ritual prayers is to wash oneself in a process called *wudu*. Prior to reciting the prayers in private or in a mosque, the faithful are to undergo a ritual washing so as to remind themselves of the importance of obtaining purification as a part of their duty of praying to God.

Along with the *wudu* rituals, Muslims are conscious of God's desire to purify them from the pollutions of their errant ways. The second half of Qur'an 33:33 speaks to this desire when it says, "God only wishes to take away the abomination from you, People of the House, and to purify you completely." In the context of this verse, the chief source of impurity is the former idolatry practiced by the audience.

However, one's state of purity can also be compromised by coming into contact with things deemed impure. Things such as ill-gained money, eating the flesh of donkeys or pigs, alcohol, sexual intercourse, and emission of bodily fluids are sources of impurity. The guidance of the Qur'an and the *Sunnah* prescribe various remedies for such impurity, most of

---

7. John Renard, ed., *Islamic Theological Themes: A Primary Source Reader* (Oakland, CA: University of California Press, 2014), 21.

which involve partial washing (*wudu*), or ritual baths (*ghusul*) involving washing the entire body.

Redemption and Salvation

While the words "redemption" and "salvation" function differently in the context of Islam than they do in Christianity, the concepts appear in both faiths. Comparing the biblical idea of salvation to the Qur'an, Mark Anderson writes, "In contrast to the Bible . . . the Qur'an depict[s] God's part in salvation as simply sending guidance and granting forgiveness."[8] In other words, salvation in Islam comes by following God's guidance to obtain forgiveness and purification. It is explicitly not substitutionary, and any idea of propitiation is totally alien to the concept of salvation in Islam.

From a Muslim perspective, Mahmoud Ayub confirms and expands upon this contrast. In his book *A Muslim View of Christianity*, Ayub compares the accounts immediately following the first sin of Adam in the Bible and the Qur'an. He counters the biblical idea of original sin, stating that in the Qur'an, "Adam was saved because he received words from his Lord. . . . Redemption, then, in Islam begins with Adam."[9] Ayub goes on to conclude that, in Islam, "Redemption is what men and women do with their own sin through repentance and through expiation through prayers, fasts, sharing their wealth with the poor, and so on."[10] In other words, though guidance and reminder come from God, men and women are responsible for redeeming themselves by following God's commands.

Summary

Christian theology views humans as creatures designed for an intimate, personal relationship with God. Human sins make this relationship untenable apart from God's provision of a means of atonement. In other words, the solution to this estrangement must be a divine act in which God redeems humanity, taking away their sin and impurity, and restoring them to a state of righteousness. The Bible teaches that this salvation requires both the satisfaction of God's justice and the extension of his mercy. It requires a divinely initiated act of sacrificial substitutionary atonement whereby God bears sin's punishment and achieves redemption.

The reality of human estrangement from God is clearly taught in Isaiah 59:1–2, which states, "Behold, the LORD's hand is not shortened, that it cannot save, or his ear dull, that it cannot hear; but your iniquities have made a

---

8. Mark Anderson, *The Qur'an in Context: A Christian Exploration* (Downers Grove, IL: IVP Academic, 2013), 313.
9. Mahmoud Ayub, *A Muslim View of Christianity: Essays on Dialogue* (Maryknoll, NY: Orbis, 2007), 93–94.
10. Ayub, *Muslim View of Christianity*, 94.

separation between you and your God, and your sins have hidden his face from you so that he does not hear." In other words, the sin of God's people has separated them from him in such a way that they require his intervention.

However, the same chapter promises that God will yet send a redeemer to save his people from their sins. Isaiah 59:20 concludes with this hope, saying, "'And a Redeemer will come to Zion, to those in Jacob who turn from transgression,' declares the LORD." The concept of God's redemption of his people is central to the Christian understanding of salvation.

Within Islam, however, the relationship between God and humanity is not so intimate that it would require God to provide anything beyond knowledge of his law. The human-divine relationship is one of master and servant, lord and slave. Therefore, the responsibility falls on humans to live in accordance with God's commands. Salvation or redemption, then, is not an issue of being restored into relationship, but rather functioning properly in light of one's status as servant. As such, guidance is the Islamic solution to the problem of the frailty of human memory.

REFLECTION QUESTIONS

1. Why might it be more appropriate to compare the Jesus of Christianity with the Qur'an of Islam than it would be to compare him with Muhammad?

2. Based upon the last chapter's depiction of the sin problem, what is the Islamic solution?

3. How did God save Adam, according to the Qur'an?

4. How does the idea of redemption in the Qur'an differ from the idea of redemption in the Bible?

5. Why is it that Islam can speak of salvation from sin without including a Savior?

What Is the Islamic View of the End Times?

The weighing on that Day (will be) the true (weighing). Whoever's scales are heavy, those—they are the ones who prosper, but whoever's scales are light, those are the ones who have lost their (own) selves, because of the evil they have done to Our signs.
~Qur'an 7:8–9

Islamic eschatology is rife with cryptic imagery. The end of the age is precipitated by the coming of a terrifying apocalyptic character (*ad-Dajjal*) and hordes of vicious cannibals who will overrun vast swaths of territory following two characters known as *Yajuj* and *Majuj*. In contrast, a savior figure known as the *mahdi* will arrive to lead Muslims back to the true practice of Islam. At the same time, 'Isa—the qur'anic Jesus figure—will return to do battle with *dajjal*.[1] These events announce the imminence of the final, universal judgment before God.

While speculation regarding the meaning of such enigmatic images is as rampant in Islam as it is in Christian eschatological interpretation, the final judgment before God is a clear and unavoidable reality. As stated by Badru Kateregga, "There will be a resurrection and a final judgment in which God

---

1. Jane Smith and Yvonne Haddad, *The Islamic Understanding of Death and Resurrection* (Albany: State University of New York Press, 1981), 68–69.

will determine who should go to hell and who should go to heaven."[2] Thus, while the details are variously understood, Islam anticipates a day in which God will once and for all declare human destiny, sending some into paradise and others into hellfire.

Christians and Muslims share a common understanding of human responsibility before God. Both faiths anticipate a day of judgment, and both envision God's justice as the final arbiter of eternal rewards and punishments. However, despite basic conceptual similarity, the eschatological expectations of each faith diverge at key points, exposing essential dissimilarity.

The following section will consider Islamic eschatological expectations according to the proposal of Islamic scholars Jane Smith and Yavonne Haddad in their book *The Islamic Understanding of Death and Resurrection*. Smith and Haddad divide Islamic eschatology into four segments: (1) apocalyptic signs, (2) the sounding of the trumpet, (3) the reckoning, and (4) the crossing of the bridge.[3] While much remains to be said regarding the Islamic eschaton, these four segments provide the reader with a basic understanding of Muslim expectation.

The Apocalyptic Signs

In almost any faith tradition that anticipates a final judgment, speculation regarding the timing of its advent is unavoidable. For Islam, though the Qur'an provides the reader with many indications that the hour of judgment is near, it remains silent regarding the precise timing of the eschaton's arrival. In a verse that bears remarkable similarity to Jesus's words in Matthew 24:36, Qur'an 33:63 warns, "The people ask you about the Hour. Say: 'Knowledge of it is only with God. What will make you know? Perhaps the Hour is near.'" As is true for Christians, then, one does well to avoid believing sources that propose a timetable for the day of judgment.

However, despite such a warning, the Qur'an has much to say in describing the final hour and the events that lead up to it. Smith and Haddad list several signs of the coming judgment, affecting both the natural world and the moral order.[4] Not only are the sun, stars, and sky subjected to disruption of their natural order, but also human behavior exhibits an alarming descent into moral decay.[5]

One component of this moral decay is the rogue leadership of a character named *dajjal*. This character is expected to lead many within the Ummah astray, multiplying innovations to Islam (*bid'a*) and drawing Muslims to

2. Badru Kateregga and David Shenk, *A Muslim and a Christian in Dialogue* (Scottdale, PA: Herald, 1997), 111.
3. Smith and Haddad, *Islamic Understanding of Death*, 65.
4. Smith and Haddad, *Islamic Understanding of Death*, 66.
5. See Qur'an 81.1–14.

himself as the ruler of a new kingdom. This *dajjal* is often compared to the biblical figure of the antichrist.

During the time of false leadership of *dajjal*, two figures named *yajuj* and *majuj* (often understood to be references to the biblical Gog and Magog) are expected to emerge from a place of containment to wreak havoc on the earth. These characters are referenced in Qur'an 21:95–100, though in A. J. Droge's comments on this verse, their exact nature is debated. Droge writes of *yajuj* and *majuj* that "they are variously understood as men, super-natural beings, peoples, or lands. [In Qur'an 21:96] they will be released shortly before the Day of Judgment."[6] Regardless of their true nature, these creatures pose a threat to humanity—Muslims and non-Muslims alike.

In contrast to the moral and physical destruction represented by *dajjal*, *yajuj*, and *majuj*, two savior figures are also expected to precede the blowing of the final trumpet. First of all, the *Sunnah* includes an expectation that 'Isa will return to earth in order to fight the enemies of Islam, break the symbol of the cross, and call Jews and Christians alike to submit to Islam.[7] Furthermore, 'Isa is expected to confront *dajjal* and kill him, thus ending his distortion of Islam.

Following 'Isa's defeat of *dajjal*, a figure known as the *mahdi* will appear to usher in a season of peace and prosperity for the Ummah. For Shiite Muslims, this *mahdi* is often understood to be the Twelfth Imam who has been hidden since shortly after his birth in 869 CE. For Sunnis, however, the *mahdi* will be a Sunni ruler who will establish peace and the proper expression of Islamic practice prior to the day of judgment.[8]

The Trumpet and Gathering

The first event that marks the actual day of judgment is the blowing of a trumpet and the resurrection of the dead. According to the Qur'an, this final trumpet blast comes from an angel who is awaiting God's command to signal the final judgment.[9] Though this angel is not named in the Qur'an, Islamic traditional literature identifies the angel as Israfil.[10]

What the Qur'an does discuss, however, is the effect of the trumpet blast. As recorded in Qur'an 39:68, "There will be a blast on the trumpet, and whoever is in the heavens and whoever is on the earth will be thunderstruck, except for those whom God pleases. Then there will be another blast on it,

6. A. J. Droge, trans., *The Qur'an: A New Annotated Translation* (Bristol, CT: Equinox, 2015), 212n92.

7. Gabriel Said Reynolds, *The Emergence of Islam: Classical Traditions in Contemporary Perspective* (Minneapolis: Fortress, 2012), 115. Reynolds notes that this expectation does not appear in the Qur'an.

8. Reynolds, *Emergence of Islam*, 211.

9. For example, see Qur'an 6:73; 27:87; 39:87–89; 69:13–17.

10. Richard Webster, *Encyclopedia of Angels* (Woodbury, MN: Llewellyn Worldwide, 2009), 97.

and suddenly they will stand up, looking around." This trumpet blast causes the resurrection of the dead and gathers all the living together in preparation for the reckoning.

The early Islamic commentator Ibn Taimiyah provides more detail as he writes of this day: "People will rise from their graves, barefooted, naked, and uncircumcised for Allah, the Lord of the worlds. The sun will come close to them; they will be drenched in sweat. Then the Balance will be erected and through it the deeds will be weighed."[11] In other words, as the reckoning begins, all will be drawn together to witness the judgment of God.

The Reckoning

Once all of humanity has been gathered together, the reckoning begins with each person's book of accounts being laid open. Describing the process, Qur'an 17:13–14 states, "And every human—We have fastened his fate to him on his neck, and We shall bring forth a book for him on the Day of Resurrection, which he will find unrolled. 'Read your book! You are sufficient today as a reckoner against yourself.'" Each book provides a record and rehearsal of each one's deeds.

The first creature to undergo the judgment will be Iblis (the Satan figure of the Qur'an) because, "as the exemplar of disobedience to the commands of God, Iblis is doomed to ultimate destruction as a kind of figurative first step in the unfolding drama of judgment."[12] Following the judgment of Iblis, every individual person will face judgment for his or her deeds.

Further developing the Qur'an's description of the day, Qur'an 18:49 records, "And the Book will be laid down, and you will see the sinners apprehensive because of what is in it, and they will say, 'Woe to us! What (kind of) Book is this? It omits nothing small or great, but it has counted it?' And they will find what they have done presented (to them), and your Lord will not do anyone evil." Expanding on this, Ibn Taimiyah includes the detail that when those who have believed in God's oneness receive their book, they will take it in their right hands and happily return to the others. However, those who are disbelievers will receive their record in their left hands, and by this they will know their destination is hell.[13]

As the book of one's record is disclosed, so too will one's deeds be put on display as one's life is weighed on a scale (*mizan*) of divine justice. Likewise, the Qur'an speaks of each individual being questioned regarding his or her life. Both the weighing of deeds and the questioning of individuals are discussed in Qur'an 7:6–9 which promises,

11. Muhammad Khan, trans., *Sharh Al-Aqeedat-il-Wasitiyah* (Riyadh, KSA: Darussalam, 1996), 166.
12. Smith and Haddad, *Islamic Understanding of Death*, 68.
13. Khan, *Sharh Al-Aqeedat-il-Wasitiyah*, 169.

> We shall indeed question those to whom (a messenger) was sent, and We shall indeed question the envoys. We shall indeed recount to them with knowledge, (for) We were not absent. The weighing on that Day (will be) the true (weighing). Whoever's scales are heavy, those—they are the ones who prosper, but whoever's scales are light, those are the ones who have lost their (own) selves, because of the evil they have done to Our signs.

While these passages focus on rewards and punishments according to one's deeds, Islam does not actually teach that one is saved on the basis of one's works. Rather, everyone depends on God's mercy to grant them final admittance into paradise.

The Crossing of the Bridge

According to Islamic tradition, God's decision to admit a Muslim into paradise is finally ratified in the crossing of a bridge (*siraat*) that stretches over the fires of hell and leads into the gardens of paradise. The final test on the day of judgment involves each person crossing the *siraat*. The Qur'an predominantly uses the word *siraat* to refer to the straight path of living according to God's laws.[14] During one's life, then, one can walk on the straight path of obedience to God or the wayward path of disobedience and disbelief, which leads to hell.[15]

Some Islamic tradition expands on the idea of a path, proposing that the final step for humanity on the day of judgment is to continue along the straight path, which becomes the *siraat* that leads into paradise. One Shiite explanation of the *siraat* is that "Siraat is finer than hair and sharper than sword. Some would pass over it like a flash of lightning and some would gallop over it like a horse, some would crawl over it on their four limbs and chests; some would traverse it on foot; some would be hanging from it; sometimes the fire of Hell would apprehend them and sometimes it would leave them."[16] Thus, in some traditions, the crossing of the *siraat* is the final demonstration of one's standing in eternity. If one successfully passes, paradise is the reward.

At any point in the process of traversing the bridge, however, hooks from hellfire might snatch a person off of the bridge. Yet, before the closing of paradise, tradition anticipates God extending additional mercy to some who are in hell, drawing them up based solely on his mercy.[17] Therefore, despite the

---

14. See, for example, Qur'an 3:51; 6:126, 161–2; 36:60–61; 38:26.
15. Qur'an 37:22–23.
16. Ayatullah Ibrahim Amini, Resurrection in the Qur'an, trans. Sayyid Rizvi (Qum, Iran: Ansariyan, 2011), https://www.al-islam.org/resurrection-maad-quran-ayatullah-ibrahim-amini/siraat-bridge#fref_f61ca6b8_5.
17. *Sunan an-Nasa'i*, book 12 (§112), https://sunnah.com/nasai/12/112.

effects of one's deeds in this life, crossing the *siraat* is not based solely on works. Rather, entry into paradise ultimately depends on God's protection and mercy.

Summary

As has been true of the previous four chapters, there are many striking similarities between Christian and Muslim expectations regarding the day of judgment. Both Christianity and Islam teach that humans will be held responsible before God for their deeds. Yet, the two faiths part ways when unpacking the details and foundations of this judgment.

For Christians, the judgment that will determine one's eternal destiny hangs solely on one's connection to the person and righteousness of Jesus Christ. One is determined to be "in Christ" by virtue of faith in his life, death, resurrection, and ascension. This faith credits the believer with Christ's righteousness and thereby provides the right standing by which believers enter into their reward. This reward consists most centrally of dwelling in the new heavens and new earth with God himself in the midst of the believing community.

For Muslims, however, each person's deeds fall only to their own account.[18] There is no system of substitution allowed within Islam, thus each one's deeds—good and bad—determine the balance of their individual scales before God. The knowledge of how to satisfy God's justice in Islam remains outside of human speculation, so the distribution of his mercy ultimately remains an issue of his sole discretion.

The greatest difference between the two conceptions of eternal rewards, however, is not just the means by which one receives the mercy of God. Rather, the reward itself presents a distinction within the two faiths. For Muslims, paradise is variously described as a garden of delights including multiple physical pleasures and an environment filled with everything the believer could have wanted while on earth.[19]

For Christians, however, Revelation 21:1–5 speaks of God's presence descending to dwell among his people in a restored material world. God's presence among his people is the ultimate hope of Christianity. Thus, in the same way that Moses recognized that the Promised Land would be undesirable without God's presence among his people, so too a description of the pleasures of the new creation devoid of the presence of God is not a Christian understanding of reward.[20]

---

18. See, for example, Qur'an 6:164; 17:15; 39:7; 58:38.
19. Bernard Lewis and Buntzie Churchill, *Islam: The Religion and the People* (Upper Saddle River, NJ: Wharton, 2009), 209.
20. See Exodus 33:12–16.

Former Muslim Nabeel Qureshi explains this different conception of paradise as a result of the Islamic concept of *tawhid*. In his book *No God but One*, Qureshi writes,

> As a part of our understanding of *tawhid*, we need to include a balanced understanding of Allah's self-revelation. Allah intends man to pursue the relationship of a servant to his master, but not the relationship of a child with his father. Nothing in the Qur'an suggests that Allah desires intimacy with humanity. . . . According to Christian teachings, God is our Father. He loves us as a perfect Father, and will always love us so. He wants us to have an intimate relationship with him, turning to him with our feats and failures, with our dreams and victories. He wants us to rejoice with him and in him.[21]

God's desires intimate relationship with his people, both in this mortal life and in eternity. Far beyond the descriptions of pleasures, crowns, and rewards, the Christian hope is dwelling in the unveiled presence of the Triune God. The Qur'an, however, anticipates an eternity for the faithful that reinforces its different understanding of creation, sin, and salvation.

REFLECTION QUESTIONS

1. What are the similarities and differences between Islamic and Christian eschatology?

2. Who is the *dajjal* character, and what role does he play in Islamic eschatology?

3. What is 'Isa's role in Islamic eschatology?

4. How does Islamic eschatology fit in the Islamic metanarrative?

5. What is the essential difference between Islamic and Christian views of eternity?

---

21. Nabeel Qureshi, *No God but One: Allah or Jesus?* (Grand Rapids: Zondervan, 2016), 62–63.

PART 4

The Practice of Islam

What Happens in the Mosque?

A mosque founded from the first day on the
(obligation of) guarding (oneself) is indeed
(more) worthy for you to stand in. In it
(there are) men who love to purify themselves,
and God loves the ones who purify themselves.
~Qur'an 9:108

To an uninitiated observer, a mosque can present itself as a mysterious and perhaps even imposing architectural phenomenon. From pictures of the Taj Mahal to the Hassan II mosque of Casablanca, images of the world's most iconic mosques can lead observers to believe that they provide the standard design for a Muslim place of worship. Soaring towers known as "minarets" pierce the skyline and stand adjacent to ornate domes stretched high above the heads of worshippers inside. The idea of entering such an austere and grandiose environment as an outsider is understandably intimidating.

Yet, more often than not—particularly in urban environments—a local mosque takes the form of a simple, dedicated room or nondescript building, in which Muslims gather for worship, community events, and religious education.[1] In Western countries, many mosques also include visitor centers and offer tours in an effort to promote community understanding and extend hospitality. This chapter, then, intends to remove some of the mystery and intimidation around a mosque visit in order to encourage more Christians

---

1. Colin Chapman, *Cross and Crescent: Responding to the Challenge of Islam* (Downers Grove, IL: InterVarsity, 2003), 50.

to consider visiting a local mosque in order to become acquainted with the Muslim populations living within their communities.[2]

Ablution Room

One of the first acts for a Muslim coming to the mosque for prayer is to perform the ritual washings known as "ablutions" (*wudu*). These washings are connected to the ritual of self-purification noted in the verse cited at the head of this chapter. Some mosques will include a separate, often ornate room for ritual washing. Most, however, will provide more modest access to a dedicated space wherein worshippers might perform the ritual washings required before prayer.

The ablution requirement comes from a variety of sources, though perhaps the clearest instruction comes from the *Sunnah*. One instance, found in *Sunan ibn Majah*, states, "The Messenger of Allah used to perform ablution for every prayer and we used to perform all of the prayers with one ablution."[3] Following this example, Muslims wash their hands, forearms, feet, heads, ears, and nose in order to effect purification prior to prayer.

Again, Ibn Majah provides the believer with rationale for this process, as he records Muhammad saying, "Verily, when a servant (of Allah) washes his hands, his sins fall to the ground from his hands, then as he washes his face, his sins fall to the ground from his face, then as he washes his arms and wipes his head, his sins drop from his arms and head; then when he washes his feet his sins pour down from his feet."[4] As a believer's sins fall away, then, he or she is in a state of readiness to pray. After leaving the ablution room, believers file into the main hall of the mosque. Before entering the prayer hall, however, shoes are to be removed and placed in a storage area outside of the main room. This is a reminder to the worshipper that they are entering a pure and sacred place of worship and prayer.

Prayer Hall

Upon entering the prayer hall, several features will likely stand out to a first-time visitor. Each of these physical aspects of the environment of the mosque is connected to the values of the community and the activities that occur within. Perhaps the first feature one will notice is the separation of the sexes.

---

2. Some Christians may recoil at the idea of visiting a non-Christian place of worship. While I do not recommend that anyone violate their conscience on these matters, I think there are multiple reasons to encourage a mosque visit as a way of connecting with the Muslim population within the local community, breaking down barriers, and initiating meaningful relationships.
3. Ibn Majah, *Sunan Ibn Majah*, https://sunnah.com/urn/1255080, book 1 (§549).
4. As quoted in Edward Hoskins, *A Muslim's Mind: What Every Christian Needs to Know about the Islamic Traditions* (Colorado Springs: Dawson, 2011), 61. Hoskins cites this *hadith* from *Sunan Ibn Majah*, vol. 1 (§283).

Men and Women

If you are visiting a mosque, you will want to know ahead of time that men and women do not normally intermingle in the prayer hall. Usually, men enter the mosque and take their places in the central space, while women go to a side room or an area in the rear that is screened off from the main prayer hall.[5] Depending upon the structure of the mosque building, men and women may even enter the prayer hall through different doors.

This separation intends to protect the modesty of the community gathered for prayer and to orient each one's focus toward undistracted worship.[6] Despite the physical separation, men and women in prayer follow the same directives and movements (*rakat*) simultaneously. The prayer ritual is the same for a man and a woman, even if the location is different. Likewise, it is often the case that there will be more men present than women, as women usually pray at home.

Facing Mecca

Another feature that one will notice is that the physical layout of the prayer room naturally orients attention toward a specific direction. This may not seem unusual, as most public venues present a unidirectional focus through the configuration of the seating options that are available. However, the prayer hall is unique in that most do not include chairs or pews, except perhaps in the rear of the room. That is because the mosque is a place of prostration, and seating would only inhibit the movements of the ritual prayers.

Without seating to indicate the direction of the hall, however, one will still find the room organized toward a specific focal point. This orientation may be indicated by lines on the carpet that direct worshippers where to stand, or it could be accomplished by individual prayer rugs arranged across the floor. Regardless of how it is constructed, the uniform direction is due to the fact that all Muslim prayers (*salat*) must be directed toward Mecca.

This direction is so important to Muslim prayers that it has its own name: *qibla*. Oftentimes hotels in the Middle East will include an arrow in each room pointing travelers toward the *qibla* in order to help facilitate their prayers while away from their community. Likewise, mobile phones purchased in the Middle East often feature a *qibla* indicator, or one can download an app, so as to be able to pray in the proper direction no matter where one is at any given time.

In the mosque, however, the uniformity of direction physically and observably reinforces the corporate nature of the Islamic faith. During the five daily prayers, row upon row of worshippers perform the same movements at the

---

5. Chapman, *Cross and Crescent*, 52.
6. It may be helpful for non-Muslim women visiting a mosque to know that they will likely be asked to wear a headscarf to cover their hair while inside the mosque, out of respect.

same time facing the same direction. A local mosque thus provides a glimpse of the Ummah as Muslims perform their devotional acts of prayer in unison.

Things to See
Despite the lack of furniture in the mosque, one will likely observe some sort of pulpit (*minbar*) and perhaps an indentation in the front wall (*mihrab*) of the prayer hall. The pulpit may take the form of a simple lectionary, or it may be an ornate, wooden structure including a lofted seat with a number of stairs leading up to it. This *minbar* is used on Fridays when the local mosque leader gives the weekly sermon (*khutba*).

The *mihrab*, however, is the architectural reminder of the uniform orientation toward Mecca—specifically toward the Ka'ba.[7] While the imam faces the community as he addresses them through the *khutba*, when it comes time to lead the prayers, he turns to face Mecca with them, offering his prayers in the exact same fashion as his fellow worshippers. This reminds the Muslim community that wherever their local mosque is meeting, the Ummah is united in its appeal to the first and primary place of monotheistic worship: the Ka'ba.[8]

Activities in the Mosque

As noted in Question 11, the word "mosque" is an Anglicization of the Arabic word *masjid*, which simply means a place of prostration. As such, the primary function of any given mosque is merely to be a place for Islamic prayer. However, a mosque often serves a variety of secondary purposes and hosts a number of additional activities.

Qur'an Studies
Many mosques host programs for qur'anic education and Arabic lessons. The focus on Arabic lessons is especially prevalent in non-Arabic speaking countries. However, even within the Middle East, qur'anic Arabic and Qur'an memorization regularly feature as educational programs offered by the mosque. Often children will attend their lessons on the Qur'an for an hour or more before or after their public-school day.[9]

Marriage Contracts
Much like Western weddings that include a ceremony and a reception, Islamic weddings often include two components. The celebration and festivities of a wedding may take place in an external venue, but traditional

7. Gabriel Said Reynolds, *The Emergence of Islam: Classical Traditions in Contemporary Perspective* (Minneapolis: Fortress, 2012), 211–12.
8. Reynolds, *Emergence of Islam*, 211.
9. Chapman, *Cross and Crescent*, 52.

marriages begin with a formal signing of the marriage contract in the mosque. As Bernard Lewis points out, "In Islam, marriage is a contract agreed [upon] between the bridegroom and the legal guardian of the bride, who would normally be her nearest ascendant male relative."[10] Thus, the marriage certificate is often signed by both the bride and groom and their fathers.

In contrast to Western weddings, the signing of the contract is usually restricted to a small group of immediate family members. While this ceremony takes place in the mosque with the imam presiding over it, extended family and friends gather at a different venue in anticipation of the reception festivities.

Civic Center

Most Westerners are accustomed to a sharp division between the sacred and the secular, the church and the state. However, within Islam, the mosque often provides a platform for political initiatives, campaigns, and announcements.[11] This is especially true in rural communities where the mosque may be both the religious center and a de facto city hall. As such, the mosque often serves as a locus for political rallies and as a major factor in effecting political and ideological change at the state level.

Summary

This chapter has briefly sought to prepare the reader for what they might encounter during a visit to a mosque. The idea of entering an unfamiliar religious environment is understandably uncomfortable.

Yet, while many mosques do present an imposing and austere exterior, one can almost presume upon a warm reception by the people who are inside. In fact, a visit to a mosque may prove to be a valuable step toward helping Christians to bridge the relational distance between themselves and their Muslim neighbors.

REFLECTION QUESTIONS

1. What is the purpose of an ablution room in a mosque?

2. Why does every modern mosque orient worshippers in the same direction?

---

10. Bernard Lewis and Buntzie Churchill, *Islam: The Religion and the People* (Upper Saddle River, NJ: Wharton, 2009), 113.

11. Lewis and Churchill, *Islam*, 43. Here Lewis and Churchill show the historical precedent for the conflation of the mosque and state including the fact that the *khutba* was originally a sort of political platform by which rulers addressed their people. They go on to say, "In modern times, the Khutba has become a favorite medium of ideological, political, and similar declarations."

3. What kinds of activities occur in the mosque throughout the week?

4. As a visitor to a mosque, what might be some culturally important things to consider upon entering?

5. Why might it be helpful in building relationships with Muslims to visit a local mosque?

How Do Muslims Observe Marriage, Birth, and Death?

Aqiqa is to be offered for a (newly born) boy, so slaughter (an animal) for him, and relieve him of his suffering.
~Sahih al-Bukhari[1]

There are a few events in life that are common to nearly all of humanity. Birth and death are inescapable realities that confront everyone. Likewise, most cultures recognize and celebrate some form of marriage as the joining of two lives together. Though these events occur throughout the world, the manner in which they are observed varies. Oftentimes, consideration of how a particular culture celebrates and mourns reveals something of its underlying worldview.

For our purposes, each of these events provides fertile ground for investigating the Islamic worldview as it is embodied and practiced. While the global nature of Islam opens the door to a variety of different manifestations of such practices, the Qur'an and *Sunnah* provide some orienting principles regarding Islamic marriage, birth, and death. Unpacking those principles reinforces several of the theological commitments considered in part 2.

Furthermore, even for cultural outsiders who are beginning to connect with local Muslim communities, it is likely that one will receive invitations to attend such events. Having a basic understanding of the customs and practices commended by the Qur'an and *Sunnah* provides an outsider with helpful cultural

---

1. Al-Bukhari, *Sahih al-Bukhari*, https://sunnah.com/bukhari/71/7, book 71 (§7).

orientation to these events. Likewise, being able to ask informed questions of the hosts and community during such events demonstrates a loving desire to understand the community through its important events and celebrations.

Marriage

In Islam, marriage transcends the husband and wife. Extending well beyond the couple, marriage binds the extended families together socially and legally by contract.[2] As such, marriage exerts considerable impact on the local Muslim community. In light of this impact, Islamic law is replete with instructions as to how marriage is to be conducted and governed.

Engagement and Mahr/Sadaq

Islamic law begins to exert its influence on marriage long before one's wedding day. Throughout the *Sunnah*, one finds reference to *mahr/sadaq*, two terms used to describe a gift given by the man to his future bride.[3] Traditionally this gift consists of gold or precious metal of significant value, though Islamic law does not provide a clear stipulation for the exact amount.

This concept is sometimes caricaturized as a bride price paid to the bride's father in order to affect his decision to agree to the marriage. However, as Qur'an 4:4 makes clear, it is intended to be a gift given to the bride, which becomes her sole possession.[4] If the couple ultimately divorces, this gift remains the property of the bride.[5] The *mahr/sadaq* is intended to provide her with a financial safety net independent of her husband's wealth.

If the patriarchs of the two families are amenable to the marriage, the *mahr/sadaq* is agreed upon as a part of the engagement contract, and a wedding date is determined.[6] Usually marriage is a transaction between the legal guardian of the bride—her father or an elder male relative—and the groom. However, the bride usually retains the right to refuse the marriage.[7] This process reinforces patriarchal authority, while yet maintaining protection for brides.

Marriage and Divorce

Islamic scholar John Esposito highlights the importance of marriage in Islam when he cites a *hadith* in which Muhammad is said to have

---

2. Bernard Lewis and Buntzie Churchill, *Islam: The Religion and the People* (Upper Saddle River, NJ: Wharton, 2009), 113.
3. Al-Bukhari, *Sahih al-Bukhari*, https://sunnah.com/bukhari/67/49, book 67 (§49).
4. Qur'an 4:4, "Give the women their dowries as a gift. If they remit to you any part of it on their own, consume it with satisfaction (and) pleasure." Cf. Lewis and Churchill, *Islam*, 114.
5. If the divorce is the result of confirmed adultery on the bride's part, however, she forfeits her right to the *mahr/sadaq*.
6. John Esposito, *Islam: The Straight Path* (New York: Oxford University Press, 2011), 117.
7. Lewis and Churchill, *Islam*, 113.

proclaimed, "There shall be no monkery in Islam."[8] Esposito explains this *hadith*, writing, "Marriage is incumbent on every Muslim man and woman unless they are financially or physically unable."[9] Since marriage ensures the growth and stability of the Muslim community, it is unsurprising that it would be so prioritized.

As a social institution, the agreement between families shapes the process of engagement more dramatically than the actual wedding ceremony. The pre-engagement negotiations serve to determine whether or not the two families, their goals, and their societal roles fit well together. Once both sides affirm such a fit, the engagement contract is ratified, announced, and celebrated. In some societies, the engagement party outstrips the wedding celebration.

As a legal institution, the actual wedding exhibits very little flair, consisting mainly of the signing of the marriage contract in the mosque, witnessed by representatives from each family.[10] Today, many Muslim wedding ceremonies are followed by receptions that look very similar to Western weddings. However, strictly speaking, Islamic law views the marriage as the contractual event that occurs in the mosque.

Since marriage is foundational to Islamic society, it is not to be taken lightly or dissolved thoughtlessly. Despite this ideal, however, divorce is permitted within Islam and can be achieved with relatively little difficulty. A husband is permitted to divorce his wife merely by intentional repudiation (*talaq*) by which he declares his intent to divorce her.[11] While women may not pronounce divorce in the same way, they are given recourse to the courts to appeal for divorce.[12]

Arranged Marriages and Polygamy

For many Westerners, the two issues that come to mind immediately when thinking about Islamic marriage are arranged marriages and polygamy. A brief note to place these practices in context is in order before moving on to Islamic celebration of birth and observance of death.

Arranged Marriage

Arranged marriages—considered primitive by Western ideals—continue to be practiced in some Muslim communities. In such marriages, the family of the bride and the family of the groom determine that their children will marry irrespective of the wishes of the bride and groom. Sometimes this

---

8. Esposito, *Islam*, 116.
9. Esposito, *Islam*, 116–17.
10. Esposito, *Islam*, 117.
11. See Qur'an 65, which is a whole chapter dedicated to divorce. See also Lewis and Churchill, *Islam*, 114; Esposito, *Islam*, 119; Carole Hillenbrand, *Introduction to Islam: Beliefs and Practices in Historical Perspective* (New York: Thames & Hudson, 2015), 251.
12. Esposito, *Islam*, 120.

decision is made while the children are infants. This approach to marriage, however, is not required by Islamic law. More often it is a cultural feature that transcends Islam.

At the same time, and as stated above, Muslim families are often far more involved in the engagement process than are most families in Western societies. For Westerners enamored with stories of star-crossed soul mates marrying for love alone, the imposition of the families of the bride and groom in the process of engagement seems egregious. Yet, comparing the divorce rates between these different approaches to marriage may provide reason to curtail Western critique.

Polygamy

Another flagrant offense to Western ideals is the concept of polygamy, which is allowed by the Qur'an. In the first half of Qur'an 4:3, Muhammad is told, "If you fear that you will not act fairly toward the orphan girls, marry what seems good to you of the women: two, three, or four." Most interpreters have taken this to mean that a man is allowed to marry up to four women at once.[13]

At the same time, many contemporary exegetes contend that the Qur'an's teaching on this matter intends to limit and eventually eliminate the polygamy that was common in seventh-century Arabia. The second half of Qur'an 4:3 continues on to say, "But if you fear that you will not be fair, (marry only) one, or what your right (hands) own. That (will make it) more likely that you will not be biased." By introducing the idea of fairness, the Qur'an makes it plain that polygamy is only admissible when one is capable of equal treatment of each of the wives.[14]

Regardless, most Muslims view the polygamy of Muhammad's day positively, as it afforded women a means of financial protection that they would otherwise be unable to provide for themselves. Additionally, in patrilineal societies, polygamy allows men a higher chance of producing male offspring to carry on their family name. This leads us into our discussion of how Muslims recognize and celebrate childbirth.

Birth

As with marriage, Muslims also follow specific rituals to celebrate childbirth. While the Qur'an is silent regarding how one should celebrate birth, the *Sunnah* provides the Islamic community with instructions for performing a ritual called *aqiqa*. This ritual is prescribed in *hadith* such as the one quoted at

---

13. Cf. A. J. Droge, trans., *The Qur'an: A New Annotated Translation* (Bristol, CT: Equinox, 2015), 47n7.

14. Later in the same chapter, Qur'an 4:129 indicates that it is impossible to maintain fairness between multiple wives. Thus, some contemporary writers argue that the Qur'an actually argues against polygamy.

the beginning of this chapter, and it involves sacrifice offered seven days after the child is born.[15]

Such sacrifices must follow approved Islamic practice. This practice involves reciting the name of Allah over the animal, slitting its jugular vein with a single knife stroke, and allowing the animal to bleed out.[16] Many Muslims believe that the early jurists prescribed this method of sacrifice in order to spare the animal excessive suffering.

The prescribed sacrifice for a male child is two sheep; for a female, one sheep.[17] In Islam, sacrifices are not necessarily atoning. Rather, sacrifice is a mere act of piety. Qur'an 22:36–37 clarifies the purpose of Islamic sacrifice when it states the following:

> The (sacrificial) animals—we have appointed them for you among the symbols of God: there is good for you in them. So mention the name of God over them, (as they stand) in lines. Then, when their sides fall (to the ground), eat from them, and feed the needy and the beggar. In this way We have subjected them to you, so that you may be thankful. Its flesh will not reach God, nor its blood, but the guarding (of yourselves) will reach Him from you. In this way he has subjected them to you, so that you may magnify God because he has guided you. Give good news to the doers of good.

These verses show that the Islamic God does not receive sacrifice, but that it is merely a means of offering thanksgiving that results in an opportunity to give charity to the poor and the beggar.

For a Muslim family, then, the sacrifice of *aqiqa* provides a tangible, visible means by which they can express their gratitude to God for granting them a child. These sacrifices could be likened to the thanksgiving sacrifices prescribed in the Old Testament. As the birth of a child is viewed as a God-ordained gift to be celebrated, so too the death of a family member or friend is believed to be the sovereign plan of God. Therefore, death must be observed with reverence and deference to God's wisdom.

Death

As with all other major elements in life, Islam understands the day of one's death to be determined by God. Thus, upon hearing the news that a

---

15. Edward Hoskins, *A Muslim's Mind: What Every Christian Needs to Know about the Islamic Traditions* (Colorado Springs: Dawson, 2011), 74.
16. Amir Toft, trans., Muhammad Taqi Usmani, *The Islamic Laws of Animal Slaughter* (Santa Barbara, CA: White Thread, 2006), 27–31, 35.
17. Hoskins, *A Muslim's Mind*, 74.

loved one has died, it is common for a Muslim's first words to be, "Praise God (*Hamdillah*)." To the outside observer, this may seem a calloused and inappropriate response. However, to one who is convinced that the events of one's life are determined by God, it is an appropriate, humble recognition that God's wisdom in ordaining this death surpasses one's own grief.

When a Muslim dies, Islamic law demands that the body be buried as quickly as possible following the death. Prior to burial, the body is ritually washed three times and shrouded in a white sheet.[18] When the body is laid in the grave, the head of the deceased must be facing Mecca.[19] All of this is done in anticipation of an eventual resurrection on the day of judgment.

Throughout the Middle East, it is common to follow a person's death with a community-wide period of mourning. This often involves erecting large tents in the street outside of the family's home. The members of the family—especially the males—sit in the auditorium-like tents while friends, neighbors, and extended family members come to give their condolences.

Often these tents will remain in the street, blocking traffic and access to nearby shops, for two or three days while the mourning takes place. Likewise, a *sheikh* (Islamic leader; community elder) is usually employed to read the Qur'an over a loudspeaker while guests mill about and sit in mourning. The Muslim community does not usually see this as the inconvenience that a Western reader might initially recognize it to be. Rather, it is an opportunity to remember loved ones, praise God who is sovereign over our days, and encourage the family members who have lost a loved one.

Summary

In each of these three important moments in Islamic life, one can glimpse certain underlying worldview commitments and community values. First of all, each one of these events highlights the importance of community. Weddings and engagements involve the entire family from the first moments through the signing of the marriage contracts. Likewise, births are celebrated with sacrifices, the meat of which is distributed to those in need, allowing the thankfulness of the family to extend to the broader community. And finally, observing a funeral and the public mourning tents display the importance of trusting God's sovereignty as a community and bearing the grief of loss together.

In addition to this, marriage, birth, and death are occasions to turn back thanks to God. Since God's will is binding on human experience, even mourning is to be conducted under the knowledge that God is directing each person's days according to wisdom that is beyond human understanding. As Christians, there

---

18. Al-Muslim, *Sahih Muslim*, https://sunnah.com/muslim/11/51, book 11 (§51).
19. See detailed instructions for Muslim funerals available on the website of the funerary company Everplans: "Muslim Funeral Traditions," https://www.everplans.com/articles/muslim-funeral-traditions.

are at least some ways that we can appreciate and learn from our Muslim friends and neighbors as they regularly turn their attention to the communities that they depend upon and the God who is sovereign over all things.

REFLECTION QUESTIONS

1. What are the differences and similarities between Islamic and Christian observance of the three life events of marriage, birth, and death?

2. What do we learn about the Islamic worldview from observing the way that Muslims sometimes celebrate marriage, birth, and death?

3. What are potential positive reasons for arranged marriages and polygamy?

4. How does the process of burial depict and reinforce Islamic theology?

5. What is the purpose of the *aqiqa* sacrifice?

QUESTION 21

What Are the Important Festivals in Islam?

And proclaim the pilgrimage among the people. Let them come to you on foot and on every lean animal. They will come from every remote mountain pass, so that they may witness things of benefit to them.
~Qur'an 22:27

Almost every religion observes special days that are set apart and recognized as sacred or holy. Such holidays establish annual rhythms for the community of believers and direct the minds of the adherents toward things beyond their present concerns. Islam recognizes two such festivals, both of which are important for both the theology and practice of the faith.

Though some expressions of Islam commemorate Muhammad's birthday or days associated with various Muslim saints, the Islamic community is divided over whether or not this is an act of unlawful innovation (*bid'a*).[1] In light of this dispute, this chapter will restrict itself to analysis of the two universally recognized festivals: Eid al-Fitr and Eid al-Adha.

---

1. For example, see "Fatwa 1563," *The Fatwa Center*, http://www.islamweb.net/emainpage/printarticle.php?id=156744&lang=E. This Fatwa rules that the earliest Islamic community did not celebrate Muhammad's birthday; thus, any later commemoration of his birth is an unlawful act of innovation that distracts from the worship of Allah (Qur'an 3:31).

The Feast of Breaking the Fast (Eid al-Fitr)

Every year, Muslims around the world participate in thirty consecutive days of fasting during the month of Ramadan. Due to the fact that Islam recognizes a lunar calendar, these thirty days of fasting occur at different times, according to the Gregorian calendar. Thus, depending upon the time of year and the location of the observer, a month of daytime fasting can be quite severe.[2] The severity of Ramadan is relieved, however, when the thirtieth day is completed.

The Practice of Ramadan and Eid al-Fitr

In order to properly observe the Ramadan fast, one must abstain from food, drink, tobacco, and sexual intercourse between sunrise and sunset.[3] However, at the end of each day, when the sun has set, the community breaks the fast together in celebration of another day's faithfulness. Usually the local mosque will signal the breaking of the fast (*iftar*) each day with a call to prayer from the minaret or loudspeakers.

Following the final day of Ramadan, Islam prescribes a three-day festival known as the Feast of Breaking the Fast (Eid al-Fitr). During this time, Muslims usually do not work so that they can gather as families to celebrate the completion of another year's Ramadan. This affords the family time together to reflect on the importance of the month to Islamic theology.

The Theology of Ramadan and Eid al-Fitr

The theological importance of Ramadan is most clearly seen in Qur'an 2:185, where the reader is given the rationale for observing the month of Ramadan as holy:

> The month of Ramadan, in which the Qur'an was sent down as a guidance for the people, and as clear signs of the guidance and the Deliverance: so whoever of you is present during the month, let him fast in it, but whoever of you is sick or on a journey, (let him fast) a certain number of other days. God wishes to make it easy for you, and does not wish any hardship for you. And (He wishes) that you should fulfill the number (of days), and that you should magnify God for having guided you, and that you should be thankful.

---

2. Bernard Lewis and Buntzie Churchill, *Islam: The Religion and the People* (Upper Saddle River, NJ: Wharton, 2009), 16–18. Lewis and Churchill include a story of some eighteenth-century Muslim seamen who found themselves on a ship in the Arctic during the month of Ramadan. Despite their shipmates' pleas to eat, they observed their fast, waiting for a sunset that never happened. Reportedly these men starved to death.

3. The prescriptions for Ramadan's are most clearly recorded in Qur'an 2:183–87.

In other words, Muslims must observe the month annually as an act of reverence and gratitude.

In addition to the importance of the entire month of Ramadan, the last ten days are exceedingly hallowed. One of these ten days is believed to be what is called the Night of Power (*Laylat al-Qadr*), during which one's prayers are weightier, more likely to be answered, and able to remit sins.[4]

Eid al-Fitr, then, as the festival that follows Ramadan, is a time for gratitude. It is a time to recall God's blessings and provision. It is also time to thank him for the guidance that has been given in the Qur'an and to celebrate the good deeds (*hasanat*) that have been accumulated through the fasting, prayer, and piety of Muslims and their communities observing Ramadan.

The Feast of the Sacrifice (Eid al-Adha)

Approximately seventy days after Ramadan, Muslims celebrate another festival called the Feast of the Sacrifice (Eid al-Adha). This festival lasts four days, and it occurs during the annual pilgrimage to Mecca (*hajj*). As indicated by the name of the feast, the central component of this Islamic holiday involves an animal sacrifice.

The basis for this sacrifice is found in Qur'an 37:99–111, where Ibrahim receives a vision that instructs him to sacrifice his son.[5] The Qur'an's account of this story lacks detail, so most Islamic commentators draw on the biblical story of the binding of Isaac from Genesis 22 to fill in the narrative gaps.[6] In so doing, one understands that God provided an animal as an alternative sacrifice.

With Genesis 22 in mind, Qur'an 37:106–111 establishes Ibrahim as an exemplar of faith whose obedience serves as the model for contemporary practice of Eid al-Adha:

> "Surely this—indeed it was a clear test." And we ransomed him with a great sacrifice, and left (this blessing) on him among the later (generations). "Peace (be) upon Abraham! [Ibrahim] In this way we repay the doers of good. Surely he was one of Our believing servants."

4. Ayman and Emily Ibrahim, "The Night of Power during Ramadan," *The Zwemer Center*, http://www.zwemercenter.com/the-night-of-power-during-ramadan/.
5. I have chosen to refrain from naming Abraham's son because the earliest Islamic commentators are divided over the issue of which son was involved. However, contemporary Islamic commentary almost universally determines the son to be Ismail, who is believed to be the biblical Ishmael, Abraham's son from Hagar.
6. Cf. Abdullah Yusuf Ali, *The Qur'an: Text, Translation, and Commentary* (Elmhurst, NY: Tahrike Tarsile Qur'an, 2005), 1205n4101; A. J. Droge, trans., *The Qur'an: A New Annotated Translation* (Bristol, CT: Equinox, 2015), 297n52; Gabriel Said Reynolds, *The Qur'an and the Bible* (New Haven, CT: Yale University Press, 2018), 681.

Thus, today, as they observe the sacrifice of Eid al-Adha, Muslims rehearse Abraham's obedience, hoping to obtain the same commendation that he received from God.

The Practice of Eid al-Adha

The Feast of the Sacrifice begins around the world at dawn with the slaughtering of the sacrificial animals. Since the Qur'an does not explicitly identify the type of sacrifice, a variety of animals are permitted. Occasionally, several families in a neighborhood will pool their money to purchase a cow or a camel as a collective sacrifice. More commonly, however, a family will sacrifice a sheep or a goat.

After the slaughter, the animals are butchered, and the meat is divided into thirds. One third of the meat belongs to the family to eat. One third is given to extended family or friends. The final third is given to the poor as a means of charity. In so doing, the participants are reminded that, as God cares for them, so too does he care for the poor in their midst.

While Muslims celebrate Eid al-Adha wherever they are around the world, it is important to note that this feast takes place on the tenth day of the month of Hajj (Dhu al-Hajja), which is the final day of the pilgrimage to Mecca (*hajj*). For those who are participating in the *hajj*, they are also required to perform additional rituals connected with Abraham and his family. Question 29 will address some of these connections in greater detail, but for our current purposes it is theologically important to note that the ritual is focused on Abraham.

The Theology of Eid al-Adha

One of the questions that Eid al-Adha often raises concerns the meaning of sacrifice in Islam. Islam rejects substitutionary atonement in Qur'an 35:18. Likewise, Qur'an 22:37 explicitly denies that God receives the blood or meat of a sacrificial animal. If that is true, what is the function of sacrifice in Islam? The answer is found just three verses earlier in Qur'an 22:34a, which says, "For every community We have appointed a ritual." In other words, each faith community has been given its own rituals as signs of authentic divine dispensation.

Despite such apparent approval of other religious communities, the Qur'an declares that other dispensations have come to an end with the arrival of Islam. Near the end of Qur'an 5:3, one reads, "Today I have perfected your religion for you, and I have completed My blessing on you, and I have approved Islam for your religion." It is clear that this verse intends to communicate that Islam supersedes Christian and Jewish religion because the surrounding context discusses how to interact with those who have previously received revelation.

Another interpretive clue emerges from the preceding verses that contain instructions regarding the *hajj* and the Feast of the Sacrifice. In light of this context, Islamic scholar Michel Cuypers identifies Eid al-Adha as "the feast *par excellence* . . . [that] will be the celebration of Islam's day of completion for all, not just the Muslims, but also the Jews and Christians."[7] This particular feast provides the Muslim community with a ritual that both supersedes and precedes other religions. As a sacrificial rite revealed to Muhammad and prescribed for his community, Eid al-Adha is specifically Islamic. It marks the final dispensation of divine religion.

However, since its sacrifice is predicated upon Abraham's faithfulness, it also connects the Islamic community into a story that predates Judaism and Christianity. Highlighting this fact, Qur'an 3:67 states, "Abraham was not a Jew, nor a Christian, but he was a *hanif*, a Muslim. He was not one of the idolaters."

Thus, as they celebrate Eid al-Adha, Muslims lay claim to both the final and the original religion revealed from God. Abraham is viewed as a proto-Muslim, and imitation of his obedience is a means of returning to the one true faith toward which God has always been guiding his people. The theological importance of Eid al-Adha is not connected with atonement, as is the case with many biblical sacrifices. Rather, it indicates Islamic authority and finality.

Summary

By inspecting the festivals above, one gains insight into the central beliefs of Islam. As Muslims celebrate Eid al-Fitr, they complete their annual fast with a feast of gratitude. This feast celebrates the return to normal rhythms of life after fasting throughout the month of Ramadan. Additionally, it celebrates the memory of God's provision of guidance through the Qur'an. God's provision of nourishment for the body and guidance for the will elicits the gratitude celebrated during this feast.

Likewise, observing Eid al-Adha causes the Islamic community to recall its roots and to reassert its place as the final dispensation of religion. Through remembering Abraham's obedience, Muslims connect themselves to an exemplar of faith who precedes both Judaism and Christianity. Furthermore, by observing the sacrifice of Eid al-Adha as commanded by Muhammad, Muslims lay claim to the final form of religion, as stated in Qur'an 5:3: "Today I have perfected your religion for you, and I have completed My blessing on you, and I have approved Islam for your religion."

Through these two festivals, Muslims remember the guidance of God through the Qur'an. Within its pages, the Qur'an recognizes Islam as both the primordial and final form of divinely approved religion. Thus, the festivals that Muslims participate in rehearse and reinforce the central claims of Islam.

---

7. Michel Cuypers, *The Banquet: A Reading of the Fifth Sura of the Qur'an* (Miami, FL: Convivium, 2009), 87. See also page 454, wherein Cuypers connects Qur'an 5:114 with the annual pilgrimage and thus its sacrifice.

REFLECTION QUESTIONS

1. How does Ramadan reinforce central tenets of Islamic thought and theology?

2. How does Eid al-Fitr connect to Ramadan, and what is its purpose?

3. What role does Eid al-Adha play in Islamic theology?

4. Why is Abraham's sacrifice so important to Muslims? Why aren't the sacrifices prescribed by Moses important to Muslims?

5. What are the differences between the Islamic practice of animal sacrifice and the biblical commands to sacrifice given in the Old Testament?

Are Women Required to Wear a Veil (*hijab*) in Islam?

---

*And say to the believing women (that) they (should)
lower their sight and guard their private parts,
and not show their charms, except for what
(normally) appears of them. And let them draw
their head coverings over their breasts.*
~Qur'an 24:31a

Muslim women can often be identified in a crowd by means of their traditional head coverings (*hijab*). While some Western Muslims have abandoned traditional Muslim apparel, viewing it as a relic of seventh-century patriarchy, the majority of Muslim women wear a *hijab* in order to comply with the qur'anic verse cited above.[1] This practice has stirred significant controversy in modern times—particularly in Western countries.[2]

Though today Muslims are often at the center of discussion regarding head coverings, such practices are not entirely unique to Islam. To this point, Gabriel Said Reynolds notes that Qur'an 24:31 finds a precedent in the

---

1. Ziauddin Sardar, *What Do Muslims Believe? The Roots and Realities of Modern Islam* (New York: Walker, 2007), 78–79.
2. Matthew Weaver, "Burqa Bans, Headscarves, and Veils: A Timeline of Legislation in the West," *The Guardian*, May 31, 2018, https://www.theguardian.com/world/2017/mar/14/headscarves-and-muslim-veil-ban-debate-timeline.

Didascalia, a third-century Syriac Christian text.[3] Likewise, in some Western churches Christian women cover their hair during worship in an effort to follow Paul's instructions in 1 Corinthians 11:2–16.

Since the Islamic practice extends beyond worship settings, however, one must address the *hijab* on its own terms. The following chapter will briefly address some of the underlying issues related to the *hijab* as they appear in the Qur'an, the *Sunnah*, and contemporary discourse.

The *Hijab, Abaya, Burqa*, and *Niqab*

Before proceeding, it will be helpful to define four terms one will encounter in discussion of Islamic clothing: (1) *hijab*, (2) *abaya*, (3) *burqa*, and (4) *niqab*. These words often appear in Western media, though the precision with which they are used varies from one source to another.

Hijab

The Arabic word *hijab* is often translated into English as "veil." The *hijab* is a scarf that is worn around the head, neck, and hair. The face is exposed, though the hairline is concealed. *Hijab* scarves come in a variety of colors and designs, and the manner of wrapping the hair varies based on the region of the world and its current fashion trends.

Abaya

The word *abaya* is used to refer to a traditional overgarment that some Muslim women wear. It is usually a loose-fitting material that covers a woman from her wrist to her neck and flows down to her feet. As with the *hijab*, there is no regulation on color or pattern for the *abaya*. However, most women who wear the *abaya* do so as an act of modesty, and thus shy away from bright colors or attention-garnering adornment.

Burqa and Niqab

The *burqa* and the *niqab* are perhaps the most controversial kinds of Muslim apparel. The *burqa* is a head covering that flows over the rest of the body. Often associated with places like Afghanistan, Saudi Arabia, and Yemen, the *niqab* is an additional face covering that is often paired with a *burqa*. Some face coverings overlay the eye-slits with a transparent tulle that

---

3. Gabriel Said Reynolds, *The Qur'an and the Bible: Text and Commentary* (New Haven, CT: Yale, 2018), 549–50. Reynolds reveals this parallel as he cites chapter 3 (§26) of the *Didascalia*: "If you want to become a faithful woman, please your husband only. And when you walk in the street, hide your head with your garment, that because of your veil your great beauty may be hidden. And adorn not the countenance of your face but have downcast looks and walk being veiled."

further obscures the woman's eyes. Often, women dressing in a *niqab* will also wear gloves to cover their hands.[4]

Modest Dress in the Qur'an

In Qur'an 24:30–31, both men and women are commanded to seek modesty, particularly in relation to members of the opposite sex. Male clothing is not addressed in the Qur'an, but females are instructed to cover their charms—their hair, neck, and breasts—with a head covering, so as to conceal their beauty from the general public, preserving it for their husbands. These principles of modesty pervade the Qur'an, but the details of how one should dress are often determined more by the specific culture in which Muslim women live.

Furthermore, the Qur'an is also concerned to protect women from harassment. For instance, Qur'an 33:59 states, "Prophet! Say to your wives, and your daughters, and the believing women, to draw some of their outer clothes over themselves. That is more appropriate for their being recognized and not hurt." Thus, the Qur'an instructs a woman to cover as a preservation of her beauty and as a protective measure to keep her safe from unsolicited sexual attention.

At the same time, a helpful observation is made by a male Muslim human rights advocate named Qasim Rashid. Rashid points out that the qur'anic commands regarding modesty begin with instructions directed at men. Before calling women to cover themselves, Qur'an 24:30 commands a Muslim man to avert his eyes from a woman that is not his wife.

In Rashid's words, "In Islam, men have an obligation to God and to women to observe hijab."[5] Viewing "hijab" as a call to modesty rather than a specific type of clothing, Rashid goes on to challenge his male Muslim audience, saying, "The Qur'an keeps us accountable. Only after the Qur'an thoroughly commands men to observe hijab by being modest, not staring, and reforming ourselves, does the Qur'an address women."[6] Though some argue that the *hijab* is to protect men from illicit temptation, Rashid shows that the burden of responsibility for one's actions falls first on men who are to respect the chastity of the women around them.

Modest Dress in the *Sunnah*

As has been the case elsewhere, where the Qur'an lacks detail regarding observance of modesty, it is supplied more readily by the *Sunnah*. Again,

---

4. Carole Hillenbrand, *Introduction to Islam: Beliefs and Practices in Historical Perspective* (London: Thames & Hudson, 2015), 266.
5. Qasim Rashid, "Muslim Men Need to Understand That the Qur'an Says That They Should Observe the Hijab First, Not Women," *Independent*, March 29, 2017, https://www.independent.co.uk/voices/muslim-men-hijab-forcing-women-islam-teaching-mohammed-quran-modesty-a7655191.html. It should be noted that, while Rashid's argument is valid and appropriate, it represents a minority position in practice.
6. Rashid, "Muslim Men."

though the particular expressions of Islamic dress are most affected by the cultural norms of a particular region, the *Sunnah* includes elements that have developed into what we see today in the *hijab, abaya, burqa*, and *niqab*.

One example is found in *Sahih al-Bukhari*, which records a *hadith* in which 'Aisha, one of Muhammad's wives, states, "When (the Verse): 'They should draw their veils over their necks and bosoms,' was revealed, (the ladies) cut their waist sheets at the edges and covered their heads and faces with those cut pieces of cloth."[7]

From this *hadith*, one can see how the *hijab, niqab*, and *burqa* became associated with proper Islamic dress. Though the verse cited merely calls for the covering of a woman's neck and chest, the *hadith* provides a precedent for covering both the head and face. Such a precedent provides some jurists with rationale for requiring a covering that conceals the hair, neck, and also the face.[8]

Edward Hoskins, in his book *A Muslim's Mind*, cites another *hadith* that explains the occasion of revelation of the veil: "'Righteous as well as immoral people come in on you. So command your wives to wear the veil (*hijab*).' Then Allah revealed the verses of al-hijab."[9] This verse provides rationale for prescribing the veil even in one's own home in order to avoid exposure to those who may visit.[10]

This is by no means an exhaustive list of *hadith* that discuss the prescribed apparel for Muslims. Nor is it the case that the rulings developed from these precedents are taken as obligatory throughout the Ummah. However, it is helpful to consider some of the textual and traditional foundations for the various expressions of Islamic dress that one may encounter. Having considered these foundations, it remains to consider how issues of Muslim dress codes are discussed in contemporary society.

Modest Dress in Modern Society

In addressing the variety of expressions of Islamic dress, it is common to read anecdotes about a Muslim woman in a miniskirt walking arm in arm down the street with a Muslim woman who is covered from head to toe.[11] Such diversity highlights the sometimes difficult process of contextualizing

---

7. Al-Bukhari, *Sahih al-Bukhari*, https://sunnah.com/urn/44370, book 65 (§4759).
8. The Permanent Committee, "Ruling on Hijab as Prescribed by Islam," *Kingdom of Saudi Arabia: Portal of the General Presidency of Scholarly Research and Ifta'*, http://www.alifta.net/fatawa/fatawaDetails.aspx? languagename=en&View=Page&PageID=6425&PageNo=1&BookID=7, fatwa 667. See also Muhammed ibn 'Abdullah as-Subayyal, "Wearing the Niqaab," *Fatwa Online*, July 24, 2010, https://www.fatwa-online.com/wearing-the-niqaab.
9. Edward Hoskins, *A Muslim's Mind: What Every Christian Needs to Know about the Islamic Traditions* (Colorado Springs: Dawson, 2011), 76.
10. Permanent Committee, "Ruling on Hijab," fatwa 16444.
11. Hillenbrand, *Introduction to Islam*, 267–68.

Islam for the modern world. Early Islamic jurists were exclusively male and often sought to enforce strict interpretations of the injunctions for female modesty.[12]

However, an influential translator of the Qur'an, Muhammad Asad, has argued that the phrase "what normally appears of them" from Qur'an 24:31 is intentionally vague and imprecise about what parts of a woman should be covered. As such, "the very vagueness of the phrase allows for time-bound changes to occur and therefore for different interpretations to be possible at different periods in history."[13] Thus, from Asad's perspective, a Muslim woman may exhibit her modesty in a multitude of ways, depending upon her context.

The diversity of expression of Muslim dress reveals some of the struggle involved in applying seventh-century religious injunctions in twenty-first-century environments. As the *Sunnah* was compiled and began to exert influence over the Ummah, early Muslims acquired access to a Muslim way to live their lives. Down to some of the minutest details, such as brushing one's teeth and keeping one's beard, the *Sunnah* provides a precedent for how to imitate Muhammad's exemplary life.[14]

While initially helpful in instructing the community regarding how to apply Islam, such detailed instructions regarding one's life can at times be very difficult to apply in contemporary society. Modern Muslims find themselves asking whether they are to follow the explicit instructions given throughout the *Sunnah* and the subsequent history of interpretation and application, or if they are to merely seek to honor the principle of the law in a way that is in keeping with contemporary cultural expectations. This struggle is most pronounced in Western countries that are not majority Muslim, though cities like Beirut, Tunis, Cairo, and Amman exhibit wide diversity within the Middle East as well.

Summary

This chapter seeks to address the question, "Are women required to wear the veil within Islam?" With the variety of different interpretations included even in this brief treatment, it is apparent that one can't answer this question absolutely. The Qur'an and the *Sunnah* both instruct women to cover their hair and neck, though the *Sunnah* goes further to include indications that women should also cover their faces. Regardless of the specific details regarding how much is to be covered, throughout the Islamic world most interpretations call for some form of head covering.

However, as recent interpreters such as Muhammad Asad have attempted to demonstrate, there is at least some reason to think that the Qur'an might

---

12. Hillenbrand, *Introduction to Islam*, 252.
13. Hillenbrand, *Introduction to Islam*, 252.
14. Hoskins, *A Muslim's Mind*, 20.

be more open to cultural expression than traditional interpreters have taught. Regardless of the ultimate answer, there are myriad reasons that Muslim women wear the *hijab*. Most Muslim women will gladly engage another woman in conversation about their head covering, and there are a variety of reasons that a woman might give for her apparel. Since asking an individual Muslim why she either wears or does not wear the *hijab* opens the door for a personal conversation, it may be best to leave the answer to this chapter's question open.

REFLECTION QUESTIONS

1. What is your first thought when you see a woman wearing a head covering?

2. Is the head covering inextricably bound up in seventh-century Arab patriarchy, or are there alternative motivations for Muslim women wearing the *hijab*?

3. Where does the idea of the *burqa* and *niqab* come from?

4. What does the Qur'an say to men about modesty? How does the way the Qur'an speaks of male modesty challenge some of the stereotypes associated with head covering?

5. Why do some women feel obligated to wear the head covering while other practicing Muslim women do not?

What Does Islam Teach about Holy War (*jihad*)?

*Those of the believers who sit (at home)—other than
the injured—are not equal with the ones who struggle
[perform jihad] in the ways of God with their wealth
and their lives. God favors the ones who struggle
[perform jihad] with their wealth and with their lives
over the ones who sit (at home). To each God has
promised the good (reward), but God favors (with)
a great reward the ones who struggle [perform jihad]
over the ones who sit (at home): (higher) ranks
from Him, and forgiveness and mercy. Surely
God is forgiving, compassionate.*
~Qur'an 4:95–96

During the 1980s, a war raged in Afghanistan between the Soviet Union and the Afghani people. As a predominantly Muslim country, Afghanistan viewed the largely atheistic Soviet Union as both a national and religious enemy. The fact that this dual threat faced a Muslim nation motivated the global Ummah to provide support to their Afghani kin.

Throughout the war, fighters from all over the Muslim world came to fight shoulder to shoulder with the Afghani army against the Soviet incursion. These fighters were known by an Arabic name: *mujahideen*. This word made its way into English by way of news coverage of the war, thus becoming a relatively well-known way to refer to religiously motivated Muslim guerilla fighters who fight for the purposes of protecting the Ummah.[1]

While the *mujahideen* of the Soviet-Afghani war fought in a place far removed from immediate Western concerns, the events of September 11, 2001, brought religiously motivated Islamic violence home to the United States in jarring fashion. As a result, the West learned another related Arabic word: *jihad*.

Having seen the willingness of the *mujahideen* to fight in the name of Islam and learning about the concept of *jihad* in the context of religiously motivated terrorism, many in the West have asked if Islam is inherently violent. In order to answer that question, it behooves us to inspect the concept of *jihad* as it appears within Islamic theology and teaching.

The Greater *Jihad*

The qur'anic verse cited at the head of this section provides an instance of the Qur'an's teaching on the concept of *jihad*. As seen above in A. J. Droge's translation of the Qur'an, the English rendering of the word *jihad* is "struggle." This translation has a lot of merit in that it allows room for both of the interpretations of *jihad* that are offered by Islamic scholars.

First of all, most Muslim writers divide *jihad* into the categories of the greater and lesser *jihad*. This division can be seen in an open letter to the Islamic State (ISIS/DAISH) that has been written and signed by Islamic scholars from around the world. The letter states, "There are two kinds of jihad in Islam: the greater jihad, which is the jihad (struggle) against one's ego; and the lesser jihad (struggle) against the enemy."[2] In other words, the greater struggle (*jihad*) is against one's own human inclinations to deviate from the straight path of Islam.

Such a division between greater and lesser *jihad* finds precedent in the *Sunnah*. The authors of the open letter cite a *hadith* in which Muhammad says that he has returned from the lesser *jihad* to the greater *jihad*, referring to his return home from battle to practice his faith and fight internally to remember the ways of Allah.[3] Furthermore, Qur'an 25:52 seems to support the idea that a great *jihad* is the internal struggle to bring one's heart under obedience to the Qur'an: "So, do not obey the disbelievers, but struggle mightily against them by means of [the Qur'an]."[4]

---

1. For a fascinating and informative treatment of the Soviet-Afghan war and its relationship to September 11, see Lawrence Wright, *The Looming Tower: Al-Qaeda and the Road to 9/11* (New York: Vintage, 2006).
2. "Open Letter to Dr. Ibrahim Awwad Al Badri, Alias 'Abu Bakr al-Baghdadi', and to the Fighters and Followers of the Self-Declared 'Islamic State,'" September 19, 2014, http://www.lettertobaghdadi.com, 10.
3. "Open Letter," 10. The *hadith* that the authors cite is admittedly weak.
4. Lit. "against them by means of it." A. J. Droge, trans., *The Qur'an: A New Annotated Translation* (Bristol, CT: Equinox, 2015), 236n64. Droge identifies the Qur'an as the "it" to which this verse refers.

Thus, for many Muslims, the concept of the greater *jihad* might be compared to a Christian understanding of fighting against the sinful flesh. For example, the spiritual warfare imagery that Paul employs in Ephesians 6:10–20 to describe the fight against sin is not radically different than the way in which the greater *jihad* functions in Islam.[5] However, while Paul teaches that the Holy Spirit is active in helping a Christian fight toward Christlikeness, Islam sees the Qur'an as sufficient guidance and reminder from God to aid the Muslim in *jihad*.

The Lesser *Jihad*

While the previous section has discussed nonviolent forms of *jihad* as preferable, it does not necessarily exclude armed struggle as an implication of the lesser *jihad*. In fact, there is significant material throughout the Qur'an and *Sunnah* that admits of and even instructs Muslims to engage in various forms of lesser *jihad*.

One qur'anic example commending such external, armed struggle comes from Qur'an 9:20, where one reads,

> Those who have believed, and emigrated, and struggled [waged *jihad*] in the way of God with their wealth and their lives are higher in rank with God. Those—they are the triumphant. Their Lord gives them good news of mercy from Himself, and approval, and (there are) Gardens for them in which (there is) lasting bliss, there to remain forever. Surely God—with Him is a great reward.

Commenting on these verses, Ayman Ibrahim notes that "a strict interpretation of this passage believes that *jihad* here cannot mean only to live a pious life—it refers to earning a higher rank by defending Allah against infidels."[6]

A few verses later, Qur'an 9:29 instructs Muslims to "fight those who do not believe in God or the Last Day, and do not forbid what God and His messenger have forbidden, and do not practice the religion of truth—from among those who have been given the Book—until they pay tribute out of hand, and they are disgraced." Despite the teaching to the contrary by some contemporary Muslims, neither this passage nor its context are qualified by any time

---

5. In fact, the word *jihad* appears in the Arabic translation of the Bible in Ephesians 6:13 where Paul says, "Our battle (*jihad*) is not against flesh and blood." See the discussion by Ayman Ibrahim, "What Does the Quran Say about Fighting Non-Muslims?," in *Islam and North America: Loving Our Muslim Neighbors*, eds. Micah Fries and Keith Whitfield (Nashville: B&H, 2018), 85.
6. Ibrahim, "Fighting Non-Muslims?," 85.

constraint or condition that would indicate that its instructions should be restricted to a specific occasion or time period.[7]

Likewise, the *Sunnah* provides many instances in which lesser *jihad* is commended. For instance, Ibn Majah records the following *hadith*: "'O Messenger of Allah, which Jihad is best?' He said: '(That of a man) whose blood is shed and his horse is wounded.'"[8] This authentic *hadith* cannot be interpreted to mean mere internal struggle against sin, but indicates a situation in which one's life and even one's horse is engaged in warfare.

Another such *hadith* found in *Sahih al-Bukhari* not only commends violent *jihad*, but promises rewards—eternal and temporal—for those who fight for the cause of Allah:

> Allah guarantees to the person who carries out Jihad for His Cause and nothing compelled him to go out but the Jihad in His Cause, and belief in His Words, that He will either admit him into Paradise or return him with his reward or the booty he has earned to his residence from where he went out.[9]

That this *hadith* endorses *jihad* as warfare can be seen in the reference to the acquisition of "booty" as the result of one's *jihad* endeavors. Likewise, the phrase "going out" shows that this is not an internal battle against sin but rather an instance of waging the lesser *jihad*.

Thus, though an apparent difference in value exists between the two forms of *jihad*, the concept of lesser *jihad* in the name of God remains as one of the canonical teachings of Islam. Since the vast majority of Muslims will never engage in the lesser *jihad*, it remains to consider the variety of interpretations that Muslims offer for understanding how to apply *jihad* today.

The Application of *Jihad*

Islam is a lived and living faith. Though it has canonical texts and systems of determining authorized interpretation, it is ultimately a faith that is individually expressed through the lives of its adherents. Having looked at some of its texts that commend both types of *jihad*, we are wise to take the advice of Ayman Ibrahim, who writes, "Non-Muslims are in no position to decide which Islamic interpretation is right for their Muslim neighbors."[10] This final

---

7. Ibrahim, "Fighting Non-Muslims?," 78. Ibrahim narrates an encounter with a Muslim friend who made the oft-repeated claim that the violence of the Qur'an was limited to the authorized fighting that Muhammad and his near successors engaged in and it is no longer applicable today.

8. Ibn Majah, *Sunan Ibn Majah*, https://sunnah.com/urn/1276430, book 24 (§2900).

9. Al-Bukhari, *Sahih al-Bukhari*, https://sunnah.com/bukhari/97/83, 97 (§83).

10. Ibrahim, "Fighting Non-Muslims?," 81.

section turns, then, to some of the interpretations and applications of *jihad* offered throughout the Islamic Ummah.

Spiritual Jihad

Perhaps the most common understanding of *jihad* among Western Muslims is that the priority of the greater *jihad* has eclipsed the lesser *jihad*. This opinion often emerges from a belief that armed *jihad* was appropriate for the first generation of Muslims, but no longer is part of Islamic practice.[11] Today, *jihad* is waged personally and internally against sin.

A related opinion concerning how to interpret and apply *jihad* is that warfare imagery is allegory. *Sunan ibn Majah* records a *hadith* that says, "The best of jihad is a just word spoken to an unjust ruler."[12] In this sense, *jihad* looks less like taking up a sword and more like taking up a microphone or a pen to stand up in the face of public injustices.

This rendering of *jihad* as an ideological fight for justice is explained by Seyyed Hossein Nasr, who writes, "In the same way that in English one says that such and such an organization is carrying out a crusade to eradicate poverty or disease, in Islamic languages one can say that this or that group of government agency is carrying out a *jihad* to say, build houses for the poor."[13] Interpreted in this manner, *jihad* becomes a nonviolent battle for personal piety and public social justice.

Defensive Jihad

While many Muslims—especially those in Western countries—will describe *jihad* in terms similar to those sketched above, the majority of traditional interpreters admit that there is clear evidence in the Qur'an and *Sunnah* that commends defensive warfare in the service of God.[14] In the words of Muhammad Abduh, a nineteenth-century Muslim commentator, "Fighting has been made obligatory in Islam only for the sake of defending the truth and its followers."[15] Such *jihad* as armed warfare, then, should be limited by several factors, chief among the condition that this armed *jihad* is defensive rather than aggressive.[16]

---

11. Ibrahim, "Fighting Non-Muslims?," 78.
12. Ibn Majah, *Sunan Ibn Majah*, https://sunnah.com/ibnmajah/36/86, book 36 (§86).
13. Seyyed Hossein Nasr, *The Heart of Islam: Enduring Values for Humanity* (New York: HarperOne, 2004), 257.
14. Cf. Qur'an 2:190–193; 4:95–96; 9:5.
15. Rashid Rida, "Tafsir Manar of Abduh," *Al Manar* 10 (1905): 332. As cited in Afsaruddin, "Jihad and Martyrdom," n. 42.
16. See Qur'an 60:7–8 and Qur'an 8:61 and the comments of al-Tabari recorded by Asma Afsaruddin, "Jihad and Martyrdom in Islamic Thought and History," March 2016, *Oxford Research Encyclopedias: Religion*, http://oxfordre.com/religion/view/10.1093/acrefore/9780199340378.001.0001/acrefore-9780199340378-e-46.

Likewise, declaring a state of *jihad* is not the unbridled prerogative of individuals, but should be determined by the criteria established by the *'ulama* (scholars of Islam). Armed conflict must meet a variety of criteria in order to be considered just-*jihad*: (1) legitimate cause, (2) legitimate goals, (3) legitimate purpose, (4) legitimate methodology, and (5) legitimate intention.[17] Despite these criteria, however, the Ummah lacks a single governing body that can authoritatively declare a state of *jihad* to be justified or unjustified. Thus, both those who limit *jihad* and those who view it as a means of service to God appeal to the Qur'an for support.

Aggressive Jihad

As has been demonstrated through the rising number of terrorist groups such as al-Qaeda, ISIS, and Boko Haram, a minority of Muslims view aggressive, violent *jihad* as a means of establishing an Islamic society. In order to espouse such a view, however, one must excise the verses that call for peaceful relations with nonaggressive outsiders.

Two problem verses for the proponents of aggression are Qur'an 2:190 and 256. The first verse instructs Muslims to "fight in the way of God against those who fight against you, but do not commit aggression. Surely God does not love the aggressors." The second verse clearly states, "(There is) no compulsion in religion." In other words, one can neither attack an enemy nor force someone to convert to Islam under threat of death.

In light of these verses, one might wonder how the blatant aggression and violent executions of non-Muslims have been such widely endorsed tactics used by contemporary radical groups.[18] To understand this apparent contradiction, one must consider the Islamic concept of abrogation. Abrogation occurs when an earlier command is nullified by a later revelation.

Therefore, radical Muslims claim that the peaceful verses of the Qur'an belong to an earlier time, and thus can be abrogated by later, more aggressive verses such as the so-called "sword verse" of Qur'an 9:5:

> Then, when the sacred months have passed, kill the idolaters wherever you find them, and seize them, and besiege them, and sit (in wait) for them at every place of ambush. If they turn (in repentance), and observe the prayer and give the alms, let them go their way. Surely God is forgiving, compassionate.

---

17. "Open Letter," 10–13.
18. Afsaruddin, "Jihad and Martyrdom." He also says there that advocates of defensive *jihad* take into account the entire corpus of Islamic literature and determine that "the critical verses which forbid the initiation of war by Muslims and which uphold the principle of non-coercion in religion categorically militate against the conception of an offensive jihad to be waged against non-Muslims *qua* non-Muslims."

This verse and others like it provide radical Islamist groups with qur'anic support for unbridled aggression against non-Muslims.[19]

Summary

The word *jihad* has entered into Western vocabulary by way of the Western news media's coverage of radical Islam and horrendous acts of terrorism. Put in its proper place in Islamic theology, however, this chapter has shown that *jihad* is not a monolithic concept. Most of the Islamic world would define the role of *jihad* in contemporary Muslim life in terms of the greater *jihad*. Greater *jihad* refers to the daily personal struggle to remember the ways of God and strive to submit to his will.

Additionally, many would also contend that there is a place for the lesser *jihad* of armed resistance. However, the obligation to participate in this lesser *jihad* only obtains when fighting in the name of God is done against those who have first attacked the Ummah. Likewise, it must be bound to certain just-*jihad* criteria including a refusal to harm noncombatants, children, and the elderly.[20]

Finally, there is a small minority of Muslims who believe that the verses that call for limiting *jihad* have been abrogated by those that command it in an unrestricted manner. Such groups take literal and selective readings of the Qur'an as their marching orders. The following question will provide further investigation into the legitimacy of such radical expressions.

REFLECTION QUESTIONS

1. Is Islam inherently violent? Why or why not?

2. How do members of violent strains of Islam justify their position textually?

3. Is Islam supposed to be spread by the sword or by peaceful means?

4. What is the difference between the greater *jihad* and the lesser *jihad*?

5. What are the different ways of understanding the call to *jihad*?

---

19. Syed Manzar Abbas Zaidi, "Eclipse of the Greater Jihad," *Journal of Religion, Conflict, and Peace* 3, no. 1 (Fall 2009), http://www.religionconflictpeace.org/volume-3-issue-1-fall-2009/eclipse-greater-jihad.
20. "Open Letter," 12.

Is Islamicist Violence a Valid Expression of Islam?

Say: "Do you wait for anything in our case except for one of the two good (rewards)? But we are waiting in your case for God to smite you with punishment from Him or at our hands. (Just) wait! Surely we shall be waiting with you."
~Qur'an 9:52

The verse cited above is part of the extended call throughout the ninth *Sura* of the Qur'an for *jihad* to be directed at the enemies of Islam.[1] The two good rewards mentioned in the first line are the equally desirable results of *jihad*: either victory in battle or martyrdom leading to paradise.[2] In other words, one fighting for Islam maintains confidence that whether in death or in life, reward is secure.

---

1. Cf. Qur'an 9:2, 5, 12–13, 17, 19, 24, 29, 36, 41, 44, 73, 81, 123. These verses use the words *jihad* and *qital*. As the previous chapter discussed, *jihad* can mean an armed struggle against an enemy or an internal struggle against one's own human tendencies to stray from the path of God. The word *qital*, however, is used exclusively to refer to physical fighting. Both words are used interchangeably throughout Qur'an 9, making it evident that the focus is on physical fighting and armed conflict. See Ayman Ibrahim, "What Does the Qur'an Say about Fighting Non-Muslims?," in *Islam and North America: Loving Our Muslim Neighbors*, eds. Micah Fries and Keith Whitfield (Nashville: B&H, 2018), 84.
2. A. J. Droge, trans., *The Qur'an: A New Annotated Translation* (Bristol, CT: Equinox, 2015), 118n76.

In the fifteenth volume of ISIS's propaganda magazine, *Dabiq*, Qur'an 9:52 was the verse chosen to conclude the introduction.[3] Specifically targeting Christians, this volume is entitled *Break the Cross*. In the final paragraph of the introduction, just prior to citing this verse, it threatens:

> We call you to reflect on these questions as the bloodthirsty knights of the Caliphate continue to wage their war of just terror against you. And have no doubt that the war will only end with the black flag of Tawhid (Islamic monotheism) fluttering over Constantinople and Rome, and that is not difficult for Allah.[4]

Such violent aggression in the name of Islam is often bewildering to Westerners, who are accustomed to hearing from their neighbors and friends that Islam is a religion of peace and tolerance.[5] This chapter will investigate the historical and hermeneutical background to groups like ISIS in an effort to understand whether or not they represent valid expressions of Islam.

Historical Precedent

Throughout the history of Islam, various schools of thought have prevailed during different stages of development. Question 10 addressed the reality of multiple different schools of Islamic jurisprudence and the various sources of authority each one permits to influence their rulings. Some schools permit individual reason a role in determining law. Other schools of thought take a strictly traditional and conservative approach, allowing only the Qur'an, *Sunnah*, and established precedents to influence their rulings.

One such conservative group known as the Kharjites arose during the Rashidun Caliphate (the rule of the first four Caliphs) and paved the way for later extremist expressions of Islam. According to Ziauddin Sardar, "The Kharjites believed that the Qur'an should be interpreted literally, that no compromise, deviation, or alternative can be permitted to this literal interpretation, and that all those who disagreed with them were legitimate targets for violence."[6] While this particular group enjoyed little lasting influence, its legacy has inspired cycles of similar qur'anic interpretation throughout later Islamic history.

---

3. Introduction, *Dabiq* 15, http://clarionproject.org/wp-content/uploads/islamic-state-magazine-dabiq-fifteen-breaking-the-cross.pdf, 7.
4. Introduction, *Dabiq* 15, 7.
5. Gardiner Harris, "Obama, in Mosque Visit, Denounces Anti-Muslim Bias," *New York Times*, Feb 3, 2016, https://www.nytimes.com/2016/02/04/us/politics/obama-muslims-baltimore-mosque.html. Harris states, as a point of fact, "Islam is a religion of peace."
6. Ziauddin Sardar, *What Do Muslims Believe?* (New York: Walker, 2007), 101.

One of the most influential scholars to promote this interpretive posture was Ibn Taimiyah (1263–1378). Ibn Taimiyah taught in the Hanbali school of jurisprudence, where he was often in conflict with other scholars.[7] He is known for wanting to wage *jihad* against the Mongols even though they had already converted to Islam. Taimiyah rationalized this aggression by labeling the Mongols as infidels because they failed to immediately begin governing by Sharia law.[8]

Modern groups such as the Salafis and Wahhabis—prevalent in Saudi Arabia, Pakistan, and Indonesia, among other places—owe much of their hermeneutical approach to both the Kharjites and to Ibn Taimiyah.[9] More recently, the writings of Hassan al-Banna (1906–49)—founder of the Muslim Brotherhood—and of Sayyid Qutb (1906–66)—a radical Salafist inspired by al-Banna—have laid the foundation for what is known as Jihadi Salafism.[10]

Jihadi Salafism combines a rigid, literal interpretation of the Qur'an with an unflinching rejection of contemporary interpretation as innovation (*bid'a*). One such rejection is any teaching that would prefer the greater *jihad* of internal struggle to the lesser *jihad* of fighting in the name of God. This posture can be seen in an online *jihadi* manifesto:

> We believe that jihad will last until judgment day, between the just and unjust, in every time and place, with the presence of a supreme leader or not. This jihad is accomplished by a single individual or by more, and will not be stopped by the tyranny of oppressors or the defeatist talk to the demoralizers.[11]

Jihadi Salafism has produced terrorist organizations throughout the world, including al-Qaeda and ISIS. As they have publicly stated, ISIS intends to reinstate a contemporary expression of the utopic Islamic state of Muhammad's day by leading the Ummah toward a new caliphate politically, militarily, and religiously.[12]

Hermeneutical Foundations

In defining the term *jihad* and determining its proper application, the previous chapter discussed the concept of abrogation. When two verses appear

---

7. William Shepard, "Salafi Islam: The Study of Contemporary Religious-Political Movements," *The Bloomsbury Companion to Islamic Studies* (New York: Bloomsbury, 2015), 166.
8. Shepard, "Salafi Islam," 166.
9. Though both of these groups reject the label, some refer to Salafis and Wahhabis as neo-Kharjites. See Shepard, "Salafi Islam," 177. See also Sardar, *What Do Muslims Believe?*, 102.
10. Shepard, "Salafi Islam," 176.
11. As quoted by Shepard, "Salafi Islam," 177.
12. "The Concept of Imamah: Parts 1–5," *Dabiq*, http://clarionproject.org/wp-content/uploads/islamic-state-magazine-dabiq-fifteen-breaking-the-cross.pdf, 21–29.

in tension with one another in the Qur'an, authority is given to the later of the two verses. Stated differently, the earlier verse is abrogated—nullified— by the more recent verse.[13] This concept of abrogation is vitally important to understanding how interpreters of the Qur'an can vary so widely on how to understand and apply *jihad*.

Yet, applying abrogation is not as simple as granting authority to the verses that appear later in the canon of the Qur'an. The Qur'an is not organized in a chronological fashion, and it provides very little internal evidence as to the specific historical setting in which any given verse was revealed. Thus, in order to apply abrogation correctly, one is dependent upon extra-qur'anic materials from the *Sunnah* to determine when a verse was revealed.

Some of the materials that prove most influential in providing a chronological orientation to the Qur'an are the biography of Muhammad's life (*Sira*) and commentaries by early Muslim writers. According to Syed Zaidi, these commentaries help to explain "the sometimes cryptic symbolism in the Qur'an, which uses the Arabic system known as *asbab an-nuzul*, or the occasions for God revealing particular Qur'anic verses. Without this spatial grounding, the Qur'anic verse may be subject to various interpretations."[14] If one rejects these commentaries, however, there is no foundation for determining when a specific verse was revealed. In a situation where two verses are in conflict with one another, there is then no way of knowing which verse should abrogate the other.

An example will highlight the interpretive dilemma. In Qur'an 16:125, *jihad* is rejected as a means of propagating the Islamic faith. At the same time, Qur'an 9:5—the so-called "sword verse"—commends unrestricted warfare. Radical Islamist groups, then, contend that Qur'an 9:5 postdates and thus abrogates Qur'an 16:125. By rejecting the commentaries and their assessment of chronology, one might view the endorsement of unrestricted *jihad* to be binding while the limitation of *jihad* is nullified by the doctrine of abrogation.[15]

Not only do radical groups such as ISIS endorse such a reading of the Qur'an, but many reject what they view to be the innovative category of spiritual *jihad*. This rejection has its roots in the fact that most of the standard scholarly opinion regarding greater and lesser *jihad* is established on a dubious *hadith*. In this *hadith*, Muhammad returns from battle and says, "We have returned from the lesser *jihad* to the greater *jihad*."[16] This is interpreted

---

13. Clinton Bennett, "A–Z Index of Key Terms and Concepts," 327–374 in *The Bloomsbury Companion to Islamic Studies*, ed. Clinton Bennett (New York: Bloomsbury, 2015), 357.

14. Syed Manzar Abbas Zaidi, "Eclipse of the Greater Jihad," *Journal of Religion, Conflict, and Peace* 3, no. 1 (Fall 2009), http://www.religionconflictpeace.org/volume-3-issue-1-fall-2009/ eclipse-greater-jihad.

15. Zaidi, "Eclipse of the Greater Jihad."

16. "Open Letter to Dr. Ibrahim Awwad Al Badri, Alias 'Abu Bakr al-Baghdadi' and to the Fighters and Followers of the Self-Declared 'Islamic State,'" http://www.lettertobaghdadi.com, 10.

by most scholars to mean that the fighting he is returning from is of lesser value than the spiritual struggle to daily submit to God's will in all things.[17]

While this *hadith* lays the foundation for moderate, mainline interpretations of *jihad*, it was rejected outright by Ibn Taimiyah—the commentator who wields a great deal of influence over many of today's radical expressions of Islam. He rejected this *hadith*, saying,

> This *hadith* has no sources and nobody whosoever in the field of Islamic knowledge has narrated it. *Jihad* against the disbelievers is the most noble of actions and moreover it is the most important action for mankind.[18]

Therefore, radical groups such as ISIS reject the concept of the greater *jihad* while also adopting a desire to reinstate their understanding of a seventh-century Islamic utopia by way of *jihad* in the name of God. Their rejection of standard hermeneutical practice allows them to ground their theological claims in the Qur'an, but it invites resounding rejection from among their more moderate brethren throughout the Ummah.

Opposing Views

Despite the historical and textual basis that ISIS claims as precedent for its radical interpretations, countless rejections of radicalism have been issued by various more moderate Muslim scholars and communities.[19] One widely endorsed rejection was issued in September of 2014, when an open letter was posted online and addressed to Abu Bakr al-Baghdadi, the leader of ISIS. Numerous Muslim scholars, teachers, and leaders have since signed this letter publicly as a way of stating their displeasure with ISIS. Chief among the complaints listed is the manner in which al-Baghdadi is reading and applying the Qur'an.

The open letter contends that al-Baghdadi and ISIS have chosen to selectively apply certain verses without taking into account verses that provide counterbalance. It argues that proper exegesis requires one to compile all relevant verses, then, "once all relevant scriptural passages have been gathered, the 'general' has to be distinguished from the 'specific,' and the 'conditional' from the 'unconditional.' Also, the 'unequivocal' passages have to

---

17. "Open Letter," 10.
18. Ibn Taimiyah, *Al-Furqan*, 44–45. As cited by Zaidi, "Eclipse of the Greater Jihad."
19. Cf. Seyyed Hossein Nasr, *The Heart of Islam: Enduring Values for Humanity* (New York: HarperOne, 2004), 263. Nasr summarizes the majority opinion, writing, "Those who carry out terror in the West or elsewhere in the name of *jihad* are vilifying an originally sacred term, and their efforts have not been accepted by established and mainstream religious authorities as *jihad* in the juridical and theological sense of the term."

be distinguished from the allegorical ones."[20] In order to distinguish which verses are currently binding upon the community, the open letter appeals to the principles of interpretation given in the commentaries and the *asbab an-nuzul*. However, as noted above, these sources have largely already been rejected by ISIS.

Another complaint that the open letter raises is the oversimplification of the Qur'an's teaching as exhibited by ISIS. The letter states, "It is also not permissible to say: 'Islam is simple, and the Prophet and his noble Companions were simple, why complicate Islam?'"[21] The letter goes on to claim, "Practical jurisprudence (*fiqh al-waq'i*) considers the texts that are applicable to people's realities at a particular time, and the obligations that can be postponed until they are able to be met or delayed based on their capabilities."[22]

While these complaints derive from the standard, accepted sources of mainline Islamic theology, it is clear from what has been seen of the history and hermeneutic of radical Islamists that the foundations for mainline theology have been rejected by ISIS. The plain and clear teaching of the text is to be applied strictly and literally. Thus, from the perspective of radical Muslims, any claim that the Qur'an lacks perspicuity is viewed merely as an attempt to shirk the responsibility to obey its commands. Likewise, to argue for contextually appropriate application of the Qur'an is to capitulate to the trends of modern society.

Finally—and perhaps most pointedly—the open letter accuses ISIS of warmongering and criminality in the name of *jihad*. A legitimate state of *jihad* requires proper cause, goals, purpose, methodology, and intentions.[23] ISIS has repeatedly targeted civilians, noncombatants, Christians, Jews, Yazidis, and Muslim communities they deem to be apostate. All of these actions are condemned by the open letter by appealing to the Qur'an, the *Sunnah*, and the majority opinion of respected scholars of Islam.

Yet, despite all of these rejections and repudiations of ISIS and its terrorist activities, the open letter comes short of declaring ISIS members to be non-Muslims. The letter is bound by its own injunction against ruling self-proclaimed Muslims to be guilty of apostasy (*takfir*) when it explicitly states, "Quintessentially in Islam, anyone who says: 'There is no god but God; Muhammad is the Messenger of God' is a Muslim and cannot be declared a non-Muslim."[24] Thus, even Muslims who vehemently reject the activities of ISIS as improper applications of Islamic teaching should refuse to condemn the members of ISIS as apostates.

---

20. "Open Letter," 4.
21. "Open Letter," 6.
22. "Open Letter," 8.
23. "Open Letter," 10.
24. "Open Letter," 14. For another ecumenical document that rejects *takfir* see, *The Amman Message*, http://ammanmessage.com, Summary Points 1–3.

Summary

Western media often presents radical Islam from one of two poles. On one hand, some sources portray Islam as a religion of peace, rejecting the idea that radical Muslims have any connection to historical or hermeneutical legitimacy. On the other hand, some sources present radical Islam as the natural conclusion that a Muslim will inevitably reach if given enough time. Careful investigation avoids either of these two conclusions.[25]

This chapter has shown that the vast majority of scholars and individual Muslims reject radical *jihadi* interpretations. From a Christian point of view, I believe this is an example of common grace causing interpreters to choose peaceful, nonviolent verses to define Islam over and against those that prescribe violence. However, the same scholars are often forced to maintain that the members of ISIS, al-Qaeda, Boko Haram, and others are in fact Muslims.

Likewise, though violence is by no means the inevitable consequence of Islam, it does have historical precedent and textual warrant. Though most Muslims would never dream of engaging in aggressive *jihad*, those who do are not without predecessors who have arrived at the same conclusions. In the words of one Muslim author,

> Most Muslims do not regard the terrorists as genuine Muslims, arguing that the Qur'an and various schools of Islamic law forbid the killing of innocent civilians. However, the terrorists are Muslims not simply because that's how they describe themselves, but also because they justify their barbaric acts by reference to the same history and a particular strand of its tradition. And they, too, are a part of the ummah.[26]

It may be worth the redundancy to say again that the majority of Muslims despise the gruesome horrors and appalling bloodlust of groups such as ISIS. However, as this chapter has shown, although Islamic scholars may deem the interpretive methods and application of *jihad* exhibited by ISIS as irregular and inappropriate, they do recognize the members of ISIS as authentic Muslims.

REFLECTION QUESTIONS

1. How do the rewards promised to those participating in *jihad* inform an understanding of *jihad* itself?

---

25. Bernard Lewis and Buntzie Churchill, *Islam: The Religion and the People* (Upper Saddle River, NJ: Wharton, 2009), 145.
26. Sardar, *What Do Muslims Believe?*, 101.

2. Is it proper to see ISIS as the inevitable consequence of Islam? Why or why not?

3. Is it proper to say that ISIS is not a valid expression of Islam? Why or why not?

4. How are Muslim leaders fighting ISIS and violent ideologies?

5. What role does the doctrine of abrogation play in determining one's understanding of the Islamic teaching on violence?

PART 5

The Qur'an and the Bible

Does the Qur'an Overlap with the Bible?

Say: "People of the Book! Come to a word (which is)
common between us and you: 'We do not serve
(anyone) but God, and do not associate
(anything) with Him, and do not take each other
as Lords instead of God.'" If they turn away, say:
"Bear witness that we are Muslims."
~Qur'an 3:64

The Qur'an is a document that regularly and self-consciously connects it-self to prior revelation. As can be seen in the reference to "the People of the Book" in the verse cited above, the Qur'an presents itself as a testimony derived from and concerning the same God to whom Jews and Christians offer their worship.[1] The Qur'an claims to be a continuation of the essential message revealed to the Jews and Christians, thus significant and sustained references to biblical characters, ideas, and ethics permeate its pages.

For a Christian engaged in conversation with a Muslim, then, it is helpful to note some of the overlap between the Qur'an and Bible for the purposes of parsing out that which is mere superficial similarity and that which is truly shared between the two faiths. While the following question addresses some of the central divergences between the Bible and the Qur'an, this question intends to explore several areas of apparent conceptual, ethical, and historical overlap.

---

1. The next question will clarify who the Qur'an includes as "the People of the Book," but for now it suffices to state that this reference is to Jews and Christians, along with another somewhat mysterious group known as the Sabians.

Conceptual Overlap

Several points of apparent conceptual similarity arise when comparing the Bible and the Qur'an. Three of the most important similarities are the ideas of monotheism, creationism, and judgment. While these concepts are explored in greater depth in other questions addressed throughout this book, we will pause to consider them briefly here.

Monotheism

In Qur'an 3:62 we read, "Surely this—it is indeed the true account. (There is) nothing of (the nature of) a god but God. Surely God—He is indeed the Mighty, the Wise." Comparing this claim about the uniqueness of the nature of God with the biblical account, one might find a nearly identical idea in reading Jeremiah 10:6: "There is none like you, oh LORD; you are great, and your name is great in might." Thus, the incomparability of the one true God is a common concept shared by the Qur'an and the Bible.[2]

Creationism

The Qur'an is committed to the idea that the material world is the product of God's creative activity. Question 15 addresses the Qur'an's view of creation in greater depth, but it is worth noting here that Qur'an 7:54 records,

> Surely your Lord is God, who created the heavens and the earth in six days. Then He mounted the throne. The night covers the day, which it pursues urgently, and the sun, and the moon, and the stars are subjected, (all) by His command. Is it not (a fact) that to Him (belong) the creation and the command? Blessed (be) God, Lord of the worlds!

Gabriel Said Reynolds suggests in his monumental work *The Qur'an and the Bible* that this verse reflects the teaching of Jeremiah 31:35, which states,

> Thus says the LORD, who gives the sun for light by day and the fixed order of the moon and the stars for light by night, who stirs up the sea so that its waves roar—the LORD of hosts is his name.[3]

Judgment

Finally, the concept of judgment for one's deeds emerges on nearly every page of the Qur'an. The manner by which one lives life will be judged as to

---

2. See Questions 29 and 35 for more in-depth analysis of whether or not the God referred to in the Qur'an is the same God as discussed in the Bible.
3. Gabriel Said Reynolds, *The Qur'an and the Bible* (New Haven, CT: Yale University Press, 2018), 262.

how closely it conforms to the revealed will of God. To this point, the Qur'an views itself as a warning and a guide provided to lead people to the straight and narrow path of ethical living.

One example of such teaching that has biblical parallels is found in Qur'an 21:47, which warns, "We shall lay down the scales of justice for the Day of Resurrection, and no one will be done any evil. (Even) it there is (only) the weight of a mustard seed, We shall produce it, and We are sufficient as reckoners." Thus, just as the Bible teaches that on the day of resurrection, everyone will give an account for their deeds and no one will be served injustice by God, so too does the Qur'an anticipate a final day when God's justice will be meted out to all people.[4]

Ethical Overlap

In light of the impending judgment mentioned above, the Qur'an is filled with instructions issued to believers as to how they are to live in accord with God's will. Many of these ethical commitments are shared with—if not derived from—Judeo-Christian teachings. Several areas of ethical overlap are the importance of following God's truth, chastity and modesty, and submission in all things to God.

Following God's Truth

The Qur'an concerns itself in many places with the importance of confirming and conforming to God's revealed will. Qur'an 57:19 highlights the necessity of affirming the truth revealed by God when it states,

> Those who believe in God and His messengers, those—they are the truthful and the martyrs in the sight of their Lord—they have their reward and their light. But those who disbelieve and call Our signs a lie—those are the companions of the Furnace.

Since God's revelation is taken as a trustworthy guide for life, Islamic teaching calls followers to believe and bear testimony to the truth, to deal honestly as those informed by the truth, and to live out of the conviction that God's word in the Qur'an is true.[5]

One familiar with the biblical teaching regarding how God's revealed truth has implications on one's life might hear echoes of Joshua 1:8, which states,

> This Book of the Law shall not depart from your mouth, but you shall meditate on it day and night, so that you may be careful to

---

4. Cf. Romans 14:12: "So then each of us will give an account of himself to God."
5. Cf. Al-Bukhari, *Sahih al-Bukhari*, https://sunnah.com/bukhari/96/9, book 96 (§9): "Honesty descended from the Heavens and settled in the roots of the hearts of men (faithful believers), and then the Qur'an was revealed and the people read the Qur'an, (and learnt it from it) and also learnt it from the Sunna." This *hadith* connects the Qur'an as revelation of truth that inspires followers of the Qur'an to live honest lives.

> do according to all that is written in it. For then you will make
> your way prosperous, and then you will have good success.

One finds the same idea in the New Testament in places such as James 1:22, which reads, "be doers of the word, and not hearers only, deceiving yourselves." Thus, for both Christians and Muslims, their holy books function both as a source of that which is ultimately true and as a divinely inspired guide to living.

Chastity and Modesty

The Qur'an—and Islam—is concerned to urge people to protect their honor in matters concerning sexuality. Qur'an 23:5–7 provides a clear example of such teaching, stating, "[The believers are those who] guard their private parts, except from their wives of what their right (hands) own—surely then they are not (to be) blamed, but whoever seeks beyond that, those—they are the transgressors."

Beyond merely prohibiting fornication, the Qur'an is also concerned with modesty. Qur'an 33:35 reinforces such modesty and chastity for both men and women, promising that "the men who guard their private parts and the women who guard (them), the men who remember God often and the women who remember (Him)—for them God has prepared forgiveness and a great reward."

The Bible, likewise, connects modesty and chastity to the appropriate use of one's body as a temple of God. First Corinthians 6:18–20 exemplifies this, urging believers,

> Flee from sexual immorality. Every other sin a person com-
> mits is outside the body, but the sexually immoral person
> sins against his [or her] own body. Or do you not know that
> your body is a temple of the Holy Spirit within you, whom
> you have from God? You are not your own, for you were
> bought with a price. So glorify God in your body.

Thus, for Christians in whom the Holy Spirit dwells, sexual immorality sullies the very temple of God and is thus anathema. Likewise, for Muslims, sexual immorality is a dishonor not only to the participants, but also to their families and communities.

Submission to God

The very word "Muslim" is etymologically related to the Arabic word meaning "to submit." Thus, a common understanding of a Muslim is one who is submitted to God in all things. This derives from the qur'anic appellative used to describe a number of model Muslims, not the least of which is Ibrahim. In Qur'an 3:67 one reads, "Abraham was not a Jew, nor a Christian, but he was a Hanif, a Muslim. He was not one of the idolaters." Likewise referring to Ibrahim and his son, Qur'an 37:99–111 commends submission as the proper response to God's commands.

So too does the Bible prize submission to God. First Peter 3:22 states, "[Jesus Christ] has gone into heaven and is at the right hand of God, with angels, authorities, and powers having been subjected to him." Immediately following this claim, Peter lists a number of ethical ramifications for those who are living as those submitted to Christ's total authority.

Historical Overlap

In mentioning Ibrahim, we encounter an instance of the final point of similarity discussed in this chapter: historical overlap. Throughout the Qur'an, one finds references that indicate the fact that it views itself as the continuation and completion of biblical history. For instance, Qur'an 5:44–50 endorses the Torah and the Gospel as books of truth. Most Muslims take this to mean that these portions of the Bible were once valid forms of revelation that have now been corrupted.

In the context of such endorsement, verse 49 calls Muslims to assess Jews and Christians based upon their sacred texts, saying, "(So) judge between them and by what God has sent down, and do not follow their (vain) desires, and beware of them in case they tempt you (to turn away) from any part of what God has sent down to you." Thus, the revelations are viewed as heaven-sent, though the Jewish and Christian application thereof needs assessment.

Other points of apparent historical overlap that one encounters in the Qur'an are the many references to biblical characters. While Adam, Abraham, Moses, David, and Jesus present themselves as the most notable inclusions, the Qur'an includes references that appear to connect with many other biblical characters, including Lot, Zechariah, Jonah, and John.[6]

Yet, as the Qur'an takes up various biblical historical narratives, it becomes clear that the Qur'an's appeal to shared history results in a very different telling of that history. Thus, when Mark Anderson discusses the qur'anic use of the Bible, he writes, "Divorced from the Bible's grand narrative—as they are in the Qur'an—the biblical narratives are very plastic, taking on whatever form or meaning they are given. That is, they are easily repurposed in the service of another form of monotheism."[7] In other words, though references to biblical characters and narratives appear in the Qur'an, they serve to reinforce the qur'anic metanarrative. As such, the characters and stories themselves take on different contours of meaning, include previously unattested details, and are made to say things that accord with Muhammad's message.[8]

---

6. For a wonderful, concise treatment of many of these points of overlap that includes references to the Islamic sources in which they appear, see John Kaltner and Younus Mirza, *The Bible and the Qur'an: Biblical Figures in the Islamic Tradition* (London: T&T Clark, 2018).
7. Mark Anderson, *The Qur'an in Context: A Christian Exploration* (Downers Grove, IL: IVP Academic, 2016), 40.
8. This claim will be treated in detail by looking at the characters of Abraham and Jesus in the Qur'an in Questions 29 and 30 respectively.

Summary

In many ways, the Qur'an exhibits a great deal of similarity to the Bible. Concepts, ethical principles, characters, and narratives that appear first in the Bible are gathered into the Qur'an and its teaching. Many Muslims are thus happy to commend the Bible as a message from God, albeit corrupted and misunderstood. But from a Christian perspective, it is necessary to consider whether or not the overlap between the Qur'an and the Bible is more than superficial.

Though there are many apparent similarities conceptually, ethically, and historically between the Qur'an and the Bible, the Qur'an sets these similarities in the context of an alternative worldview. In so doing, the apparent similarities dissolve into rather different and divergent programs. Therefore, even though the Qur'an claims to extend and continue the divine revelation given through the Bible, it weaves biblical references together with its own concerns in such a way as to fundamentally alter the function of the Bible as the revelation of God.

To this point, Mark Anderson writes, "The qur'anic use of biblical and other monotheistic materials, however, recombines their elements in such a way that it redefines the entire divine-human relationship: the basic human problem is no longer sin (i.e., moral deficiency), requiring salvation, but rather a simple lack of guidance calling for revelation."[9] The following question will address some of the underlying points of divergence that can be obscured by the preceding points of surface-level similarity.

REFLECTION QUESTIONS

1. What is the Qur'an's stance regarding the Bible? How does the Qur'an view itself in relation to the Bible?

2. What are the concepts that appear to be shared between the Qur'an and the Bible?

3. How does the Qur'an present its ethical teaching? What is the purpose of the ethics taught by the Qur'an, and does the Bible share that purpose?

4. Does the Qur'an share historical material with the Bible? What does the Qur'an do with that history?

5. With all of this apparently shared material, why is it that this chapter concludes that the Qur'an and the Bible have different trajectories?

---

9. Anderson, *Qur'an in Context*, 38.

What Are the Differences between the Qur'an and the Bible?

Alif Lam Ra. Those are the signs of the clear Book.
Surely we have sent it down as an Arabic Qur'an,
so that you may understand. We shall recount
to you the best of accounts in what We have inspired
you (with of) this Qur'an, though before it you
were indeed one of the oblivious.
~Qur'an 12:1

As noted in the previous chapter, the Qur'an and the Bible seem to exhibit some similarities. First of all, they are both the sacred scriptures of major world religions. Second, they are viewed as a means of moral guidance to the communities to whom they were sent. Finally, they both contain references to characters that are intended to be understood as the same historical figures.

If one does not take the time to critically assess the differences between the Bible and the Qur'an, the similarities might lead to the assumption that a Muslim reads the Qur'an in the same way and for the same purposes as a Christian reads the Bible. However, noticing the ways that the Qur'an and the Bible differ is perhaps more important to understanding how and why a Muslim takes up the Qur'an. These differences can often be overlooked in dialogue between Christians and Muslims, resulting in significant misunderstanding.

In an attempt to mitigate such misunderstanding, this chapter will address three significant differences between the Qur'an and the Bible. First, for a reader accustomed to the structure and genre of biblical texts, the format of the Qur'an will immediately appear foreign. Second, though both books claim to be divine revelation, the content revealed by each book differs significantly. Third, in the life of a faithful Muslim, the Qur'an functions differently than does the Bible for Christians.

The Structure of the Qur'an

Traditional Islamic accounts teach that Muhammad recited verses of the Qur'an to his followers little by little over a twenty-two-year period.[1] These followers committed the Qur'an to memory and recorded some of it in writing, using whatever materials were at hand whenever Muhammad experienced occasions of revelation. When Muhammad died, however, the Ummah lacked a written and codified version of the Qur'an. Much of it had yet to be recorded in writing, and what was written down had not been gathered into a centralized collection.

Compilation of the Qur'an

Therefore, one of the first acts of the community was to begin the process of recording the Qur'an in writing. The necessity of this task was made all the more urgent when many of the Muslims who had memorized the Qur'an were killed during the early battles in which the Muslim armies fought.

In light of these deaths, Gabriel Said Reynolds comments, "Abu Bakr accordingly became concerned that some of the divine revelation might soon be lost forever, so he commissioned a council to record the entire text."[2] This council included Muhammad's scribe, Zayd ibn Thabit, along with several Meccan scholars. The council gathered all those who had memorized the Qur'an and collectively determined the correct and authoritative reading.

Organization of the Qur'an

Islamic tradition teaches that during the occasions of revelation, Muhammad received not only verses (*aya*) of the Qur'an, but entire chapters (*sura*). Since Muhammad died before the collection of his recitations, however, the ordering of these chapters appears to have been determined by the Ummah as they compiled the Qur'an.

Since these chapters present themselves as individual literary units, many contemporary scholars argue that one must attend to the chapter-level context in order to interpret meaning.[3] Such attention requires a sensitivity to ancient

---

1. Gabriel Said Reynolds, *The Emergence of Islam: Classical Traditions in Contemporary Perspective* (Minneapolis: Fortress, 2012), 97–98. Some traditions teach that Muhammad received the entire Qur'an in the cave. Yet, all traditions teach that Muhammad transmitted the Qur'an over an extended period of time and through occasional revelations.
2. Reynolds, *Emergence of Islam*, 100.
3. Raymond Farrin, *Structure and Qur'anic Interpretation: A Study of Symmetry and Coherence in Islam's Holy Text* (Ashland, OR: White Cloud, 2014), xiv–xv.

Semitic rhetoric and literary conventions uncommon to Western readers.[4] Thus, first-time readers of the Qur'an—especially Westerners reading English translations—will almost certainly struggle to grasp or appreciate its message.[5]

Whether or not one can establish a plausible rhetorical case for interpreting the Qur'an at the chapter level, the arrangement of the chapters themselves poses a barrier to understanding. Generally speaking, with the exception of the opening *sura*, the Qur'an moves from the longest chapter to the shortest.[6] An implication of this arrangement is that the Qur'an is not chronological.[7] In fact, it reads as an ahistorical document, admitting very little evidence of the context in which it was written, in part due to the fact that the genre of the Qur'an is poetry.

Genre of the Qur'an

One of the chief reasons that Muslims claim inspiration for the Qur'an is due to its inimitable beauty. This claim finds its foundation in Qur'an 17:88, which states, "Say: 'If indeed humankind and the jinn joined together to produce something like this Qur'an, they would not produce anything like it, even if they were supporters of each other.'" Other verses throughout the Qur'an make the same point: its perfection cannot be imitated; thus, it is from God.[8]

The claim is also reinforced with accounts of those who, upon hearing the Qur'an's beautiful poetry, experience spontaneous conversion. Raymond Farrin offers an example of such a conversion, citing the words of the second caliph, 'Umar, writing, "When I heard the Qur'an, my heart was softened and I wept, and Islam entered into me."[9] Therefore, on the basis of the perceived perfection

---

4. Michel Cuypers, *The Banquet: A Reading of the Fifth Sura of the Qur'an* (Miami: Convivium, 2009), 1. Cf. Farrin, *Structure and Qur'anic Interpretation*, xv. Some interpreters labor to show that the entire canon of the Qur'an exhibits evidence of an intentional, rhetorical design, which should be considered in the process of interpretation. Farrin claims, "The whole Qur'an, including all its arranged parts, possesses a magnificent design."

5. Farrin, *Structure and Qur'anic Interpretation*, xiii. Farrin quotes Voltaire as having written, "The Qur'an is a rhapsody without liaison, without order, without art; it is said nevertheless that this boring book is a very beautiful book—I am referring here to the Arabs who pretend it is written with an elegance and a purity that no one has approached." He also quotes Thomas Carlyle's opinion: "I must say, it is toilsome reading as I ever undertook. A wearisome confused jumble, crude, incondite; endless iterations, long-windedness, entanglement."

6. John Kaltner and Younus Mirza, *The Bible and the Qur'an: Biblical Figures in the Islamic Tradition* (New York: T&T Clark, 2018), 3.

7. Most scholars believe that Qur'an 96:5 is the first verse that was revealed, while the last verse to be revealed is often said to be Qur'an 5:3.

8. Cf. Qur'an 2:23; 10:38; 11:13; 52:33–34. One might be excused for finding such an argument less than convincing. Beauty as a subjective category cannot provide proof of the claims of divine revelation. All the more so, the claim that it cannot be imitated cannot be substantiated due to the subjective nature of the claim.

9. Farrin, *Structure and Qur'anic Interpretation*, xiii. Farrin also offers the reflections upon hearing the Qur'an of a poet from Muhammad's lifetime, "It was a gentle and soulful

of the poetry of the Qur'an, read in its original Arabic, Seyyed Hossein Nasr can claim, "The greatest miracle of Islam is said to be the eloquence of the Qur'an."[10] Even more than the actual words themselves, then, the Arabic poetics that comprise the Qur'an provide proof of its inspiration for many faithful Muslims.[11]

That the Qur'an is poetic, however, exacerbates the difficulty for Westerners wanting to understand its message. Such poetic use of language is often intentionally ambiguous and metaphorical. Likewise, adequately translating such culturally bound metaphor into any common language is rarely achieved. Thus, appreciation of its texture and meaning is all but impossible in translation. As seen above, the structure of the Qur'an takes a very different shape than that of the Bible. So, too, does its content differ.

The Content of the Qur'an

In Christian theology proper, the doctrine of revelation has as its object God himself. As Michael Bird puts it, revelation is "God's self-disclosure of himself."[12] While Christians recognize that we do not know God exhaustively, we do claim to know him personally. Ultimately, we gain this knowledge most fully through the incarnation, though we view and interpret it through the lens of the Bible. For Christians, the content of revelation is God himself.

Revelation of God's Will

Though it may initially seem an insignificant distinction, the content of the Qur'an's revelation is not God himself but rather God's will. The Qur'an rejects the idea that anyone can know God personally. The person of God—if one can so speak of Allah in Islam—is wholly transcendent and unknowable. Perhaps the closest thing that can be known about God's essence is simply that God is one.[13] The Qur'an instead occupies itself with revealing how human creatures are to follow God's will.

Revelation of Guidance

Corroborating the claim above in his influential book *Major Themes in the Qur'an*, Fazlur Rahman writes, "The Qur'an is no treatise about God and

---

recital. It bewitched the heart and caressed the mind. Such an attraction was in the recitation that no man of poetry and letters could resist. In it, he found a wave of tenderness and a spiritual wealth in its meaning, which he had never heard in human speech before."

10. Seyyed Hossein Nasr, *The Heart of Islam: Enduring Values for Humanity* (New York: HarperOne, 2004), 24.

11. Nasr, *Heart of Islam*, 224. Nasr writes, "In traditional Islamic society one never hears the Word of God except in beautiful chanting, which moves the very depth of the soul of even those Muslims who do not know Arabic and do not comprehend the message of what is recited. . . . In the eyes and ears of Muslims the central theophany of their religion, namely the Qur'an, has always been associated with beauty."

12. Michael Bird, *Evangelical Theology* (Grand Rapids: Zondervan, 2012), 164.

13. Fazlur Rahman, *Major Themes of the Qur'an* (Chicago: Chicago University Press, 2009), 1.

His nature: His existence, for the Qur'an, is strictly functional—He is Creator and Sustainer of the universe and of man, and particularly the giver of guidance for man."[14] As such, a reader approaching the Qur'an should be conscious of the fact that it does not invite personal knowledge of God, but rather it provides guidance for faith and life as a creature submitted to the creator.

The Function of the Qur'an

Since the Qur'an and Bible reveal different content, it follows that the primary reason a Christian reads the Bible is different than the reason a Muslim reads the Qur'an. Both Christians and Muslims read scripture for the purpose of conforming their lives to its commands. However, such commands in the Bible are inextricably connected to the person and character of the Triune God who has revealed himself in and through its pages. Ultimately, then, Christians read the Bible in order to know God himself. In contrast, most Muslims primarily read, memorize, and recite the poetry of the Qur'an as an act of devotion and in order to obtain blessing.[15]

An Act of Devotion

Among the laity throughout the Ummah, study of the Qur'an is more directed at memorization and recitation than to personal interpretation. Interpretation is a task left to scholars and clerics. Thus, though the Qur'an is read and memorized by individuals, apprehension of its meaning and application depends more upon the local imams, traditions, and commentaries.

The priority given to memorization follows from the belief that the Qur'an is not a creative work of Muhammad, but is itself a product of Muhammad's recitation. Islamic tradition teaches that the very first instruction Muhammad was given in the cave of Hira was, "Recite!"[16] Thus, in most Islamic communities, one who has memorized the Qur'an (*hafiz*) is viewed admirably as extremely pious.[17]

An Object of Blessing

Finally, many Muslims believe the Qur'an itself to be a source of blessing. One way to obtain such blessing, as noted by Carole Hillenbrand, is by developing proficiency as a reciter of the Qur'an, which "is a skill highly valued in Muslim societies and one said to bring both spiritual and material rewards."[18] The Qur'an, then, both guides the Muslim and provides a means of blessing.

---

14. Rahman, *Major Themes of the Qur'an*, 1.
15. Carole Hillenbrand, *Introduction to Islam: Beliefs and Practices in Historical Perspective* (London: Thames & Hudson, 2015), 77.
16. Qur'an 96:5.
17. Hillenbrand, *Introduction to Islam*, 78.
18. Hillenbrand, *Introduction to Islam*, 77.

Less frequently—and as is the case in certain syncretistic Christian environments—some Muslims read verses from the Qur'an as incantations or to ward off evil in certain situations. Additionally, some Muslims display copies of the Qur'an in their homes, cars, and places of business because its very presence is considered to bring luck and protection. Thus, in certain Muslim cultures, the book itself is viewed as a talisman or charm.

Summary
Though the Bible and the Qur'an are both sacred texts that offer guidance and instruction, this chapter has shown that there is a great deal of difference between the two books. The Qur'an, as a book of poetic guidance, provides the Muslim community with a window through which to view God's will for their lives. Following its instruction, memorizing its words, and reciting its message display pious devotion and invite spiritual and material rewards.

The biggest difference, however, between the Qur'an and the Bible is that the Qur'an reveals only God's will and instructions for how to order one's life. It does not reveal God himself. Having investigated the essential differences between the Qur'an and the Bible, many of the similarities highlighted by Question 25 prove to be rather superficial in the light of such distinct purposes and functions of both books in their respective faiths.

REFLECTION QUESTIONS

1. Are the Qur'an and the Bible the same kind of book? Why or why not? What difference does it make?

2. Why does the Qur'an seem to be jumbled and out of order? Is there a narrative progression throughout the Qur'an?

3. How would you describe the Qur'an's presentations of previous prophets and their message?

4. If you were to compare the content of the Qur'an with the content of the Bible, what would be the major differences? What appears to be the distinct purpose of the Qur'an?

5. If the Qur'an is a book of revelation, what does it reveal? How does the answer to this question affect our understanding of Islamic theology?

What Does the Qur'an Teach about Jews and Christians?

Say: "O People of the Book! You are (standing) on nothing until you observe the Torah and the Gospel, and what has been sent down to you from your Lord." But what has been sent down to you from your Lord will indeed increase many of them in insolent transgression and disbelief. So do not grieve over the people who are disbelievers. Surely those who believe, and those who are Jews and the Sabians, and the Christians—whoever believes in God and the Last Day, and does righteousness—(there will be) no fear on them, nor will they sorrow.
~Qur'an 5:68–69

Throughout the Qur'an one encounters repeated reference to groups of people who are addressed as "People of the Book." At first glance, one might assume that this phrase refers to the immediate audience reading the Qur'an. However, with a bit more exploration, it becomes apparent that "People of the Book" extends beyond the community formed by the Qur'an.

In this brief chapter, we will discuss the people to whom this phrase refers. Likewise, we will consider what book or books are in view. Finally, we will investigate what implications this phrase has for our understanding of the context of the Qur'an.

What People?

The verse that is cited at the head of this chapter calls the People of the Book to attention. It is a summons to pay attention to the revelation before them in the pages of the Qur'an, but then it expands by the end of the passage to include—alongside those referred to as believers—three distinct groups of people that are also considered "People of the Book." Two of these groups are easily identifiable, while one remains a mystery.

Jews

Popular understanding of Jewish-Muslim relationships tends to derive from the discord between the two groups as evidenced by the ongoing conflict between Israel and Palestine. Thus, for many contemporary readers who are unfamiliar with the Qur'an, it may come as a surprise to find that some of the Jews are counted among the People of the Book whom the Qur'an commends. In fact, at least some of the Jewish community is identified as those who have followed their revelation from God and who need not fear the final judgment.

Christians

Likewise, for those who are acquainted with stories of Christians persecuted by Muslims around the world, many readers may again be surprised to find that the Qur'an speaks rather highly of Christians. Again, some Christians are included among the People of the Book alongside of Jews, and again, as indicated by the verse cited above, they need not fear the judgment day. As Islamic literature developed, the phrase "People of the Book" came to be a technical appellative reserved for Jews and Christians especially.[1] However, in the Qur'an there is yet another group included among the People of the Book.

Sabians

The third group that the Qur'an includes as People of the Book are referred to as the Sabians. However, Islamic scholarship is divided over the identity of this group. Citing such division, Gabriel Said Reynolds points out that the early Muslim commentator al-Tabari lists eight different opinions on this matter. He writes,

> The [Sabians] are either those who have left a religion, or those who have no religion, or a group "between" the Zoroastrians and the Jews, or a tribe in the Sudan, or a religion based in Mesopotamia that teaches the belief in one God but has no prophets and no book, or a religion that teaches the worship

---

1. Gabriel Said Reynolds, *The Emergence of Islam: Classical Traditions in Contemporary Perspective* (Minneapolis: Fortress, 2012), 209.

of angels, or a group of believers who pray in the direction of Mecca and use the Psalms as their scripture, or simply a group from the People of the Book.[2]

Thus, one is left with mere speculation as to whom this word refers. Etymologically, "Sabian" could refer to a group that has left their religion or homeland. At the same time, it could serve as the name of a specific tribe, nation, or religion. Resolution of this mystery is all but impossible with the current data available, and the later Islamic traditions that restrict the use of People of the Book to Jews and Christians demonstrates a willingness to leave the issue unresolved.

What Book?

The Arabic word *kitab* can be translated simply as "book." However, as the word functions in the Qur'an, it could also be translated as "scripture."[3] Illustrating the qur'anic understanding of previous books or scriptures as true divine revelation, noted Muslim scholar Fazlur Rahman states, "It is quite obvious from the Qur'an that from the beginning to the end of his prophetic career, Muhammad was absolutely convinced of the divine character of the earlier revealed documents and of the divine messengership of the bearers of these documents."[4] Thus, it is helpful to consider what books of scripture are intended to qualify people as People of the Book.

Torah (Tawrah)

The Qur'an not only refers to the Torah in its discussion of previous revelation, but it also connects it to the people of Israel. For instance, explicit reference to the Torah as revelation comes in Qur'an 5:44 which states, "Surely We sent down the Torah, containing guidance and light." Thus, the Torah is viewed as divine guidance—the same term used for the Qur'an itself.[5]

Further connecting the Qur'an and the Torah, Qur'an 2:40–41 summons the Israelites to believe in the message of the Qur'an as a confirmation of the message of the Torah sent to them, saying, "Sons of Israel! Remember my blessing which I bestowed on you. Fulfill My covenant (and) I shall fulfill your covenant, and Me—fear Me (alone). Believe in what I have sent down, confirming what is with you, and do not be the first to disbelieve in it." The reference here to "what is with you" is understood to be the Torah given to

---

2. Gabriel Said Reynolds, *The Qur'an and Its Biblical Subtext* (New York: Routledge, 2010), 20n71.

3. Paul Loffler and Mark Swanson, "Islam and Christianity," in *Islam: A Short Guide to the Faith*, eds. Roger Allen and Shawkat M. Toorawa (Grand Rapids: Eerdmans, 2011), 128.

4. Fazlur Rahman, *Major Themes of the Qur'an* (Chicago: University of Chicago Press, 2009), 163.

5. Cf. Qur'an 2:2 and 31:3.

Moses, and it demonstrates the Qur'an's claim to completion and confirmation of that which was previously revealed.[6]

Psalms (Zabur)

In addition to the Torah, the Qur'an also speaks of the Psalms as a book of divine revelation given to David. Qur'an 4:163 states, "Surely We have inspired you as We inspired Noah and the prophets after him, and as We inspired Abraham, and Ishmael, and Isaac, and Jacob, and the tribes, and Jesus, and Job, and Jonah, and Aaron, and Solomon, and We gave David the Psalms." Thus, along with a substantial list of biblical characters whom the Qur'an recognizes as inspired prophets, it also specifically refers to David's reception of the Psalms.[7]

Gospel (Injil)

Finally, the Qur'an explicitly endorses the Gospel as divine revelation.[8] It is worth quoting a somewhat lengthy passage from Qur'an 5:44–47 in order to display the Qur'an's posture toward the role of previous revelation and the interrelationship between the Torah, Gospel, and Qur'an:

> Surely We sent down the Torah, containing guidance and light. By means of it the prophets who had submitted rendered judgment for those who were Jews, and (so did) the rabbis and the teachers, with what they were entrusted of the Book of God, and they were witnesses to it. . . . And in their footsteps We followed up with Jesus, son of Mary, confirming what was with him of the Torah, and We gave him the Gospel, containing guidance and light, and confirming what was with him of the Torah, and as guidance and admonition to the ones who guard (themselves). So let the people of the Gospel judge by what God has sent down in it. Whoever does not judge by what God has sent down, those—they are the wicked.

---

6. Interestingly, the Torah is never explicitly connected directly to Moses in the Qur'an, though Qur'an 2:87 connects Moses with divine revelation in a book or scripture, such that most commentators, such as A. J. Droge, trans., *The Qur'an: A New Annotated Translation* (Bristol, CT: Equinox, 2015), 5n53, explicitly tie the Torah to Moses.

7. Another such instance occurs in Qur'an 17:55. Furthermore, Qur'an 21:105–6 states, "Certainly we have written in the Psalms, after the Reminder: 'The earth—my righteous servants will inherit it.' Surely in this there is a delivery indeed for a people who serve."

8. As noted in previous chapters, there is some debate as to whether the Injil is a long-lost book given to Jesus or if it refers to the Synoptic Gospels of the Bible. Most Muslims believe this is a reference to the biblical books, though they have since been corrupted from their original form.

In this passage, one sees that the Qur'an understands the Gospel given to Jesus to confirm the authenticity of the Torah. Likewise, the Qur'an itself claims to confirm the Gospel, and by extension the Torah and Psalms.[9]

Book or Books?

Having glimpsed qur'anic affirmation of at least three different sections of the Bible, it may seem apparent that the Qur'an views such books as independent, self-contained sources of divine guidance. However, a closer reading of the Qur'an's assertions regarding previous revelation produces a slightly different understanding.

Citing Qur'an 5:15, Gabriel Said Reynolds highlights the final sentence of the verse, which he renders, "There has come to you from God a light, and a Book Manifest."[10] Explaining this sentence, Reynolds contends that "the Qur'an seems to mean that Jews and Christians are 'People of the Book' because they are nations whom God has already given revelation—a chapter of the heavenly 'book'—in the past."[11] Thus, the designator "People of the Book" should be understood to refer to those who have received parts of the one heavenly book rather than distinct books unto themselves.[12] The Torah, Psalms, and Gospel then could be understood to derive from the same heavenly source from which the Qur'an hails.

The Context of the Qur'an

Perhaps one of the most frustrating aspects of Islamic studies is the lack of material available to give verifiable historical context to the Qur'an. The Qur'an presents past narratives and some of their context. Yet, details are not forthcoming when one asks about the immediate context surrounding the writing of the Qur'an itself. Thus, Mark Anderson remarks, "The Qur'an [is] singularly unhelpful as a historical source when taken on its own."[13]

Nearly all of the material available to provide such context is written at a much later date than the Qur'an and almost exclusively by Muslim authors. Thus, if one is in search of information about the first two centuries of Islam that would pass standard tests of historical criticism, the search comes up empty.[14]

However, one thing that our discussion regarding the People of the Book indicates about the Qur'an's surrounding context is that the author of the Qur'an was either acquainted with Jewish and Christian scriptures

---

9. Droge, *Qur'an*, 68–69n93.

10. Reynolds, *Emergence of Islam*, 155.

11. Reynolds, *Emergence of Islam*, 155.

12. Rahman, *Major Themes in the Qur'an*, 163–64.

13. Mark Anderson, *The Qur'an in Context: A Christian Exploration* (Downers Grove, IL: IVP Academic, 2016), 2.

14. Karl-Heinz Ohlig, "Islam's 'Hidden' Origins," in *The Hidden Origins of Islam*, ed. Karl-Heinz Ohlig and Gerd-R. Puin (Amherst, NY: Prometheus, 2010), 9.

or with Jews and Christians themselves—or both. The Qur'an's apparent familiarity with the stories, characters, and claims of the Jewish and Christian scriptures bears at least some internal evidence to the fact that it was written in a religious milieu wherein both Jews and Christians were known, if not immediately present.

Summary

In various places, the Qur'an addresses a group of people known as the "People of the Book," among whom are Jews and Christians. They gain this designation by receiving chapters of the heavenly book, disclosed to their messengers in the Torah, Psalms, and Gospel. Though many of the Jews and Christians are chastised by the Qur'an for their negligence in following the revelation given them, the various books of revelation are yet viewed as authentic.

REFLECTION QUESTIONS

1. Why does it matter that the Qur'an discusses Christians and Jews as those who have received revelation?

2. How does the Qur'an understand itself in relation to prior books?

3. If the Qur'an endorses the revelation entrusted to Jews and Christians, how does it view Jews and Christians themselves?

4. Is the Qur'an a book of history? Why or why not? How does the answer to this question affect our interpretation of its contents?

5. Why does it seem that the Qur'an is not as concerned to record the historical events surrounding its writing?

What Does Islam Teach about the Bible?

People of the Book! Why do you mix the
truth with falsehood, and conceal the truth,
when you know (better)? . . .

Surely (there is) indeed a group of them who twist
their tongues with the Book, so that you will think it
is from the Book, when it is not from the Book. And
they say, "It is from God," when it is not from God.
They speak lies against God, and they know (it).
~Qur'an 3:71, 78

The previous question demonstrated that the Qur'an endorses the Torah, Psalms, and Gospel as authentic revelation, descended from the same heavenly source as the Qur'an. However, it does not take long for a Christian in conversation with most Muslims to discover that Islamic confidence in the Bible's authority is lacking. How is it that the Qur'an can commend these books as authentic revelation, yet most Muslims reject the Bible out of hand?

The answer to this question comes in the form of a later Islamic teaching known as *tahrif*. The doctrine of *tahrif* is the teaching that the Jews and Christians have corrupted and changed their scriptures such that they can no longer be trusted. This chapter will discuss what the Qur'an says about the Jews and the Christians as they interpret and explain their holy books. It will then consider how later Islamic theology developed the doctrine of *tahrif*.[1] Finally, it will consider the tension that such a doctrine introduces between the Qur'an and later Islamic teaching.

The Qur'an's Accusation against the Jews and Christians

In various places throughout the Qur'an, one finds Jews and Christians being chastised for misusing or misinterpreting their scripture. Gabriel Said Reynolds has done the work to demonstrate that the Qur'an itself uses eight verbs to discuss such accusations of Jewish and Christian impropriety.[2] Only one of these words is etymologically related to the extra-qur'anic term *tahrif*, which has been adopted by later Islamic theology and commentary to mean that Christians and Jews have altered, changed, or corrupted the texts they were given.

The rest of the verbs used to chastise Jews and Christians focus mainly on improper interpretation, wrenching verses out of context, and obscuring parts of the scripture they have received. Likewise, in Qur'an 2:79, one reads, "So woe to those who write the Book with their (own) hands, (and) then say, 'This is from God,' in order to sell it for a small price." However, even this criticism does not indicate that the actual text of the Bible has been altered. Rather it merely emphasizes the fact that human words cannot serve as a substitute for divine words.

Having presented an exhaustive survey of this type of accusation throughout the Qur'an, Reynolds convincingly concludes, "There is no compelling reason to think the Qur'anic idea of *tahrif* involves textual alteration."[3] Instead, the Qur'an makes a far more modest appeal to Christians and Jews to read, interpret, and apply their scriptures appropriately and with sufficient integrity as to take the whole revelation into account. Yet, the vast majority of Islamic literature written from the Medieval period through to the present maintains the conviction that the Jews and Christians have so corrupted their scripture as to no longer be able to trust it. An investigation of the origins of such an argument is appropriate at this point.

---

1. For much of the material found in this chapter, I am indebted to the article by Gabriel Said Reynolds, "On the Qur'anic Accusation of Scriptural Falsification (*Tahrif*) and Christian Anti-Jewish Polemic," *Journal of the American Oriental Society* 130, no. 2 (2010): 189–202.
2. Reynolds, "Scriptural Falsification," 192–93. Those eight verbs used to accuse Jews and Christians of falsifying their scriptures are: (1) cover up (Qur'an 2:42); (2) conceal (Qur'an 2:42); (3) exchange (Qur'an 2:59); (4) write (Qur'an 2:79); (5) twist their tongues (Qur'an 3:78); (6) shift words out of their contexts (Qur'an 4:46); (7) forget (Qur'an 5:13–14); (8) hide (Qur'an 5:15).
3. Reynolds, "Scriptural Falsification," 194. For others who reach the same conclusions, see Gordon Nickel, *Narratives of Tampering in the Earliest Commentaries on the Qur'an* (Leiden: Brill, 2011); and Mark Anderson, *The Qur'an in Context: A Christian Exploration* (Downers Grove, IL: IVP Academic, 2016), 257–69.

Islamic Commentary and the Development of *Tahrif*

Turning from the Qur'an to the later texts collected in the *Sunnah*, one finds the posture toward previously revealed scripture to be much more antagonistic. For example, in a *hadith* classified as authentic, one reads,

> Why do you ask the people of the scripture about anything while your Book (Qur'an) which has been revealed to Allah's Messenger is newer and the latest? You read it pure, undistorted and unchanged, and Allah has told you that the people of the scripture (Jews and Christians) changed their scripture and distorted it, and wrote the scripture with their own hands and said, "It is from Allah," to sell it for a little gain. Does not the knowledge which has come to you prevent you from asking them about anything? No, by Allah, we have never seen any man from them asking you regarding what has been revealed to you![4]

Following this trajectory, the *Sunnah* and later commentaries often embellish the Qur'an's complaint against the Jews and Christians by accusing them of corrupting the actual text of their sacred books.

Presenting a more charitable version of this Islamic understanding of the contemporary unreliability of the Bible, Badru Kateregga writes of the Jewish and Christian scriptures, "Muslims are aware that human imperfections seem to be included in the Bible. For example, the personalities of the biblical Prophets form part of the content of biblical Scriptures. Moreover, the biblical Scriptures include both history and the Word of God."[5] In other words, rather than contending that the Bible has been overtly corrupted, Jewish and Christian tampering allowed human additions into the text of the Bible and have rendered it unreliable.

Though the Qur'an refers positively to the Torah, Psalms, and Gospel, popular Muslim opinion derives from the Islamic tradition that teaches that the Bible is unreliable because its text has been altered. In light of this tradition of biblical corruption—and since the Qur'an purports to be the complete, final, and summative revelation from God—few Muslims see reason to personally read or consult the Bible.

Introducing a Tension

Popular understanding about the reliability of the Bible relies solely upon extra-qur'anic traditions rather than the teaching of the Qur'an. In fact, most

---

4. Al-Bukhari, *Sahih al-Bukhari*, https://sunnah.com/bukhari/96/90, book 96 (§90).
5. Badru Kateregga and David Shenk, *A Muslim and a Christian in Dialogue* (Scottdale, PA: Herald, 1997), 55.

Muslims take the corruption of the Bible as established fact.[6] However, such traditions present an irreconcilable tension. The Qur'an not only recognizes the Torah, the Psalms, and the Gospel as authentic revelation; it also indicates that these very books, in uncorrupted form, were present and available to its audience.[7]

That the Gospel was understood to be accessible to the audience of the Qur'an is apparent, as Qur'an 5:47 instructs, "So let the People of the Gospel judge by what God has sent down in it." Corroborating this understanding, Reynolds notes, "If the Qur'an speaks against certain Christians, it speaks in support of the Gospel, and moreover assumes that the valid Christian revelation is still at hand in its day."[8] Anderson concurs with this conclusion, saying, "Clearly, both the Jewish and Christian scriptures were still extant in Muhammad's day, which is why the Qur'an calls Muslims to believe them (Qur'an 3:84; 4:136)."[9]

Furthermore, it appears that while the Qur'an specifically names the Torah, Psalms, and Gospel, early Muslims understood these citations to function as a reference to the entirety of the Old and New Testaments.[10] The Qur'an even instructs its readers to consult with those who have been given previous scriptures if they lack understanding. For instance, Qur'an 10:94 encourages the reader to seek understanding among the Jews and Christians: "If you are in doubt about what We have sent down to you, ask those who have been reciting the Book before you."[11]

If the Qur'an endorses the previous revelation that is apparently still available to the reader of the Qur'an, it views the Bible as reliable and uncorrupted as of the seventh century CE. For the later Islamic accusation of corruption to be true, then, such corruption would have had to have occurred after Muhammad's death. However, the many and widely disbursed extant manuscripts demonstrate the consistency of the biblical text from at least two centuries before Muhammad's birth. As Anderson concludes, "The Christians in Muhammad's day had the selfsame scripture we have today."[12]

---

6. Anderson, *Qur'an in Context*, 260n11.
7. Occasionally Muslims contend that Moses, David, and Jesus were given books—now lost to history—that are distinct from the Torah, Psalms, and Gospels of the Bible. However, as Anderson, *Qur'an in Context*, 260–69, convincingly demonstrates, this position is historically and theologically untenable, and the earliest witnesses in Islamic history contradict it. Furthermore, no earlier source recognizes this claim, which bears obvious Islamic bias.
8. Reynolds, "Scriptural Falsification," 195.
9. Anderson, *Qur'an in Context*, 265.
10. Anderson, *Qur'an in Context*, 266–67.
11. Cf. Qur'an 21:7. Commenting on Qur'an 10:94, A. J. Droge, trans., *The Qur'an: A New Annotated Translation* (Bristol, CT: Equinox, 2015), 131n197, notes that the phrase "those who have been reciting the Book before you" is a reference to Jews and Christians.
12. Anderson, *Qur'an in Context*, 267.

This evidence introduces a tension that makes the doctrine of *tahrif* untenable. If one is to maintain that the Bible is corrupt, it would then imply that the Qur'an was mistaken to commend it and to recommend that those in doubt consult with the people who are informed by it. Either the Bible is as the Qur'an says it is—and as such should be taken as true divine revelation by the Muslim community—or the Qur'an and its author were mistaken to so highly praise it.

Summary

Many Muslims are raised with the assumption that the Qur'an, Muhammad's teaching, and early Islamic tradition reinforce the claim that Jews and Christians have altered and corrupted the revelation that came to them from God. This doctrine is known as *tahrif*, and though it does not appear in the Qur'an, it has become standard Islamic belief through the writings of Muslim authors from Ibn Hizam in the eleventh century to Ahmed Deedat in the twentieth.[13] A more critical inspection of the Qur'an's claims about the Bible and appeal to biblical manuscript evidence, however, shows that the later idea actually complicates central Islamic claims regarding the total accuracy of the Qur'an. Neither the Qur'an nor any prior history lends credibility to the popular Islamic idea of *tahrif*.

REFLECTION QUESTIONS

1. What does the Qur'an accuse the Jews and Christians of doing to their scriptures?

2. What might have driven early Muslims to develop and expand the accusation of scriptural falsification to include actual change and corruption?

3. Does the Qur'an's endorsement of the Torah, Psalms, and Gospel cause problems for this doctrine of corruption? Why might this position be qur'anically untenable?

4. How does the prevalence of belief in the doctrine of *tahrif* affect conversation with Muslims regarding Christian theology?

5. What might be some ways to help a Muslim friend overcome some of this distrust?

---

13. Anderson, *Qur'an in Context*, 261n11.

What Does the Qur'an Teach about Abraham?

People of the Book! Why do you dispute about [Ibra-him], when the Torah and the Gospel were not sent down until after him. Will you not understand? There you are! Those who have disputed about what you know. Why do you dispute about what you do not know? God knows but you do not know. [Ibrahim] was not a Jew, nor a Christian, but he was a Hanif, a Muslim. He was not one of the idolaters.
~Qur'an 3:65–67

Many approaches to religious studies refer to Judaism, Christianity, and Islam using the umbrella title "the Abrahamic traditions."[1] This is because each tradition traces its history through Abraham and thus stakes its claim to Abraham as a key founder of the faith. For the Jews, Abraham is the patriarch who received the covenant and bore the promised offspring that led to the twelve tribes of Israel. For Christians, Abraham is an exemplar of salvation by faith and the recipient of a promise that all nations would be blessed through his offspring.

For Islam, the most recent of the three traditions to emerge, establishing a connection with this key figure is also vital. In fact, he is the second-most

---

1. See Irving Hexham, *Understanding World Religions* (Grand Rapids: Zondervan, 2011), 251–464.

referenced person in the Qur'an.[2] Perhaps most importantly, Ibrahim—the name by which this character is known in the Qur'an—is presented as neither a Jew, nor a Christian, but as a primal Muslim.

This chapter, then, explains the qur'anic Ibrahim and his importance to Islam. Such an investigation also serves as a test case to demonstrate how other biblical characters are assumed into the Islamic metanarrative. Not only does the Qur'an capitalize on his importance to prior religions, it also recasts him and his story according to its own purposes.[3]

Ibrahim the Muslim

As one might have already noticed, the verse quoted at the beginning of this chapter explicitly claims that Ibrahim was a Muslim who lived prior to the dawn of Judaism or Christianity. Along with the reference to Ibrahim as a Muslim, one notices an untranslated, transliterated appellative: *hanif*. This word, though debated in Islamic scholarship, is often taken in context to mean an upstanding monotheist.[4]

Ibrahim's adoption of monotheism in contrast to polytheism is made more explicit in Qur'an 6:79, where one reads Ibrahim's declaration, "Surely I have turned my face to Him who created the heavens and the earth—(being) a Hanif. Yet I am not one of the idolaters." The section goes on to show Ibrahim disputing with those who associate other gods with God, giving evidence to the polytheistic version of idolatry he rejected.

Thus, for the Qur'an, Ibrahim is exemplary as one who rejected the surrounding polytheistic pagan religions and who did so before the rise of other monotheistic religions. In addition, he serves as a prototype for Muhammad, the final Islamic prophet who would also adopt monotheism from within the context and culture of polytheism. Thus, it is instructive to consider a number of additional distinctives between the Ibrahim of the Qur'an and the Abraham of the Bible in attempting to understand his role as he features in the Islamic scriptures.

Ibrahim and Abraham

Ibrahim in the Qur'an is one of twenty-three biblical characters who serve as Muhammad's predecessors. Likewise, the Qur'an argues in many places that God's prophets are all responsible for delivering the same message,

---

2. John Kaltner and Younus Mirza, *The Bible and the Qur'an: Biblical Figures in the Islamic Tradition* (London: T&T Clark, 2018), 10.

3. Ibrahim is the same name given to the patriarch in the Arabic Bible. However, to distinguish the biblical character from the qur'anic account, I will use Ibrahim when referencing the character as presented in the Qur'an.

4. Fazlur Rahman, *Major Themes in the Qur'an* (Chicago: University of Chicago Press, 2009), 164.

and therefore should all be received and revered.[5] The implication of such a universal message proclaimed by prophets who overlap with Judaism and Christianity, then, is that the Qur'an views each prior prophet as one who serves the Qur'an's religious program and who offers worship and submission to its conception of God.

The Qur'an unflinchingly claims that Ibrahim—along with Adam, Moses, David, Jesus, and the other biblical prophets it commends—was an early Muslim worshipper of the qur'anic God. Several elements of the biblical story of Abraham are absent from the Qur'an's account, however, which raises the question as to whether or not Abraham can so easily be drawn up into qur'anic history without doing violence to his biblical role.

A Lineage Difference

First of all, in the Qur'an, one finds no reference to the fact that God made a covenant with Ibrahim that would continue through the line of Ishaq (Isaac).[6] Instead, the Qur'an only uses covenant language regarding Ibrahim when connected to Ismail (Ishmael), as seen in Qur'an 2:125–29:

> We made a covenant[7] with [Ibrahim] and [Ismail]: "Both of you purify My House for the ones who go around (it), and the ones who are devoted to it, and the ones who bow, (and) the ones who prostrate themselves. . . . Our Lord, make us both submitted to You, and (make) from our descendants a community submitted to You. And show us our rituals, and turn to us (in forgiveness). Surely You—You are the One who turns (in forgiveness), the Compassionate."

Though the Qur'an also identifies a covenant with the Sons of Israel,[8] and it views Ishaq as a prophet,[9] it avoids the idea that God intended to uniquely connect himself to Ishaq as the conduit of blessing for the nations. Instead, as

---

5. Mark Anderson, *The Qur'an in Context: A Christian Exploration* (Downers Grove, IL: IVP Academic, 2016), 143, cites Qur'an 2:136, 285; 3:84; 4:150, 152 as among the places that such unanimity of prophetic message is reinforced.

6. Cf. Genesis 17:15–21. See Anderson, *Qur'an in Context*, 144, who notes, "Although the covenant (*mithaq*) concept so prominent in the Bible appears in the Qur'an, it is never specifically related to Abraham. This is not surprising when we remember that, biblically, the Abrahamic covenant is precisely what excludes Ishmael."

7. The Arabic word here is *'ahad* which can be understood as "command" or "covenant." Both translations are represented in reputable English versions of the Qur'an, so I have chosen to follow Droge for consistency (A. J. Droge, trans., *The Qur'an: A New Annotated Translation* (Bristol, CT: Equinox, 2015). For a side-by-side comparison of translations, see https://www.islamawakened.com/quran/2/125/default.htm.

8. Cf. Qur'an 2:83–86.

9. Cf. Qur'an 19:49; 37:112.

seen above, Ibrahim and Ismail are seen praying for specific rituals to be given to them, and for a prophet to arise from their line, furthering the qur'anic presentation of Ibrahim as an anticipation and prefiguration of Muhammad.

A Geographic Difference

This same passage highlights a second difference regarding Ibrahim and Ismail in the Qur'an: an extrabiblical journey they took to the Arabian Peninsula. Not only does Qur'an 2:125–29 record the covenant between Ibrahim, Ismail, and God in Mecca, but according to most Islamic interpretations, this journey took place so that the father and son could build the holy temple known as the Ka'ba.[10]

This journey and the temple it resulted in connects Ibrahim not only with Muhammad, but also with contemporary Islamic practice. As was seen in Question 2, when Muhammad marched victoriously to Mecca around 630 CE, his first act as conqueror was to rid the Ka'ba of its idols and to restore it as a place of worship of the one true God. To this day—following the commands of Qur'an 2:144–50—contemporary Muslims are called to orient their prayers toward the Ka'ba in Mecca as the center of true monotheism. Thus, Ibrahim in the Qur'an is not as concerned with the land of promise that would be given to ancient Israel, but in fact plays a pivotal role in reinforcing the city of Mecca as the center of Islam.

A Covenant Difference

Third, the covenant God makes with Ibrahim and Ismail in the Qur'an appears to be essentially a command to build the Ka'ba. In the biblical account, however, YHWH initiates the covenant as a promise that precedes law. Furthermore, YHWH guarantees its perpetuity based upon his own eternal purposes and faithful character.[11] In the Qur'an, covenants are connected with the revelation of God's will and law without anticipation of any further divine engagement in ensuring the success of the covenant.

Such an understanding of covenant as law pervades the teaching of the Qur'an, and is reiterated in the references to covenant pertaining to the children of Israel and the Mosaic law. Illustrating this, in Qur'an 2:83 and 86 one reads,

> (Remember) when We took a covenant with the Sons of Israel: "Do not serve (anyone) but God, and (do) good to parents and family, and the orphans, and the poor, and speak well to the people, and observe the prayer and give the alms."

---

10. Kaltner and Mirza, *Bible and the Qur'an*, 13.
11. See especially Genesis 12:1–3; 15:1–21; 17:1–14. Compare the biblical account to Droge, *Qur'an*, 9n94. Droge explicitly directs the reader to compare Qur'an 2:83 with the giving of the Ten Commandments in Exodus 20:1–17.

Then you turned away in aversion, except a few of you. . . .
Those are the ones who have purchased this present life with
(the price of) Hereafter. The punishment will not be light-
ened for them, nor will they be helped.

In other words, the concept of covenant in the Qur'an appears to be more like
the concept of the law given to Israel in the Bible. While the biblical concept
of covenant does contain blessings and curses that depend upon human faithfulness, in the Bible it is YHWH who initiates the covenant with Abraham as
a promise that is founded upon YHWH's own eternal faithfulness.

Ibrahim and the Final Dispensation of Religion

The final aspect of Ibrahim's appearance in the Qur'an is one with which
non-Muslim readers might be more familiar. In Qur'an 37:99–111, one encounters a narrative that has significant overlap with the story of Abraham's
near sacrifice of Isaac. In Genesis 22, YHWH calls Abraham to take Isaac up
to Mount Moriah where Abraham is to sacrifice him. Obediently, Abraham
goes, but before he slaughters Isaac, the angel of the Lord stops him. Looking
up, Abraham sees a ram caught in the thicket, and offers it up as a burnt offering in the place of his son to the God who has provided a lamb of sacrifice
for himself.[12]

The Qur'an also references this story in Qur'an 37:99–111 and likewise lauds the faithful submission of Ibrahim and his son.[13] As in the Bible,
Ibrahim does not actually slaughter his son, but as Qur'an 37:107 states, "We
ransomed him with a great sacrifice." This great sacrifice serves a different
purpose in the Qur'an than it does in the Bible. Unlike the Bible, Islam rejects
the concept of substitutionary atonement. Rather, the Qur'an provides a non-
substitutionary rationale for this particular sacrifice that further reinforces
Ibrahim's role within the Qur'an's program.

One begins to see the Qur'an's rationale for this sacrifice in Qur'an 2:128.
Upon completing the Ka'ba, Ibrahim and Ismail pray that God would show
them their rituals. Elsewhere in the Qur'an, one reads that God has provided
rituals for every dispensation of true religion. For example, Qur'an 22:67
states, "For every community we have appointed a ritual which they practice.
So let them not argue with you about the matter, but call (them) to your Lord.
Surely you are indeed on a straight guidance." Thus, as Ibrahim and Ismail

---

12. Cf. Genesis 22:1–19. In the biblical account, then, this pre-Mosaic offering anticipates the
    Levitical sacrificial system wherein substitutionary sacrifice is required as the means by
    which YHWH would allow the priests to make atonement for Israel's sins.
13. In the Qur'an we are not told which son was nearly sacrificed, and this has caused a great
    deal of speculation for Muslim commentators. The earliest commentators were divided as
    to whether the son was Ishaq or Ismail. Contemporary Islamic scholarship favors Ismail.
    See Kaltner and Mirza, *Bible and the Qur'an*, 12.

request a ritual from God, they are asking to be identified as an authenticated community of faith.

These rituals take center stage in Qur'an 5:3, which states: "Today I have perfected your religion for you, and I have completed My blessing on you, and I have approved Islam for you as a religion." This verse comes on the heels of Qur'an 5:2, which reminds believers to not profane the symbols of God, which include the Ka'ba. Furthermore, Qur'an 5:95–97 connects the idea of pilgrimage to the Ka'ba and sacrifices that are offered there. Therefore, in Islam, both the sacred pilgrimage (*hajj*) and the Eid al-Adha sacrifice performed to this day are directly connected to the story of Ibrahim and Ismail. As an answer to Ibrahim and Ismail's petition, then, the *hajj* and Eid al-Adha provide Islam with rituals that establish Islam as the final dispensation of heavenly religion.[14]

Summary

The Ibrahim character in the Qur'an is intended to build upon the story of the biblical patriarch, Abraham. One specific point of overlap is the near-sacrifice of Ibrahim's son. However, though the Qur'an tells this story without much deviation from the biblical account, it serves a different function than it does in the Bible. In Islam, Ibrahim's sacrifice—observed to this day through Eid al-Adha—provides Islam with a ritual that confirms its authenticity as the final and perfected version of heavenly religion.

Not only does this particular ritual set Muhammad's community apart from the Jews and Christians, but it also hearkens back to a time that predates Judaism and Christianity. Thus, as the Qur'an employs Ibrahim in its program, it utilizes him as an ancient character who provides a picture of an exemplary Muslim before the dawn of competing monotheistic faiths. Therefore, Ibrahim in the Qur'an is an early prototypical Muslim who provides a sacrifice that authenticates the late faith of Islam.

In contrast to the biblical Abraham, the Qur'an focuses on Ibrahim's son, traditionally understood to be Ismail, as the recipient of divine covenant. Furthermore, Ibrahim in the Qur'an redirects attention away from the biblical promised land to Mecca, where he builds the Ka'ba. Finally, the concept of covenant connected to Ibrahim in the Qur'an is more akin to the Mosaic law than the Abrahamic covenant.

Though the Qur'an is adamant that it refers to the biblical Abraham and his God, those reading the Bible are justified in asking, "Is Ibrahim in the Qur'an the same character as Abraham in the Bible?" And even more pertinent, "Is the God of Ibrahim the YHWH of the Bible?" While Question

---

14. For a detailed and convincing discussion of this theme as it pertains to interpreting Qur'an 5, see Michel Cuypers, *The Banquet: A Reading of the Fifth Sura of the Qur'an* (Miami: Convivium, 2009).

35 will address this question in more detail, it is sufficient to conclude this chapter by saying that there are significant reasons to contend that Ibrahim is a different character than Abraham, and that the God of Ibrahim has different characteristics and purposes than the YHWH of the Bible.

REFLECTION QUESTIONS

1. Why did this chapter identify the Qur'an's character as Ibrahim and the biblical character as Abraham? Aren't these the same character? What difference does it make to identify the character differently according to the book in which he appears?

2. Why is Ibrahim such an influential character in the Qur'an and Islamic thought?

3. What role does Ibrahim's sacrifice play in Islam?

4. Does Ibrahim worship YHWH?

5. How should we approach characters in the Qur'an who purport to be the same characters as depicted in the biblical material?

Is 'Isa in the Qur'an the Same Person as Jesus in the Bible?

> *(Remember) when God said, "['Isa]! Surely I am going to take you and raise you to Myself, and purify you from those who disbelieve. And I am going to place those who follow you above those who disbelieve until the Day of Resurrection. Then to Me is your return, and I shall judge between you concerning your differences."*
> *~Qur'an 3:55*

Arguably, no character in the Qur'an is more contentious than the one named 'Isa. That is because this character is regularly understood to be Jesus. In fact, 'Isa does exhibit many similarities to the Jesus of the Bible. He is born of the virgin Mary,[1] said to be strengthened by the holy spirit,[2] and performed signs such as healing the blind and lepers and raising the dead.[3]

Throughout the Qur'an's pages, 'Isa features as a prophet, as a transmitter of God's revelation, and as one who confirms the Torah that was given before him.[4] Yet, despite these similarities with the biblical Jesus, 'Isa also speaks and acts in extrabiblical ways. Some aspects of 'Isa's story are not only extrabiblical, but they contradict the biblical account of Jesus.

---

1. Qur'an 19:20–31; 21:91.
2. Qur'an 2:87, 253; 5:110.
3. Qur'an 5:110.
4. Qur'an 61:6.

Thus, much like the previous question about Ibrahim, the present question seeks to investigate the role that 'Isa plays in the Qur'an. To do so, we must consider his qur'anic name, his qur'anic claims, and his qur'anic role. Much like Ibrahim, 'Isa in the Qur'an is employed to advance the Islamic program, and extrabiblical claims and stories are the primary means by which this character does so.

'Isa or Yasua'

The previous chapter chose to transliterate the Arabic form of Abraham's name to help the reader distinguish the figure in the Qur'an from the character in the Bible. In reality, however, the Arabic form of Abraham's name is Ibrahim whether in the Qur'an or in the Arabic Bible. Discussing the difference between Ibrahim and Abraham is merely a convenient way to distinguish the characters for an English-speaking audience.

The discussion of 'Isa may appear similar on the surface; however, there is a significant difference introduced by the fact that 'Isa is not the Arabic name for Jesus. 'Isa is the qur'anic Arabic name that is linked to the biblical Jesus. Yet, in the Arabic Bible, the name Jesus is rendered Yasua'. Before considering the material in the Qur'an that diverges from the biblical portrait of Jesus, it is important to recognize that this reality has missiological implications.

When a Christian and a Muslim find themselves in dialogue about things of faith, a discussion concerning the person of Jesus inevitably arises. Particularly if this discussion is happening in Arabic, the name by which one chooses to refer to Jesus comes loaded with baggage before any claims about Jesus are made.

Attempting to connect with Muslims and to lean into the respect that already exists for the qur'anic prophets, many missiologists recommend adopting the name 'Isa for evangelistic engagement with Muslims.[5] In fact, the Al-Sharif Arabic translation of the Bible has fully adopted qur'anic forms of the names of the biblical prophets for the purpose of engendering in the Muslim reader the respect these characters have already been given in their qur'anic context.

Such a discussion is more nuanced than this chapter can adequately cover. The following investigation of the qur'anic 'Isa should, however, give the reader pause to consider the qur'anic baggage that comes with using 'Isa before uncritically adopting it into one's evangelism.

Extrabiblical Stories and Claims

Reading through the Qur'an's account of 'Isa and his role, one notes several extrabiblical aspects that are worth investigating further. By exploring these points of divergence, the role of 'Isa in the Qur'an becomes more apparent.

---

5. See Phil Parshall, *Muslim Evangelism: Contemporary Approaches to Contextualization*, rev. ed. (Downers Grove, IL: InterVarsity, 2003), 73–74.

Son of Mary

Throughout the New Testament, Jesus is given many messianic titles. Son of David, Son of Man, Son of God, Christ, and Lord are regularly applied to him by the Gospel writers who intend to connect him with the expected messiah of the Old Testament.[6] The Qur'an, however, uses the title Son of Mary twenty-three times. In so doing, it appears to be a way of underscoring Jesus's humanity in contrast to the Christian claims.[7]

Speaking from the Cradle and Creating Clay Birds

The Qur'an also includes two stories about 'Isa that stem from extrabiblical early Christian literature. In Qur'an 19:27–36, one reads an account that bears echoes of a treatise known as the *Syriac Infancy Gospel*, wherein 'Isa speaks from the cradle as an infant about his own prophetic calling. Immediately connected to this is the claim that 'Isa is not God's son.

The second story is found in Qur'an 3:48–51, where one reads about Jesus performing a creative act whereby he fashions a bird out of clay and then brings it to life.[8] This account does not come from the New Testament, but rather appears to have its origin in a second-century extracanonical writing known as the *Infancy Gospel of Thomas*.[9] Both of these stories, though miraculous, are noted by the Qur'an as being connected to God's work through 'Isa by his permission. As such, they defend his role as a prophet, but reject the idea that 'Isa possessed personal divine power.

Preserved from Crucifixion

By nearly all Islamic accounts, the Qur'an is understood to teach that 'Isa was not crucified, nor was he killed by the Jews, but that God preserved him from what would be such a shameful fate. This understanding derives from Qur'an 4:157–58, which states,

> And for [the Jews'] saying, "Surely we killed the Messiah, ['Isa], son of Mary, the messenger of God"—yet they did not

---

6. Interestingly, the Qur'an also refers to 'Isa as *al-Masih*—the messiah. However, this term functions more like a proper name than the biblical title for the expected, anointed savior. In fact, the Qur'an simply utilized "messiah" as a referent to 'Isa without further comment. See A. J. Droge, trans., *The Qur'an: A New Annotated Translation* (Bristol, CT: Equinox, 2015), 35n65.

7. This title is used only once in the Bible, and in the context of a crowd that is disparaging Jesus and his teaching by asking, "Is this not the carpenter, the son of Mary?" (Mark 6:3). See John Kaltner and Younus Mirza, *The Bible and the Qur'an: Biblical Figures in the Islamic Tradition* (London: T&T Clark, 2018), 76.

8. This story is also referenced in Qur'an 5:110.

9. See Droge, *Qur'an*, 35n73. It is important to note that the Qur'an makes it explicit that 'Isa is not providing these birds with life of his own accord, but that God is animating these birds by giving his permission that they come to life.

kill him, nor did they crucify him, but it only seemed like (that) to them. Surely they have no knowledge about him, only the following of conjecture. Certainly they did not kill him. No! God raised him to Himself. God is mighty, wise.

What this passage unequivocally teaches is that 'Isa was not killed nor crucified by the Jews. What happened to 'Isa, and what it means that the Qur'an states that it seemed like he was crucified, however, are matters of debate.

The standard Islamic teaching on the issue is that 'Isa was raised to paradise prior to the crucifixion, and that he will return at the end of time to do battle with *dajjal* (the antichrist figure) and to die a natural death. Scholars speculate about who was crucified in his place, though many Muslims contend that Judas was made to look like (*shubbiha lahum*) 'Isa and was crucified in his place.[10] Regardless of what specific interpretation one takes, the qur'anic 'Isa does not die a substitutionary, atoning, or salvific death on behalf of his followers.

Rejecting the Trinity

Finally, 'Isa is made to be a champion of qur'anic monotheism. As such, the Qur'an argues that 'Isa is but one of many messengers who proclaim the same message. This claim can be seen in the declaration of Qur'an 4:171, which states,

> People of the Book! Do not go beyond the limits in your religion, and do not say about God (anything) but the truth. The Messiah, ['Isa], son of Mary, was only a messenger of God, and His word, which He cast into Mary, and a spirit from Him. So believe in God and His messengers, but do not say, "Three." Stop! (It will be) better for you. God is only one God. Glory to Him! (Far be it) that He should have a son! To Him (belongs) whatever is in the heavens and whatever is on the earth. God is sufficient as a guardian.

This verse specifically targets Christian monotheism, which understands God to exist as three persons in one essence.

Elsewhere, the Qur'an depicts the idea of the Trinity as the preposterous idea that includes God, Jesus, and Mary as the divine persons. In Qur'an 5:73 one reads, "Certainly they have disbelieved who say, "God is the third of three." Two verses later, in Qur'an 5:75, it continues on saying, "The Messiah, son of Mary, was only a messenger. Messengers have passed away before him. His mother was a truthful woman. They both ate food. See how We make

---

10. See the helpful discussion provided by Kaltner and Mirza, *Bible and the Qur'an*, 80–83.

clear the signs to them, then see how deluded they are?" The idea of God eating food is taken to be absurd, thus 'Isa and Mary are to be viewed merely as admirable humans.

Yet, even more explicitly, Qur'an 5:116 depicts God asking, "['Isa] son of Mary! Did you say to the people, 'Take me and my mother as two gods instead of God (alone)?' He said, 'Glory to You! It is not for me to say what I have no right (to say). If I had said it, You would have known it. You know what is within me, but I do not know what is within You." Thus, 'Isa in the Qur'an is made to declare to God that he never sought the worship of his followers, and he merely commanded them to serve God in the same way as all of the previous prophets also did.

'Isa in Muhammad's Shadow

Having seen the various differences between the Qur'an's account of 'Isa and the biblical person of Jesus, we must consider what role 'Isa plays within the overall program of the Qur'an and Islam. Though 'Isa is counted as the second most revered prophet, his character in the Qur'an plays an anticipatory role for the coming of Muhammad.

This claim is seen most clearly through the Qur'an's insistence that 'Isa is merely one of many prophets to preach the singular message of submission to God. Likewise, the Qur'an everywhere reinforces the humanness of 'Isa while rejecting all hints at divinity. 'Isa is a human messenger who proclaims an ancient message, confirming the Torah, contained in the Injil, and culminating in a coming prophet who will be the Seal of the Prophets (Qur'an 33:40).

Finally, in Qur'an 61:6 one reads 'Isa himself predicting Muhammad's arrival, as he says, "Sons of Israel! Surely I am the messenger of God to you, confirming what was before me of the Torah, and bringing good news of a messenger who will come after me, whose name will be Ahmad." Ahmad is a derivation of the name Muhammad; thus, this passage is understood to be a prediction of his coming by almost all scholars of Islam.

Summary

'Isa in the Qur'an—like Ibrahim—bears some significant similarity with his biblical counterpart, Jesus. However, the manner in which 'Isa deviates from—and even contradicts—the Jesus of the Bible, demonstrates that the character plays a different role and advances a different story in the Qur'an. 'Isa is merely a human agent advancing a singular divine message calling his audience to submit to the one and only God. He did not die a sacrificial death on the cross, and his ministry is no different in substance than the prophets and messengers who have preceded him. Ultimately, 'Isa serves to prepare the way for the ministry of Muhammad, who will serve as the Seal of the Prophets.

REFLECTION QUESTIONS

1. What are the differences and similarities between the qur'anic 'Isa and the biblical Jesus?

2. Why do Muslims insist that these two characters are the same historical person? What difference does it make?

3. What is the primary role of 'Isa in the Qur'an and in its overarching message? How does 'Isa relate to Muhammad?

4. When conversing with a Muslim in Arabic, what are the communicative effects of choosing to use 'Isa versus choosing to use Yasua'? What are the effects of a Muslim-sensitive translation of the Bible choosing to use 'Isa rather than Yasua'?

5. When using language that has been indelibly shaped by a nonbiblical worldview, what dangers does one encounter? How does one communicate while mitigating misunderstanding?

PART 6

The Development of Contemporary Critical Scholarship

A Brief Disclaimer

The following section intends to expose the reader to some contemporary strands of critical scholarship within the discipline of Qur'anic and Islamic studies. However, some of the following material, wielded unlovingly, could potentially be destructive to healthy engagement with Muslim friends and neighbors. Before we begin, let me establish my purpose and posture.

Purpose

This section is included for the purpose of alerting the reader to research trajectories current in the field. Such research challenges the historicity of the traditional accounts of Islam on the basis of the fact that they were first committed to writing two hundred years removed from the death of Muhammad and largely uncorroborated by non-Muslim sources. It is not intended to be exhaustive, nor can conclusive arguments be presented in such limited space. The curious reader is encouraged to investigate the works and research mentioned in the footnotes.

Posture

Some of the writers who employ this material do so from a desire to paint Islam in an uncharitable light and to undermine Muslim faith. This section attempts a more dispassionate and objective approach to the material, with the result being a better approach to hearing the Qur'an speak for itself without the imposition of later bias potentially distorting our understanding. Most Muslims with whom one interacts will reject this research regarding the Islamic traditional material found in the *Sunnah*. Therefore, though interesting as a scholarly discussion, one should always keep in mind that one's Muslim friends are likely much more influenced by the traditional accounts and the worldview produced thereby.

Is Mecca Really the Birthplace of Islam?

He (it is) who restrained their hands from you, and
your hands from them, in the heart of Mecca, after he
gave you victory over them—God sees what you do.
~Qur'an 48:24

The four questions contained in this section on critical scholarship may surprise those first encountering the field of Islamic studies. To question some of the central traditions of Islamic origins may seem to be the stuff of unbridled polemics. In fact, sometimes that is exactly where one encounters such questions. Yet, following the historical-critical scholarship of John Wansbrough,[1] and especially since the 1977 publication of Patricia Crone and Michael Cook's work, *Hagarism*, many scholars have revisited early Islamic history in fresh light.[2]

In so doing, certain strands of academic study of Islam have come to raise significant doubts about some of the assumed tenets of the first two centuries of Islam. Citing the central reason for such a critical approach to the traditional narrative, Karl-Heinz Ohlig notes, "All the biographical 'information' [concerning Muhammad] we have can be found in two types of sources. The first consists of the biographical works of the early ninth and tenth centuries. . . . The second type of source consists of the six canonical

---

1. See John Wansbrough, *Qur'anic Studies: Sources and Methods of Scriptural Investigation* (Oxford: Oxford University Press, 1977).
2. Patricia Crone and Michael Cook, *Hagarism: The Making of the Islamic World* (New York: Cambridge University Press, 1977). This book was controversial because of the polemical tone of the authors who described their work as "written by infidels and for infidels." The data produced, however, remains worthy of consideration.

collections of hadith, which date from the late ninth century."[3] Thus, Ohlig concludes that if scholarship is to follow the accepted canons of historical-critical research, such late and biased records should be received as historical fact only with great reservations.[4]

In addition, the records come almost exclusively from Islamic sources prone to bias; little to no concrete corroborating data exists to reinforce the claims about their prophet, early history, or beliefs. The dearth of extra-Islamic attestation of traditional Islamic origins, then, has caused fresh critical scholarship to propose alternative origins of Islam over the last half century.[5]

The purpose of this section is simply to make the reader aware of extra-traditional endeavors to understand Islamic origins. Inclusion of research trajectories and alternative proposals is not to be understood as endorsement. Space prohibits us from conducting an investigation of these issues sufficient enough to offer such conclusions, though, as mentioned above, the curious reader is encouraged to utilize the resources in the footnotes for further investigation.

As noted above, some of these queries are picked up by those who merely aim to discredit Islam as a faith. Thus, as one is likely to encounter various renditions of these claims, it will be helpful to be introduced to some of the critical issues and to consider the motivations and scholarship of those who address them. One such issue is the question regarding the historicity of pre-Islamic Mecca as a center of trade. Thus, the first chapter of this section presents some of the critical scholarship that argues that modern-day Mecca may not be the birthplace of Islam.

Misdirected Mosques

The first place that questions began to be raised regarding Meccan antiquity comes from archeological data pointing to anomalies in the earliest mosques. In the process of excavating many of the early mosques of the Umayyad era, it became apparent that many of them do not point toward southwestern Arabia. This is abnormal because mosques are built to indicate the direction of prayer (*qibla*), pointing the worshippers to pray facing the

---

3. Karl-Heinz Ohlig, "Islam's 'Hidden' Origins," in *The Hidden Origins of Islam*, eds. Karl-Heinz Ohlig and Gerd-R. Puin (Amherst, NY: Prometheus, 2010), 8.

4. Ohlig, "Islam's 'Hidden' Origins," 8.

5. Such scholars come to the study from a variety of their own motivations. As with all reading, one should consider some of the motivations of the authors prior to uncritically adopting their conclusions. An example of a polemical approach can be found in Robert Spencer, *Did Muhammad Exist?* (Wilmington, DE: ISI Books, 2014). Others write from the posture of disaffected former Muslims, such as the prolific Ibn Warraq, ed., *What the Koran Really Says* (Amherst, NY: Prometheus, 2002). Yet others, such as Gabriel Said Reynolds, *The Qur'an and Its Biblical Subtext* (New York: Routledge, 2010), write charitably and compellingly, while yet dealing critically with the traditional accounts in light of emerging data.

Ka'ba.[6] If they intended to point toward Mecca, these early mosques are mis-directed to the north.[7]

In light of this anomaly, author Dan Gibson has examined the *qibla* of more than sixty ancient mosques that also appear to point much farther to the north than they would if rightly aligned toward Mecca.[8] In analyzing these various *qiblas*, Gibson contends that Petra seems to present itself as the likely point of orientation.

Gibson is not without his detractors, however. David King has criticized Gibson's work as being uninformed about how the *qibla* was determined by tradition and folk astronomy.[9] King argues that obtaining any singular focal point for the early *qibla*—Mecca or otherwise—is unlikely and does not nec-essarily deny Mecca as the early center of Islam.[10] Still, King himself notes a number of ancient mosque orientations that evade his method of *qibla* determination.[11]

Though Gibson is not a credentialed academic, he is also not alone in his contention that Mecca may not be the birthplace of Islam. In the late 1970s, Patricia Crone and Michael Cook raised the question of modern-day Mecca and the holy city of Islamic origins. Crone and Cook argue that northwestern Arabia appears to match the data much better than Mecca, which seems to be congruent with some of what Gibson proposes.[12] This data alone does not deny Mecca its traditional place in the Islamic story, but it is worth noting that many of the earliest mosques do point north of modern-day Mecca.

An Improbable Trade Center

A second line of inquiry that calls Mecca into question comes from the tra-ditional claim that Mecca was a bourgeoning city of trade prior to Muhammad. As noted above, in 1977 Patricia Crone and Michael Cook were among the first

---

6. Clinton Bennett, "A–Z Index of Key Terms and Concepts," 327–374 in *The Bloomsbury Companion to Islamic Studies*, ed. Clinton Bennett (New York: Bloomsbury, 2015), 359.

7. Crone and Cook, *Hagarism*, 23.

8. Dan Gibson, *Early Islamic Qiblas* (Vancouver, BC: Independent Scholars Press, 2017), 5. Gibson specifically argues that the early *qiblas* point specifically to Petra as the true center of early Islamic worship.

9. See the scathing review by David A. King, "From Petra back to Makka—From 'Pibla' back to Qibla," Muslim Heritage, https://muslimheritage.com/pibla-back-to-qibla.

10. King, "From Petra back to Makka." King writes, "In a society without serious geographical notions or mathematical science beyond commercial arithmetic, how does one locate a distant edifice to face it? The answer is astronomical alignments, of which the cardinal directions are the most obvious, less so sunrise and sunset at the winter and summer sol-stices, but also risings and settings of select qibla stars."

11. King, "From Petra back to Makka," writes of the unusual orientation of a number of Syrian mosques: "These orientations of 190°–195° are not so easily explained. What is clear is (a) that the direction was not calculated, and (b) that [it] was not derived from risings and settings of the sun at the solstices, or of a bright star."

12. Crone and Cook, *Hagarism*, 22–24.

to question modern-day Mecca as the holy city of Islamic origins.[13] A decade later, Crone's book *Meccan Trade and the Rise of Islam* continued to examine some of the central issues concerning early Islam, Mecca, and geography.

In particular, *Meccan Trade* dismantles the assumption that Mecca's strategic location along the seventh-century spice trade provided the city with wealth and importance.[14] Countering this notion, she writes, "Mecca is frequently credited with the advantage of having been located at the crossroads of all the major trade routes in Arabia . . . [but] these claims are quite wrong. Mecca is tucked away at the edge of the peninsula."[15] In reality, a stop along a trade route located where modern-day Mecca is would be an inconvenient and inhospitable wayside when compared to the lush landscape of nearby Ta'if.[16]

In fact, even if Mecca were a stop along an overland trade route, Crone convincingly shows that international maritime trade had supplanted the overland spice trade by the third century CE. Thus, Mecca should no longer be thought of as the hub of a vast trading empire that it is reported to be during Muhammad's life.[17] Rather, at best Mecca dealt in more humble, regional trade in cheaper commodities, such as leather and perfume.[18] Thus, following Crone's conclusions, it is hard to imagine modern-day Mecca being the location of the city that the Qur'an and Islamic tradition describe as the Mother of Towns.[19]

Pre-Islamic History and Mecca

A final reason to question modern-day Mecca as the birthplace of Islam is its absence from the pre-Islamic historical record. According to the traditional accounts, Mecca was not only an important economic center, but it was also a religious center for pilgrims coming to visit Abraham's temple—the Ka'ba—which had devolved into a center of pagan worship.[20]

Described as a city of such international importance, one would expect that archeological and historical reference to Mecca would be readily available. Yet reference to a trade city located in modern-day Mecca is sparse and

---

13. Crone and Cook, *Hagarism*, 22–24.
14. Crone's work takes aim at the influential work of Montgomery Watt as a representative of the many Orientalist scholars who affirm the seventh-century Meccan frankincense trade. See Patricia Crone, *Meccan Trade and the Rise of Islam* (Piscataway, NJ: Gorgias, 2004), 7.
15. Crone, *Meccan Trade*, 6.
16. Crone, *Meccan Trade*, 6.
17. Crone, *Meccan Trade*, 25.
18. Crone, *Meccan Trade*, 97.
19. See the references to the Mother of Towns (*umm al-qora*) in Qur'an 6:92 and 42:7.
20. A. Guillaume, trans., *The Life of Muhammad: A Translation of Ibn Ishaq's "Sirat Rasul Allah"* (Oxford: Oxford University Press, 1982), 3637. However, as Reynolds acknowledges this traditional reality, he also contends, "The premise that the Qur'an emerged amidst paganism has more than once left scholars confused by the fact that paganism is hardly evident in the Qur'an" (*Qur'an and Its Biblical Subtext*, 33).

increasingly questionable.[21] For example, it has long been held as consensus that Claudius Ptolemy's second-century work *Guide to Geography* identifies Mecca by using the name Macoraba.[22] However, Ian Morris has demonstrated that such a connection is based upon implausible etymology and is uncorroborated by any epigraphical texts from Arabia.[23] Furthermore, even if Macoraba is a reference to Mecca, Ptolemy merely notes the city's existence without further comment. Such a mere passing reference to a city of such apparent influence seems unbefitting and unlikely.

In light of these issues, some authors are quick to conclude that the Mecca of the traditional Islamic narrative is simply fabricated so as to provide Islam with an Arabian home.[24] Others have argued that the Qur'an and traditional history speak of a region or city that lies to the north of modern-day Mecca.[25] Yet others remain suspicious of revisionist explanations and take the traditional narrative as the best framework for inquiry.[26]

Summary

This chapter has highlighted several of the reasons some scholars question whether modern-day Mecca fits the traditional description of the birthplace of Islam. First, excavation of early mosques shows that many appear to direct prayers to a region in northern Arabia. Second, the traditional claims that Mecca was a bourgeoning center of trade seem to have no basis in history or geography beyond later Islamic documentation. In fact, even in the Qur'an, Mecca is only named one time. Finally, reference to Mecca cannot be conclusively verified within the annals of pre-Islamic history.

While none of these reasons provide indisputable proof that Mecca is not the city of Islamic origins recognized by tradition, the cluster of issues appears to at least warrant critical consideration. In light of these and other issues, Fred Donner concludes, "Even if Arabia does turn out to have been the historical context of the Qur'an, as seems likely to this author, it may be an Arabian environment vastly different from anything with which we are familiar from the *Sira*'s picture of Muhammad's Mecca and Medina."[27]

The following question will continue to consider recent critical scholarship regarding the linguistic background of the Qur'an. In so doing, we will

---

21. See Fred Donner, "The Historian, the Believer, and the Qur'an," in *New Perspectives on the Qur'an: The Qur'an in Its Historical Context*, vol. 2, ed. Gabriel Said Reynolds (New York: Routledge, 2011), 29–30.
22. Ian Morris, "Mecca and Macoraba," *Al-ʿUsur al-Wusta* 26 (2018): 3.
23. Morris, "Mecca and Macoraba," 3. See also Morris's etymological survey conducted between pages 13–50.
24. See the polemicist Peter Townsend, *Questioning Islam* (Seattle: CreateSpace, 2014), 24–50.
25. Crone and Cook, *Hagarism*, 23.
26. See Fred Donner, *Narratives of Islamic Origins* (Princeton, NJ: Darwin, 1998).
27. Donner, "Historian, the Believer, and the Qur'an," 30.

see that several scholars argue that the language, citations, and apparent dialogue partners of the Qur'an also indicate an environment different than one
would expect from reading the traditional accounts of the environment in
southwestern Arabia.

REFLECTION QUESTIONS

1. What are the most compelling reasons to doubt the traditional claim that
   modern-day Mecca is the location of Muhammad's birth and some of his
   prophetic career?

2. If the Qur'an was written in a different location, what role might its environment have played in shaping its message?

3. What are the reasons for doubting that Mecca was a booming trade city
   during the seventh century?

4. If Mecca is not the location of Islam's birth, what would cause the early
   Islamic community to choose it as the place of origin?

5. Why would the idea that Mecca might not be the birthplace of Islam be so
   disruptive and offensive to contemporary Islam?

Is the Original Qur'an an Arabic Text?

*Surely it is indeed a sending down from the Lord of
the worlds. The trustworthy spirit brought it down on
your heart, so that you may be one of the warners, in a
clear Arabic language. Surely it is indeed in the scriptures of those of God. Was it not a sign for them that
it was known to the learned of the Sons of Israel? If we
had sent it down on one of the foreigners, and he had
recited it to them, they would not have believed in it.*
~ *Qur'an 26:192–99*

R ecently the work of an interdisciplinary group of scholars going by the
name of Inarah—the Arabic word for enlightenment—has been translated
into English.[1] These scholars propose various reconstructions of Islamic origins
citing linguistic, religious, and archeological research. Perhaps their most influential work proposes that the Qur'an derives from non-Arabic sources.[2]

---

1. See Markus Gross, "Foreword to the English Edition," 7–9, in *Early Islam: A Critical
   Reconstruction based on Contemporary Sources,* ed. Karl-Heinz Ohlig (Amherst, NY:
   Prometheus, 2013), 7. Gross introduces Inarah's work and aims which are represented
   in the rest of the colume. Though Inarah is relatively new, the most influential academic
   writer to suggest that Islam borrowed directly from existing religious traditions was the
   nineteenth-century author Abraham Geiger, whose work has been translated and re-
   printed as "What Did Muhammad Borrow from Judaism?," in *The Origins of the Koran:
   Classical Essays on Islam's Holy Book,* ed. Ibn Warraq (Amherst, NY: Prometheus, 1998).
2. Gross, "Foreword," 8. Some of the impetus for this research comes from the fact that at
   least four times throughout the Qur'an one encounters the claim that the Qur'an has been

While the proposals offered by Inarah and those following their trajectory are often dismissed as the speculative work of polemicists, there is value in considering how and why the influence of non-Arabic religious language and texts can be detected in the Qur'an. In an effort to do so, this chapter will investigate some of the linguistic and textual anomalies of the Qur'an. Further, it will highlight some of the arguments posed by critical scholars that envisage qur'anic origins and dialogue partners that differ from those expected by the traditional accounts.

Non-Arabic Words and Phrases

In an effort to protect the literal interpretation of the qur'anic verses that refer to the Qur'an as a book of pure Arabic, some of the earliest Islamic commentators, such as ash-Shafi and al-Tabari, adamantly denied that the Qur'an contained non-Arabic vocabulary.[3] Today, however, almost all scholars of the Qur'an—secular and confessional alike—admit the presence of loan words from other languages.

Words originating in Hebrew, Aramaic, Akkadian, Ethiopic, and other languages have been recognized alongside of the seventh-century Arabic of the Qur'an.[4] The language that seems to have the broadest impact, however, is the Syriac dialect of Aramaic.[5] In fact, the field of qur'anic studies has been fruitfully investigating the impact of Syriac, and the religious impact of those who wrote in Syriac, on the Qur'an for the better part of the past century.

One scholar, Christoph Luxenberg, has gained notoriety for advancing the extreme view that behind the Arabic Qur'an—or at least significant parts of it—there exists an original Syriac lectionary for Christian worship.[6] While Luxenberg has been challenged on a number of points, he is not alone in his argument. As other scholars have also traced the Syriac impact on the Qur'an, it has opened up fruitful lines of inquiry regarding the religious milieu in which the Qur'an was codified.[7] Along with the Syriac language, the Qur'an also appears to be aware of and engaged with Syriac religious literature and communities.

---

revealed in Arabic. Cf. Qur'an 12:2; 16:98–105; 26:192–99; 42:7. See also 14:4 and 19:97. For some, the oddity of a text declaring its own language is actually evidence that it is attempting to obscure its non-Arabic origins and borrowings from preexisting texts. An instance of this can be seen in Ibn Warraq's introduction to *What the Koran Really Says*, ed. Ibn Warraq (Amherst, NY: Prometheus, 2002), 39.

3. Yasir Qadhi, "The Arabic Qur'an and Foreign Words," *Muslim Matters*, May 21, 2008, https://muslimmatters.org/2008/05/21/the-arabic-quran-and-foreign-words.

4. Emran Albadawi, "The Impact of Aramaic (Especially Syriac) on the Qur'an," *Religious Compass* 8, no. 7 (2014): 221.

5. Albadawi, "Impact of Aramaic," 221. Albadawi credits this fact to the philological work of Arthur Jeffrey, *The Foreign Vocabulary of the Qur'an* (Baroda, India: Oriental Institute, 1938).

6. Christoph Luxenberg, "Relics of Syro-Aramaic Letters in Early Qur'an Codices in Higazi and Kufi Ductus," in Ohlig, *Early Islam*, 337.

7. Albadawi, "Impact of Aramaic," 221–23.

Preexisting Religious Sources

Even a cursory reading of the Qur'an reveals its clear concern to acknowledge and interact with biblical characters and history. Since the Qur'an claims to be the continuation of the biblical message, the presence of biblical material should not be taken to indicate, as has been argued, that Muhammad borrowed or plagiarized religious ideas from Judaism and then attempted to pass them off as his own.[8]

Yet, the Bible is not the only religious document with which the Qur'an is familiar. For example, the account of the revolt of Satan recorded in the fourth-century Syriac document *The Cave of Treasures* appears almost verbatim as the account of Satan's refusal to worship Adam in Qur'an 7:11–18.[9] Likewise, the qur'anic accounts of 'Isa speaking from the cradle[10] and making birds from clay[11] existed in Syriac as apocryphal stories such as the *Infancy Gospel* that predate the Qur'an.[12]

The intimate relationship between the Qur'an's biblical and extrabiblical texts and traditions is highlighted by Karl-Heinz Ohlig. He notes, "Recently many authors have abdefended the opinion that most of the theological statements in the Qur'an . . . arose from Syrian traditions of Christianity."[13] Thus, as noted above, a few scholars have developed extreme theories that imagine the Qur'an to be Arabic plagiarism of Syriac-speaking Christian texts.[14] While these proposals appear to overreach their data, other scholars have taken a more modest approach in suggesting that the Syriac influence is inevitable because biblical literature had yet to be written in Arabic, and the Qur'an is intentionally engaged in inter-faith and intertextual discussion.[15]

Intentional Intertextual Polemic

Due to the traditional belief that Muhammad was illiterate, most accounts of the Qur'an's origins do not suppose that its message reflects much

---

8. See Geiger, "What Did Muhammad Borrow from Judaism?," and those who followed in his stead.

9. Ephraim the Syrian, "The Revolt of Satan," in *The Book of the Cave of Treasures*, trans. E. A. Burdge (London: Religious Tract Society, 1927), http://www.sacred-texts.com/chr/bct/bct04.htm.

10. Qur'an 19:30.

11. Qur'an 3:49; 5:109–110.

12. See A. J. Droge, trans., *The Qur'an: A New Annotated Translation* (Bristol, CT: Equinox, 2015), 35n73.

13. Karl-Heinz Ohlig, "Syrian and Arabian Christianity in the Qur'an," in *The Hidden Origins of Islam*, eds. Karl-Heinz Ohlig and Gerd-R. Puin (Amherst, NY: Prometheus, 2010), 387.

14. Karl-Heinz Ohlig, "Evidence of a New Religion 'Under Islamic Rule'?," in Ohlig, *Early Islam*, 235–40.

15. For a definitive argument for the post-Qur'an emergence of an Arabic Bible, see Sidney Griffith, *The Bible in Arabic* (Princeton, NJ: Princeton University Press, 2015).

engagement with biblical texts.[16] The apparent discrepancies between stories in the Qur'an and their biblical counterparts, then, are taken to be either the result of Muhammad's lack of familiarity with the Bible or the Qur'an's reassertion of the true testimony. For some scholars, evidence of other religious texts in the Qur'an leads to the conclusion that Muhammad was stitching together extant religious ideas.

Rather than assuming the Qur'an to be a "scrapbook of earlier religious ideas," however, Gabriel Said Reynolds has proposed that the Qur'an may in fact be a more textually aware document than is often supposed.[17] In light of this fact, Reynolds argues that "the Qur'an is in conversation with a larger literary tradition."[18] This approach recognizes the linguistic and religious influences on the Qur'an while also engaging it as a text in its own right.

An example of this approach can be seen in Reynolds's treatment of Qur'an 28:38, wherein the biblical stories of Haman, Pharaoh, and Babel coalesce into a single narrative. Reynolds argues that this ahistorical connection of biblical characters is not evidence that the author of the Qur'an was misinformed.[19] Instead, drawing these three stories together is intentional, as it highlights three stories that expose human hubris and warn of divine judgment.[20]

In other places, Reynolds's approach shows that the Qur'an's intention is to present its opposition as ridiculous, such as the inclusion of Mary within the Trinity.[21]

By reading the Qur'an as if it is consciously involved in intertextual and interreligious dialogue, one avoids the pejorative conclusions reached by some that the author is merely ill-informed about biblical history. Instead, the presence of extra-Islamic, non-Arabic material might be understood as a part of an intentionally constructed polemic or rearranged so as to advance the Qur'an's own agenda. The Qur'an, then, could be understood as a sort of midrash or homily in which familiar stories and references are brought together, not so much for the purpose of retelling history, but for the purpose of impacting the reader in a fresh way in promotion of its own distinct purposes.[22]

---

16. For a list of Islamic scholars who rely upon the traditional Islamic material in their study, see the literature review provided by Gabriel Said Reynolds, *The Qur'an and Its Biblical Subtext* (New York: Routledge, 2010), 85.

17. Reynolds, *Qur'an and Its Biblical Subtext*, 35.

18. Reynolds, *Qur'an and Its Biblical Subtext*, 24. Granting the Qur'an the dignity of being its own text, Reynolds's book both proposes this method of reading the Qur'an and then demonstrates how it illumines the meaning through a series of case studies.

19. Reynolds, *Qur'an and Its Biblical Subtext*, 146. In fact, Reynolds's whole approach dispenses with the idea that the Qur'an is attempting to present history at all, noting that when the Qur'an presents Mary the sister of Moses and Mary the mother of Jesus as the same person, it is engaging not in history but in typology.

20. Reynolds, *Qur'an and Its Biblical Subtext*, 99–106.

21. Qur'an 5:116.

22. Reynolds, *Qur'an and Its Biblical Subtext*, 232–58.

Summary

While some scholars have viewed the presence of non-Arabic language and non-Islamic narrative in the Qur'an as evidence of borrowing—or stealing—from other religious texts, this chapter contends that one need not arrive at such a pejorative conclusion. Instead, if one considers the Qur'an to be intentionally engaged with other religious communities and their sacred texts, the question becomes, "How is the Qur'an using this material to its own ends?"

Reynolds has paved an encouraging path forward that allows the Qur'an to be read and interpreted on its own terms, apart from the late Islamic traditions that force its message to fit in a narrative world for which it seems unsuited. Seen in this light, the non-Arabic and non-Islamic references lead one to ask more specific questions about the sociocultural world of the audience to whom the Qur'an addresses its message. The next question naturally, then, turns to the traditional accounts about the situation surrounding the reception of the Qur'an to ask, "What can we actually know about Muhammad?"

REFLECTION QUESTIONS

1. Why would some Muslims want to argue that the Qur'an is pure Arabic with no loan words at all? What difference does it make?

2. What are some possible reasons for the appearance of non-Arabic words in the Qur'an? Which of the options seems most plausible?

3. Why might there be so much attention to biblical and extrabiblical Jewish and Christian material in the Qur'an, while there is relatively little attention given to specific pagan practices or writings?

4. How might this chapter's attention to the language of the Qur'an also contribute to the previous chapter's contention that modern-day Mecca may not have been where the Qur'an was recorded?

5. What reason might the Qur'an have for intentionally conflating several biblical stories into a single ahistorical narrative?

What Can We Actually Know about Muhammad?

Muhammad is the messenger of God.
~ Qur'an 48:29

Famed scholar of religion Ernest Renan is often quoted as saying, "Instead of the mystery in which other religions wrapped their cradle, [Islam] was born in the full light of history."[1] Such a statement reflects the assumption that the many volumes of Islamic traditions containing stories, teachings, and biographical information about Muhammad and the early Muslims provide a generally accurate account of the first two centuries of Islam.

These accounts are used to paint a picture of the environment in which the Qur'an emerged, because the Qur'an itself lacks details about its contextual setting. As a result of the Qur'an's silence regarding its *Sitz im Leben*, Muslims depend upon the traditional material found in the *Sunnah* to understand the message of the Qur'an and the motivations of its author. This backstory, however, derived from the *Sunnah*, depends upon what one scholar describes as "conflicting Muslim traditions dated some two centuries after the events recounted."[2]

In light of this dubious data, many contemporary scholars—including some Muslims—have found reason to withhold such confidence in the accuracy of the

---

1. Ernest Renan, *Studies of Religious History and Criticism* (Charleston, SC: BiblioBazaar, 2009), 228.
2. Mark Anderson, *The Qur'an in Context: A Christian Exploration* (Downers Grove, IL: IVP Academic 2016), 15.

records of Islamic origins.[3] By calling the *Sunnah* into question, however, much of the contemporary understanding of the prophet of Islam slips out of the "full light of history" and into the shadows of speculation. This chapter, then, investigates some of the contemporary questions being raised about Muhammad.

Is "Muhammad" a Name?

Today, Muhammad is the probably most common given name in the world.[4] Yet, much to the surprise of many first-time readers of the Qur'an, the word *muhammad* appears only four times in the entire book.[5] Perhaps more surprising, since the mid-nineteenth century, scholars have questioned whether or not these occurrences should be understood as a proper name.[6]

Drawing on Aramaic, Syriac, and Greek etymologies, some suggest that *muhammad* should be understood as an adjective and translated as "the one longed for, the chosen one, or the praised one."[7] While there are strains of scholarship that take up this line of inquiry and jump to the conclusion that there never was a historical Muhammad,[8] or that the Muhammad of Islam is merely the conceptual evolution of the decidedly human Jesus of Syriac-speaking Monophysites,[9] such an extreme conclusion is not necessary.

Following any of the translations listed above, *muhammad* fits well as part of the Arab prophet's claim to fulfill the message of the People of the Book. If taken as a descriptor rather than a proper name, the author of the Qur'an could be connecting himself with Jewish messianic longing and Christian ideas of Jesus as the chosen one. In other words, *muhammad* would be an instance of the Islamic prophet's attempt to contextualize his ministry according to the language, expectations, and literature of his audience. If true, this could indicate that the audience of the Qur'an is not necessarily the polytheistic pagans of Muslim tradition, but one that is saturated with christological debates and discussions of biblical texts.[10]

---

3. Gabriel Said Reynolds, *The Emergence of Islam: Classical Traditions in Contemporary Perspective* (Minneapolis: Fortress, 2012), 91–92. Reynolds notes that there is a movement within confessional Islam, known as the Qur'anist movement, that rejects most of the *Sunnah* in favor of following only the Qur'an.
4. "Muhammad, Prophet of Islam," in *Columbia Encyclopedia*, 6th ed. (New York: Columbia University Press, 2001), https://web.archive.org/web/20090210042242/http://www.bartleby.com/65/mu/Muhammd.html.
5. Qur'an 3:144; 33:40; 47:2; 48:29.
6. See Gabriel Said Reynolds, *The Qur'an and Its Biblical Subtext* (New York: Routledge, 2010), 189–99.
7. Reynolds, *Qur'an and Its Biblical Subtext*, 189–90, 194–95.
8. See Robert Spencer, *Did Muhammad Exist?* (Wilmington, DE: ISI, 2014).
9. See Karl-Heinz Ohlig, "From *Muhammad* Jesus to Prophet of the Arabs—The Personalization of a Christological Epithet," in *Early Islam: A Critical Reconstruction based on Contemporary Sources*, ed. Karl-Heinz Ohlig (Amherst, NY: Prometheus, 2013), 252–53.
10. Reynolds, *Emergence of Islam*, 135.

Was Muhammad Illiterate?

Another inherited fact about the Arab prophet that critical scholarship has come to question is whether or not he was illiterate (*ummi*). According to tradition, this fact is understood to reinforce the miraculous nature of the Qur'an, as it would be unlikely that an uneducated person could compose such stunning poetry. Indeed, the Islamic traditional material seems to include a number of details about Muhammad's life that separate him from contact with preexisting religious texts. Two examples of this are Muhammad's Meccan origin, which separates him from the various Christian communities of the Levant[11]; and his illiteracy, which aims to make borrowing of pre-Islamic texts impossible.[12]

With these assumptions pervading the field, not many scholars have suggested that the Qur'an might exhibit a high level of textual awareness of biblical material. And yet the Qur'an seems to be rather intimately aware of and explicitly in dialogue with biblical and extrabiblical texts and traditions. As Reynolds contends,

> In its religious message, the Qur'an separates itself from both the Jewish and the Christian communities. It does not, however, separate itself from the Bible. On the contrary, through consistent references to Biblical literature the Qur'an claims a status as the proper interpreter of the Bible.[13]

One might be able to imagine that the author of the Qur'an gained familiarity with all of the extra-Islamic traditions and narratives that appear in the text of the Qur'an through oral transmission. Yet the sheer amount of references to biblical literature—and the sensitivity the Qur'an exhibits to these texts in their non-Arabic languages—seems to indicate a more textual engagement. If one grants the possibility that the author of the Qur'an was both literate and in conversation with biblical texts, the question about the Qur'an's audience appears in fresh light.

Who Was Muhammad's Audience?

One of the basic assumptions about the beginning of Muhammad's ministry is that his monotheistic message emerged as a direct challenge to the polytheists of Mecca. Furthermore, these polytheists persecuted Muhammad and his followers, causing them to flee from Mecca to Medina after twelve years of

---

11. Ibn Warraq, *Why I Am Not a Muslim* (Amherst, NY: Prometheus, 1995), 131.
12. Muslim Bhanji, "Prophet Muhammad Was Unlettered," *Ahlul Bayt Digital Islamic Library Project*, https://www.al-islam.org/authenticity-quran-shaykh-muslim-bhanji/prophet-muhammad-was-unlettered. See also, Qur'an 7:157; 29:28.
13. Reynolds, *Qur'an and Its Biblical Subtext*, 248–49.

preaching against paganism. In Medina, Muhammad engaged with both pagans and Jews. Muhammad and his army returned a decade later, marching on Mecca, and his first act was to liberate the temple from its many idols.

This is the traditional account of Islamic origins, as seen in the first section of this book. And yet, despite the key role that polytheism is said to play in the development of early Islam, the Qur'an appears to have very little to say about pagan worship, belief, and practices.[14] If one were to dispense with the idea of a pagan Mecca as derived from the traditional Islamic account, reading the Qur'an alone would produce little if any indication that its author had anything more than a cursory knowledge of pagan polytheism.

Contrast this general and occasional reference to polytheism with the consistent, specific, and clear address to those familiar with Jewish and Christian texts, and the Qur'an indicates an intimate involvement with Jews and Christians. In fact, though the traditional material admits of only a minimal engagement with a Christian population, the Qur'an seems to exhibit a high degree of awareness and interaction with Christian theological texts.

Thus, instead of believing the Qur'an to be mistaken in its recollection of biblical stories, following Reynolds and others, it appears that the Qur'an emerged in an environment that was highly aware of biblical stories; as a result, it "does not seek to correct, let alone replace, Biblical literature, but instead to use that literature for its homiletic exhortation."[15] The audience of the Qur'an, then, appears to be more Jewish and Christian than polytheistic and pagan.

Summary

Despite the amount of material available in the *Sunnah* and later Islamic commentaries to describe Muhammad's life, the historical critic is left wanting for verifiable, noncontradictory information. For scholars eager to dismantle Islam as a system of faith, such inadmissible data affords them the opportunity to deny the historicity of any Arab prophet behind the Qur'an and posit political-military impulses as the probable motivation for the writing of the Qur'an and its faith tradition.

For scholars like Reynolds, however, the doubt cast upon the historicity and veracity of the *Sunnah* provides the opportunity for a much more fruitful investigation of the Qur'an as a conversation with biblical texts. Such an approach is not only more charitable than some of the polemicists one might encounter, but it proves far more fruitful in the search for understanding the message of Islam's holy book.

This section has demonstrated that a number of significant gaps remain for the scholar seeking understanding of the first two centuries of traditional

---

14. In fact, the only specific reference comes in the controversial "satanic verses" of Qur'an 53:19–20.
15. Reynolds, *Qur'an and Its Biblical Subtext*, 239.

Islamic history. Questions remain regarding the historicity of Mecca, the level of engagement the author of the Qur'an had with non-Arabic religious texts, and the biography of the prophet of Islam. Though the traditional narratives of Islamic origins insist that they represent historical fact, their accounts appear to conflict with the historical record.

At the same time, this has opened the door for a reinvestigation of the Qur'an and its message. Following Wansbrough, Crone, Reynolds, and other scholars like them, the field of Islamic studies seems to be making progress in understanding the Qur'an's message more clearly as it engages not with a pagan world, but with an environment where the biblical material is well known and hotly debated. In such an environment, the Qur'an appears to make its own distinct contribution to discussions on Christology, human morality, and divine judgment.

REFLECTION QUESTIONS

1. What difference does it make whether Muhammad is a name or a title? If it is a title, why is this particular title chosen for the Arab prophet?

2. If the Arab prophet was literate, how might that change the way that we read the Qur'an and its references to biblical literature?

3. If the Arab prophet was literate and the Qur'an reflects intentional engagement with Syriac writings of Jews and Christians, how would that affect how we read the Qur'an?

4. If the Qur'an is more aware of the extensive literature and heated debates of Syriac-speaking Christian populations than the traditional Islamic history would indicate, what might that tell us about the culture and location in which the Qur'an was written?

5. Taken together, the last three chapters argue that the traditional account of Islamic origins is problematic. How would abandoning the traditional Islamic accounts of history (seen through the *Sunnah*) affect the way that we read the Qur'an?

What Does Islam Teach about Women?

*Your women are (like) a field for you, so come
to your field when you wish, and send forward
(something) for yourselves.*
~Qur'an 2:223

Attempts to construct a revised version of early Islam are not limited to textual criticism. In fact, a growing number of female Muslim authors have been arguing that the stereotypical portrayal of Islam as inherently misogynistic needs to be revisited.[1] An example of this can be found in the work of an Australian Muslim woman named Susan Carland, who recently published a book entitled *Fighting Hislam: Women, Faith, and Sexism*. Carland writes,

> Commonplace is the firm conviction that sexism against Muslim women is rife, most often coupled with the utter disbelief that women who challenge sexism could exist, let alone that there are many of them, that they are not a new phenomenon, and that Muslim men often support them in their efforts.[2]

---

1. See Cathy Hine, "Negotiating from the Margins," in *Dynamics of Muslim Worlds*, ed. Evelyne Reisacher (Downers Grove, IL: InterVarsity, 2017), 113–34. See also Asma Barlas, "Women's Readings of the Qur'an," in *CCQ*, ed. Jane Dammen McAuliffe (New York: Cambridge University Press, 2006).
2. Susan Carland, *Fighting Hislam: Women, Faith, and Sexism* (Melbourne: Melbourne University Publishing, 2017), ii.

While she is not naive to the plight of many women in Muslim-majority countries, some of whom are subjected to atrocities such as forced marriage, female genital mutilation, and honor killings, she contends that Islam itself does not discriminate against women.

In a review of this book, however, Adrian Williams takes issue with Carland's thesis and her methodology. Williams claims that the research pool from which Carland draws—twenty-three Muslim women from Australia and North America—is not representative of most Muslims, nor do they espouse historically accepted expressions of Islamic theology.[3] He rejects the idea that Islam and its texts, strictly followed, are capable of creating a modern society that would support an egalitarian environment as suggested by Carland.[4]

What is to be made of such divergent claims? How does one parse out the difference between the teaching of the Islamic faith and the various cultures in which it has taken up residence? Is Carland's brand of Islam more Australian than it is qur'anic? Or is it the Wahhabis of Saudi Arabia whose interpretation bears more marks of cultural influence than of proper qur'anic exegesis? This chapter will investigate three issues in an attempt to understand the picture that the Qur'an paints of women: the *hijab*, polygamy, and marriage.

The *Hijab*

As was seen in Question 22, the *hijab* and the issue of female dress in Islam is a contentious topic. By some accounts, head coverings are viewed as a means of oppressing women and reinforcing their subjugation to the male population. Others, however, view the head covering as a means of honoring and protecting the dignity of women.

As it appears in the Qur'an, the concept of the *hijab* appears to favor the latter interpretation. Qur'an 24:30–31 states,

> Say to the believing men (that) they (should) lower their sight and guard their private parts. That is purer for them. Surely God is aware of what they do. And say to the believing women (that) they (should) lower their sight and guard their private parts, and not show their charms, except for what (normally) appears of them.

While some treatments single out the command for women to cover themselves by exclusively highlighting Qur'an 24:31, the preceding verse shows that the Qur'an first addresses men and calls them to take a similar posture toward their own modesty. Thus, at least as it pertains to the Qur'an, the *hijab*

---

3. Adrian Williams, "Muhammad: Social Justice Warrior," *Quadrant*, July–August 2017: 99.
4. Williams, "Muhammad: Social Justice Warrior," 100.

alone does not necessarily appear to serve as the symbol of oppression, subjection, or female inferiority as it is sometimes understood.[5]

Polygamy

In the seventh-century world of Arabia, polygamy was not the controversial or foreign concept that it is in contemporary Western society. As such, the qur'anic permission given to men to marry up to four wives at a time is not only culturally fitting but is also viewed as a means of caring and providing for women of that day and age.

Many argue that if in seventh-century Arabia the workforce was composed of men, economic security for women was only available through their connections to men. Therefore, the Qur'an's purpose in allowing polygamy is to be understood as a means of connecting women to men who could offer them financial provision.

Others note that the Qur'an puts regulations on the practice of polygamy that are actually more restrictive than the surrounding culture.[6] By limiting men to four wives, the Qur'an argues against a Solomonic accrual of a harem of wives, ensuring that the more limited number of women would receive the care and provision they deserved.[7] Likewise, Qur'an 4:3 permits polygamy on the condition that all of the wives receive equal treatment.[8]

Polygamy, however, is often explained within Islam as a means of providing satisfaction for male sexual desires. This derives from the fact that the Qur'an focuses on permitting multiple wives to men, but no woman is encouraged or allowed to take on multiple husbands. Shaykh Muhammad al-Munajjid defends polygamy saying, "A woman may fall ill or there may be reasons that prevent her from engaging in intercourse, such as menses and nifaas (post-partum bleeding); this prevents a man from fulfilling his desire

---

5. Though the Qur'an may not present the *hijab* as a symbol of oppression, this does not preclude or negate circumstances in which the *hijab* is enforced under the banner of Islam in service of such diminution of women.

6. Azizah al-Hibri, "A Study of Islamic Herstory: Or How Did We Ever Get into This Mess?" *Women's Studies International Forum* 5, no. 2 (1982): 209. Al-Hibri records that pre-Islamic Arabs were allowed to marry up to one hundred women; thus, the qur'anic permission to marry up to four is actually a restriction of the norm.

7. Mark Anderson, *The Qur'an in Context: A Christian Exploration* (Downers Grove, IL: IVP Academic, 2016), 163.

8. Al-Hibri, "Study of Islamic Herstory," 209. The life of Muhammad, however, seems to present a difficulty for some of the points made above. First of all, Muhammad himself was economically indebted to his first wife, Khadija, who was his first employer (Al-Hibri, "A Study of Islamic Herstory," 209). While Khadija may not represent the norm, there was apparently precedent for women who were financially independent. Second, Muhammad exceeded the qur'anic limitation of four wives, having married at least eleven women throughout his life and nine of whom were his wives simultaneously (see Ghassan Ascha, "The 'Mothers of the Believers': Stereotypes of Muhammad's Wives," in *Female Stereotypes in Religious Traditions*, ed. Ria Kloppenborg and Wouter J. Hanegraaff [Leiden: Brill, 2003], 89).

with her, so he needs to have another wife with whom he can fulfill his desires instead of suppressing them or committing immoral actions."[9] This approach to explaining polygamy rationalizes the practice based upon its ability to satisfy male sexual desires in religiously permissible fashion.

The Qur'an does not supply the rationale for the practice of polygamy. Thus, one can neither say that Islam's foundational document supports or denies equality between the sexes as it pertains to polygamy. As a result, one finds presentations of polygamy that emphasize the protection and provision that it afforded to women of Muhammad's day. One can also find defenses of the practice that prioritize the satisfaction of male sexual desires, both through polygamy and through marriage in general.

Marriage

When considering how the Qur'an presents women, it is necessary to consider how men and women are to relate within marriage. One aspect that immediately presents itself is in the realm of sexual intercourse. Male priority in sexual fulfillment is reinforced by Qur'an 2:223, wherein the Qur'an appears to grant husbands the right to engage in sexual relations with their wives at any time they desire, comparing their women to a plot of land they own.

Second, according to Qur'an 4:34, husbands are given permission to punish their wives physically if they suspect that their wives are rebellious. While some contemporary writers attempt to soften this passage, few deny that it clearly permits corporeal punishment for mere suspicion of disloyalty or rebellion.[10] These injunctions can lead to an understanding of the Qur'an as a document that reinforces the inferiority of women and the priority of men in Islam.

The greatest problems for male-female equality in Islam emerge from studying the *Sunnah*. Where some construe the teaching of the Qur'an as offering a progressive vision of gender relationships in seventh-century Arabia, the *Sunnah* is significantly less flexible. For example, in *Sahih al-Bukhari*, one reads that Muhammad understood hell to be mostly filled with women who were ungrateful to their husbands and that he believed women are of inferior intelligence.[11]

At the same time, the *Sunnah* records many *hadith* that instruct men to highly revere and protect their wives and the women in their community. The

9. Standing Committee for Academic Research and Issuing Fatwas, "The Wisdom behind the Prophet's Marrying More Than Four Wives," *Islam Question and Answer*, May 14, 2013, https://islamqa.info/en/answers/127066/the-wisdom-behind-the-prophets-marrying-more-than-four-wives.

10. Nicholas Awde, ed. and trans., *Women in Islam: An Anthology from the Qur'an and Hadiths* (New York: Hippocrene, 2005), 204.

11. Al-Bukhari, *Sahih al-Bukhari*, https://sunnah.com/bukhari/6/9, book 6 (§9).

same collection of *hadith* that records Muhammad's estimation that hell is mostly filled with women includes a clear statement from Muhammad saying, "Treat women nicely."[12] Likewise, despite narratives to the contrary, other *hadith* state that Muhammad disapproved of the killing of women and children in battle.[13] In many Muslim marriages, then, one finds husbands heeding these instructions rather than taking advantage of the permission given elsewhere in Islamic texts to seek self-satisfaction without regard for their wives.

Summary

As the first chapter in this book argued, we do well to recognize that it is unhelpful to speak about Islam as if it were monolithic. Islam does not exhibit a single perspective on women. Instead, a growing number of contemporary feminist Muslims argue for an understanding of the teachings of Islam that are egalitarian, and which run contrary to traditional interpretations. Likewise, the *hijab* and polygamy—two subjects often attacked as inherently misogynistic—can be explained as means of honoring and protecting rather than oppressing and subjugating women.

Ultimately, however, the Qur'an and the *Sunnah* do exhibit evidence that seems to prioritize male perspective, value, and desires over and against their female counterparts. Thus, the roots of injustice and inequality pervasive among certain traditional expressions of Islam do trace back to the authoritative texts of the faith. The heavier burden of proof lies on the shoulders of contemporary feminist authors who challenge such traditional Islamic practice.

While one can find evidence to support a more progressive approach to male-female relationships, such evidence requires selecting and prioritizing certain texts over others. In the end, culture and worldview often predispose a reader to highlight certain passages while obscuring or reinterpreting others. Therefore, it is far more important to engage individual Muslims on the issues pertaining to women rather than expecting to discern a singular Islamic view.

REFLECTION QUESTIONS

1. How do some Muslim women argue that Islam can be interpreted to support egalitarianism between the sexes?

2. What is the most positive argument for the *hijab* and modesty? What is the most positive perspective on the Qur'an's teaching regarding polygamy?

---

12. Al-Bukhari, *Sahih al-Bukhari*, https://sunnah.com/bukhari/60/6, book 60 (§6).
13. Al-Bukhari, *Sahih al-Bukhari*, https://sunnah.com/bukhari/56/223, book 56 (§223).

3. In what ways does the *Sunnah* appear to present conflicting opinions about the treatment and value of women? What is problematic about leaning on the *Sunnah* for guidance on these issues?

4. In what ways might the Qur'an's and the *Sunnah*'s teaching about women contribute to patriarchy and even misogyny?

5. In what ways does it seem likely that certain cultural environments predispose readers to interpret the Qur'an in ways that lead to patriarchy and misogyny?

PART 7

The Christian Gospel and the Followers of Islam

Do Muslims and Christians Worship the Same God?

*We believe in what has been sent down to us, and
what has been sent down to you. Our God and your
God is one, and to Him we submit.*
~Qur'an 29:46

On December 10, 2015, a Facebook post reignited debate over a fourteen-hundred-year-old question. At the center of the debate was Dr. Larycia Hawkins, a professor at Wheaton College, who posted a message to her personal Facebook page in which she stated, "I stand in religious solidarity with Muslims because they, like me, a Christian, are People of the Book. And as Pope Francis stated last week, we worship the same God."[1] This post initiated a chain of events that led initially to Hawkins's suspension and ultimately culminated in her resignation.

This highly public incident provoked heated controversy, as those inside and outside of evangelicalism weighed in with their opinions regarding the question, "Do Muslims and Christians worship the same God?" Prompted by the controversy, the Evangelical Missiological Society issued a special edition of its *Occasional Bulletin*, inviting a variety of missiologists to present their

---

1. Kirkland An, "Summary of the Hawkins Case (Updated)," *The Wheaton Record*, January 15, 2016, http://www.wheatonrecord.com/news/summary-of-the-hawkins-case. The Pope's statements can be found in Thomas Gumbleton, "Everyone is a son or daughter of God," *National Catholic Reporter*, January 7, 2016, https://www.ncronline.org/blogs/peace-pulpit/everyone-son-or-daughter-god.

approaches to answering the question. Despite reaching various conclusions, one clear theme emerged from the contributions: the question itself is flawed.[2]

In an effort to clarify this discussion and to provide theological traction for moving forward missiologically, this chapter will approach the question from three different angles to elucidate the underlying issues that the question, as posed, obscures. We will investigate both the idea and identity of God as presented in Islam and Christianity before ultimately inverting the question to reorient our inquiry toward God's perspective on worship and gospel-driven mission.

The Idea Question: What Is Allah?

A good place to start this investigation is with the Arabic word *Allah*. While *Allah* features in Islam as the referent to God, the word itself predates Islam and has been used to refer to the God of the Bible by Arabic-speaking Christians until today.[3] While questions remain regarding the etymology of the word, *Allah* is commonly understood to be the noun "god" (*ilah*) and the attached definite article (*al*). Thus, *Allah* could be translated into English as "The God."[4]

Since Islam and Christianity are monotheistic faiths, it is conceptually appropriate to share the word *Allah* as the Arabic referent to the one entity responsible for the universe.[5] In other words, we can say that Islam and Christianity share a commitment to the idea that there is only one God. Though this shared idea provides common conceptual ground, the concept alone is no more than an impersonal idea.

The Identity Question: Who Is Allah?

In order to conclude that Muslims and Christians worship a God who is the same in any meaningful way, we must consider the identity of God in each of the systems. At first blush, the Qur'an provides us with multiple descriptions of God's activities that evangelicals affirm. Muslims believe that God is creator, ruler, revealer, and judge, and that God forgives. Still, Colin Chapman warns against prematurely concluding that we are talking about the

---

2. Robert J. Priest, ed., "Wheaton and the Controversy over Whether Muslims and Christians Worship the Same God," *Occasional Bulletin of the Evangelical Missiological Society*, Special Edition, 2016, https://www.emsweb.org/images/occasional-bulletin/special-editions/OB_SpecialEdition_2016.pdf.

3. Hanna Massad, "Do Christians and Muslims Worship the Same God, 'Allah'?," in Priest, "Wheaton and the Controversy," 20.

4. See Timothy Tennent, *Theology in the Context of World Christianity* (Grand Rapids: Zondervan, 2007), 44–46, who details several theories regarding the Aramaic or pagan roots of the word *Allah*.

5. C. S. Caleb Kim, "A Missional Response to an Ever Provoking Question," in Priest, "Wheaton and the Controversy," 17, writes, "Ontologically speaking, both Christianity and Islam seem to refer to the same God since neither of them allows the idea of the existence of more than one God."

same God, cautioning, "The issue between us is not *whether* God forgives, but *how* he forgives; not *whether* he reveals, but *what* he reveals and *how*."[6] We do well to consider that shared activity does not necessitate shared identity.

One factor that must be considered in giving the Islamic answer to the question, "Who is Allah?" is the Islamic doctrine of God's absolute unity (*tawhid*).[7] The God of Islam is a monad, undivided and singular. He is the completely other creator and judge to whom humanity owes worship and submission.[8] The result of such otherness and transcendence is that God himself is unknowable in any intimate, relational sense in Islam.[9] Ismail al-Faruqi illustrates this stark contrast with Christianity, writing that in Islam, "[God] does not reveal himself to any one in any way. God reveals only His will. . . . Christians talk about the revelation of God Himself—by God of God—but that is the great difference between Christianity and Islam."[10]

This difference is most pronounced when one considers the Christian doctrine of the incarnation. Not only did God make himself intimately immanent and knowable by taking on flesh and living among humanity, the incarnation also provides the lens by which we might understand the Trinitarian nature of God most vividly.[11] Timothy Tennent highlights the importance of this difference between the God of Islam and the God of Christianity, stating,

> It is not as if the texts of the Qur'an and the Bible differ on minor points of eschatology or the precise nature of the

---

6. For a helpful treatment of these apparent similarities, see Colin Chapman, *Cross and Crescent: Responding to the Challenge of Islam* (Downers Grove, IL: InterVarsity, 2003), 225–28.

7. Seyyed Hossein Nasr, *Ideals and Realities of Islam*, rev. and updated ed. (San Francisco: Aquarian, 1994), 18, writes, "The Divine Essence (*al-dhāt*) remains absolutely transcendent and no religion has emphasized the transcendent aspect of God more than Islam."

8. Mark Anderson, *The Qur'an in Context: A Christian Exploration* (Downers Grove, IL: IVP Academic, 2016), 63, concludes, "The Qur'an asserts [God's] untrammeled glory and utter unapproachability, making its creator-creature distinction as sharp as possible."

9. Anderson, *Qur'an in Context*, 53; cf. John Renard, *Islamic Theological Themes: A Primary Source Reader* (Oakland: University of California Press, 2014), 4–7, 13. Renard highlights verses in the Qur'an that speak of God using anthropomorphic language to indicate his hearing, seeing, and being ready to respond, yet, as indicated on page 13 in his note regarding the doctrine of *tawhid*, it is clear that the transcendent unity of God the doctrine requires trumps any reference to his immanence. Further, notes regarding his immanence are not relational, nor do they indicate intimate knowledge of God.

10. Ismail al-Faruqi, *Christian Mission and Islamic Da'wah* (Leicestershire, UK: Islamic Foundation, 1982), 47–48. As cited in Chapman, *Cross and Crescent*, 227. While some branches of Islam, such as Sufis, do speak of God in more personal terms, orthodox Islamic theology maintains a commitment to the complete otherness and unknowability of God.

11. Cf. Fred Sanders, *The Deep Things of God: How the Trinity Changes Everything*, 2nd ed. (Wheaton, IL: Crossway, 2017), 94, writes, "Tracing the line back from his appearance in Bethlehem is how we learned anything about the Trinity at all, for this is the central event in which God revealed that he had a son."

soul. They differ on central doctrines of identity such as the Trinity, the deity of Christ, the doctrine of the incarnation, the redemptive power of the cross, and the resurrection of Jesus Christ from the dead. All of these doctrines are central to what we as Christians mean when we say, "We worship God." For the Christian, the doctrine of God cannot possibly be separated from Christology.[12]

In other words, the Islamic and Christian conceptions of God are fundamentally irreconcilable because of the incarnation, which is as essential to the Christian as it is anathema to the Muslim.

Furthermore, and as it concerns the present investigation, the incarnation is an indispensable component of what Christians mean when they say that they worship God. While both testaments of the Christian Bible provide instructions on how to approach God in worship, the New Testament clearly maintains that God the Son's incarnate life, death, and resurrection is the means by which it is possible for humanity to approach God in acceptable worship.[13] Therefore, if we are curious about how to answer the question, "Do Muslims and Christians worship the same God?" we should first consider what God thinks of our respective offerings of worship.

The Inverted Question: Does Allah Receive Muslim Worship?

The central flaw in the question as posed above is that it frames what should be a theocentric investigation as an anthropocentric discussion. We end up asking about what humans think about their worship rather than what God thinks of it. By inverting the question, we might more helpfully ask, "Does God accept the worship of Muslims and Christians?" From an evangelical point of view, this question evokes a negative answer and a greater evangelistic burden.

Throughout both testaments of the Christian Bible, one finds explicit instructions pertaining to how humanity might approach God and present acceptable worship. The Old Testament prescribes the priestly tasks in meticulous detail along with the terrible consequences of bringing unprescribed worship before the Lord.[14] In the New Testament, the author of Hebrews connects the Levitical priesthood to Jesus's ministry, showing that Jesus has

---

12. Tennent, *Theology in the Context of World Christianity*, 38.
13. John 14:6 records Jesus's clear teaching that he is the only way by which humanity might approach the Father. Likewise, Paul's Areopagus speech in Acts 17:22–31 states that through the resurrection of Christ, humanity has been given the one and only key to worshipping God. And Hebrews 10–12 provides a sustained comparison between the Old Testament system of approaching God and the new way that has been opened up in Christ.
14. See Leviticus 10 and the account of the "strange fire" Nadab and Abihu brought to the tabernacle.

opened a new and eternal way to God.[15] Following this, Hebrews warns the reader not to refuse the offer that God has extended, but rather to take advantage of his invitation, and under Jesus's new covenant, to offer to God acceptable worship.[16] This corresponds with Jesus's own words in John 14:6, where he declares, "I am the way and the truth and the life; no one comes to the Father except through me." Faith in Jesus's life, death, and resurrection is the only way we can approach God in acceptable worship. This is the gospel.[17]

Most often, Christians who affirm the same-God position do so out of a missiological desire to find common ground for deepening relationship with Muslim friends. While common ground can provide some initial traction, the incompatible identities of the God of Christianity and Islam will inevitably arise if the Christian is faithful to present the biblical gospel. Thus, in friendships with Muslims, a Christian need not aggressively attack the idea that Muslims and Christians worship the same God. The gospel itself will highlight the incompatibilities. Yet, the Christian communicator must be aware that, though a Muslim is a fellow monotheist, the word "God" in Islam refers to a character that is different than the God of the Bible.

Summary

Even though our Muslim friends may be compelled by the Qur'an to affirm that Muslims and Christians worship the same God, the additional angles from which we've considered the question have shown that we cannot so quickly agree. With the late former Muslim Lamin Sanneh, we conclude that a conflation of the Islamic and Christian identities of God is "inadequate with respect to God's character, on which hang matters of commitments and identity, the denial of which would sever our ties to God."[18] With so much apparently on the line, it behooves us to recognize how and where these two perspectives diverge. Seeing such divergence, we cannot help but move past the controversy raised by this question and engage in calling our Muslim friends to understand why the gospel is good news, even when it requires abandoning Islamic ideas about who God is.

In a pluralistic world and in a culture that values breadth of embrace over depth of conviction, any claim to exclusivity will be viewed as abrasive and domineering. Such a culture will recoil in the face of a Christian claim to worshipping a God different than the God referenced in the Qur'an. Yet, if the Christian gospel is what it claims to be, it is the only remedy for a sin-stained people who were created to bring worship to the one God of creation. To

---

15. Hebrews 10:19–25.
16. Hebrews 12:18–29.
17. 1 Corinthians 15:3–5.
18. Lamin Sanneh, "Do Christians and Muslims Worship the Same God? Part 2," *Christian Century* 121, no. 9 (May 4, 2004): 35. As quoted in Tennent, *Theology in the Context of World Christianity*, 38.

present the gospel to a Muslim, then, is to maintain that there is no meaningful connection between the God of the Qur'an and the God of the Bible in terms of one's salvation and one's worship. Yet in the same breath, that exclusive gospel provides an invitation to our Muslim friends to come and know the true God of creation who has extended true mercy and forgiveness through the death and resurrection of the incarnate Son of God.

REFLECTION QUESTIONS

1. When you first read the question this chapter poses, what was your immediate reaction? Has anything changed after reading the chapter?

2. What might drive a person to claim that Muslims and Christians do in fact worship the same God? Why is this such a hotly debated question?

3. What are some of the irreconcilable differences between the Islamic conception of God and the Christian conception of God?

4. If a Muslim friend asked you whether or not you think that he is worshipping the God of the Bible, how might you winsomely respond?

5. For a Christian, what is the more pressing question that this chapter pushed us to consider? Why does that question weigh more heavily on us than the "same God" question?

What Are Some Common Objections to Christianity Made by Muslims?

People of the Book! Do not go beyond the limits in your religion, and do not say about God (anything) but the truth. The Messiah, Jesus, son of Mary, was only a messenger of God and His word, which He cast into Mary, and a spirit from Him. So believe in God and His messengers, but do not say "Three." Stop! It will be better for you. God is only one God. Glory to Him! (Far be it) that He should have a son! To Him (belongs) whatever is in the heavens and whatever is on the earth. God is sufficient as a guardian.
~Qur'an 4:171

Christians and Muslims have been engaged in theological dialogue since the earliest days of Islam. Despite more than fourteen intervening centuries of discussion, several areas of impasse remain and recur in contemporary interactions. The present chapter seeks to address three central points of debate that regularly arise when discussing theology with Muslims, along with suggested starting places for the Christian to respond to such challenges.

Prior to beginning, it is important to note that the suggested responses are merely ways to respect a Muslim's questions with an introductory answer. As Christians engaged in dialogue with Muslim friends and neighbors, we are not burdened with the task of winning an argument. We are called to prayerfully, lovingly, and winsomely hold out the word of truth as we testify to the gospel that is transforming us. Therefore, the provided responses should not be viewed as a means to end a conversation or win a debate. Rather, they are invitations to further conversation and study of the Bible whereby the Holy Spirit can illumine God's Word and soften hard hearts.

Jesus Was Not Crucified

One of the most appalling ideas to Muslims is that Jesus, a prophet and messenger of Allah, would undergo a cruel and shameful crucifixion. The Qur'an indicates that Jesus was spared from crucifixion in Qur'an 4:157:

> "Surely we killed the Messiah, Jesus, son of Mary, the messenger of God"—yet they did not kill him, nor did they crucify him, but it (only) seemed like (that) to them. Surely those who differ about him are indeed in doubt about him. They have no knowledge about him, only the following of conjecture. Certainly they did not kill him.

In light of this verse, nearly all Muslim commentators reject the idea that Jesus was crucified.[1]

The temptation arises at this point to appeal to historical data and rational proof for Jesus's death and resurrection.[2] Both of these approaches have a role in reinforcing Christian belief. However, it is important first to invite a Muslim friend to consider two biblical ideas that should precede the extrabiblical arguments: Jesus's claims and the story in which his death fits.

Regarding the first idea, the Bible records Jesus's own claims regarding his impending death. Consider Jesus's words in Luke 18:31–33:

> And taking the twelve, he said to them, "See, we are going up to Jerusalem, and everything that is written about the Son of Man by the prophets will be accomplished. For he will be delivered over to the Gentiles and will be mocked and shamefully treated and spit upon. And after flogging him, they will kill him, and on the third day he will rise."

---

1. It should be noted that Islamic Studies scholar Gabriel Said Reynolds contends that the Qur'an does not require the reader to follow traditional interpretations that deny Jesus's death in his article "The Muslim Jesus: Dead or Alive?" *Bulletin of the School of Oriental and African Studies* 72, no. 2 (2009): 237–58. While Reynolds's treatment of the Qur'an is intriguing, he himself admits that traditional Muslim scholars and even most critical scholars are of the opinion that the Qur'an teaches that Jesus was not crucified.
2. For a particularly helpful approach to discussions with Muslims regarding historical and rational arguments, see Nabeel Qureshi, *No God but One: Allah or Jesus?* (Grand Rapids: Zondervan, 2016).

Jesus makes it clear that he is willingly going to Jerusalem, according to the prophets, in order to die and rise again.[3]

Second, and even more pressing, our Muslim friends need to know what part Jesus's death plays in his ministry and mission. In other words, before arguing about whether or not Jesus *did* die, it is incumbent upon the Christian to explain *how* Jesus's death fits in the larger story that God has been telling. Such an explanation requires a biblical understanding of the role of sacrifice that precedes Jesus's sacrificial death.[4]

While there are multiple places in Scripture that one might go to begin exploring the concept of sacrifice, the book of Hebrews is an excellent option for showing how the Old Testament prepares the reader to understand Jesus's ministry. In particular, Hebrews 7–10 focuses on the priestly role that Jesus assumes, concluding that through his death, resurrection, and ascension, he serves as both an eternal high priest and a once-for-all sacrifice.[5] By presenting the larger biblical teaching on substitutionary atonement and sacrifice, the argument over whether or not Jesus died on the cross can be drawn up into the story in which it can be demonstrated to fit.

Jesus Did Not Claim to Be Divine

A second contention that is likely to arise in conversation about Christian theology is the apparent absence of Jesus's clear claim to be God. The Four Gospels present a complex vision of Jesus's ministry and teaching. By turns Jesus speaks of himself in both human and seemingly divine terms. Of course, for Western evangelical Christians this is not surprising, as we maintain that Jesus the Messiah was the incarnate Son of God who was at the same time both fully human and fully man.[6] Though it is eventually helpful to discuss the biblical and historical foundations of formal Christology, it is not best to begin with the creeds and counsels of Christian history.

Instead, one might invite a Muslim conversation partner to consider John 8:58–59, which says, "Jesus said to them, 'Truly, truly I say to you, before Abraham was, I am.' So they picked up stones to throw at him, but Jesus hid

---

3. One might also consider Jesus's words in John 10:17–18, which further demonstrate that this coming death is not inflicted upon Jesus unwillingly, but rather he actively chooses it, "For this reason the Father loves me, because I lay down my life that I may take it up again. No one takes it from me, but I lay it down of my own accord. I have the authority to lay it down, and I have the authority to take it up again. This charge I have received from my Father."

4. For a sweeping treatment of the biblical narrative of which Jesus's life, death, resurrection, and ascension provide the climax, see Trent Hunter and Stephen Wellum, *Christ from Beginning to End: How the Full Story of Scripture Reveals the Full Glory of Christ* (Grand Rapids: Zondervan, 2018).

5. David Moffitt, *Atonement and the Logic of Resurrection in the Epistle to the Hebrews* (Boston: Brill, 2013), 295.

6. Thomas Torrance, *Incarnation: The Person and Life of Christ*, ed. Robert Walker (Downers Grove, IL: IVP Academic, 2008), 83.

himself and went out of the temple." This claim comes at the end of a dispute with a crowd of Jews. The extreme reaction of the crowd encourages the reader to ask, "Why did Jesus's claim evoke such a violent response?"

When Jesus says, "I am," the English rendering obscures the Greek construction of the text. The underlying Greek reveals an intriguing phrase: *ego eimi*. This phrase is intriguing because writing "I am" in Greek only requires *eimi*. The phrase *ego eimi* adds an additional pronoun "I" (*ego*) either for emphasis or to point to something else. The latter option seems most likely when one considers that, when Moses asks God for his name prior to approaching Pharaoh, the Septuagint renders the Hebrew response "*YHWH*," using this exact construction: *ego eimi*. In light of this, many scholars conclude that John 8:58 is an instance of Jesus applying the covenant name of God to himself.[7] This conclusion also explains the reaction of the Jewish audience who immediately recognize Jesus's claim for what it is and pick up stones to carry out the prescribed punishment for blasphemy.

Following this, it would be helpful to invite a Muslim friend to consider why it is important to Christian theology that Jesus is both God and man. A helpful place to continue the dialogue is Jesus's response to John the Baptist's question, "Are you the one who is to come, or shall we look for another?"[8] Jesus's response is a list of Old Testament prophecies, many of which are recorded in Isaiah pertaining to the coming of the messianic age in which God would act to redeem his people.[9] By capitalizing on Jesus's answer to John the Baptist, one might show that Jesus conceived of his ministry and identity in terms of God's own activity in fulfilling Isaiah's prophecy.

The Trinity Is Incomprehensible

At the center of Islamic critique of Christian theology is the issue of the Trinity. The apparent illogic of saying that I believe in one God who is at the same time three persons seems an embarrassment my Muslim friends are quick to challenge. There are, however, several issues that lie under the surface of this critique.

---

7. For example, see Jeffrey Miller, "I Am Sayings," in *Lexham Bible Dictionary*, eds. John D. Barry, et al. (Bellingham, WA: Lexham, 2016), who writes, "Jesus' use of ἐγώ εἰμί (*egō eimi*) in the absolute sense ("I am") draws on Exod 3:14 and other Old Testament passages where the phrase clearly refers to God. In using the expression, Jesus seems to be explicitly identifying Himself with Yahweh, asserting His eternality, self-existence, and changelessness, and claiming to bear Yahweh's presence on Earth."

8. Matthew 11:2–6.

9. Donald Hagner, *Matthew 1–13*, WBC 33A (Nashville: Nelson, 1993), 301. The blind receive their sight (Isa. 29:18); the lame walk (Isa. 35:6); lepers are cleansed (Isa. 53:4); the deaf hear (Isa. 29:18; 35:5); the dead are raised (Isa. 26:19); and the poor hear the good news of salvation (Isa. 61:1).

First, in the Qur'an there is a verse that appears to understand the Christian doctrine of the Trinity as including God the Father, Jesus as God's Son, and Mary as the third person of the Trinity.[10] Qur'an 5:116 describes an interaction between Jesus and Allah, stating,

> (Remember) when God said, "Jesus, son of Mary! Did you say to the people, 'Take me and my mother as two gods instead of God (alone)?'" He said, "Glory to You! It is not for me to say what I have no right (to say). If I had said it, You would have known it. You know what is within me, but I do not know what is within You. Surely You—You are the Knower of the unseen."

This verse misleads many to understand that Christians believe Mary to be the third member of the Trinity. Therefore, the first component of such an interaction regarding the Trinity is to make plain what Christianity does in fact believe.

Beyond this, it is helpful to consider several passages in the New Testament that discuss the Trinity so that our Muslim friends see this doctrine emerge from the pages of Scripture rather than thinking it to be the product of the ruminations of late Christian counsels. I would suggest following Matthew's Gospel as he bookends Jesus's ministry with a Trinitarian vision. In Matthew 3:16–17, the account of Jesus's baptism includes the Holy Spirit descending like a dove, and the voice of the Father declaring from heaven that Jesus is his Son. At the end of the book, then, Matthew 28:16–20 records Jesus's commission to his disciples to baptize new disciples of all nations in the name of the Father, the Son, and the Holy Spirit.

Finally, it can be helpful to consider the fact that, both in Islamic and Christian conception, God is unchanging. As such, anything that is true of him must have been true prior to creation. This is perhaps most pertinent to the doctrine of the Trinity when Christians claim with John that "God is love."[11] As Carlos Madrigal explains, "To love entails loving someone; love needs a lover and a loved one. If God, in his unique self, did not exist as a plural personality from eternity past, he would have not been able to share

---

10. Gabriel Said Reynolds, *The Qur'an and Its Biblical Subtext* (New York: Routledge, 2010), 12, argues that the Qur'an is not interested in telling history as much as it is in utilizing biblical themes and characters to construct a literary polemic against what its author deems to be heretical in Jewish and Christian thought. Thus, applied to Mary and the Trinity, the author may not be confused as to the constituents of the Christian doctrine. Instead, the author may be attempting to paint an argument *ad absurdum* regarding what is viewed as a detestable outcome of understanding God to have a Son: that God also has a wife.
11. 1 John 4:8, 16.

his love with anyone."[12] In other words, the doctrine of the Trinity allows for a God who has always been loving, independent of that which he creates. If God was a singular monad, he would then depend on creation for the expression of any of the relational characteristics attributed to him.

Summary

Theological impasse between Islam and Christianity has been the focus of countless debates since the rise of Islam. If history tells us anything, we should not expect that intellectual argument will suffice to once and for all resolve these debates. All the more, we must not expect that winning any one of those debates equates with winning a Muslim to Christ.

Instead, while acknowledging that these perennial criticisms do have biblical and rational answers, we should see each encounter with a Muslim neighbor as an opportunity to prayerfully bear witness to the gospel of Jesus. This will involve giving an answer on the spot, but it should also include an invitation to sit under the Scriptures together, asking that the Spirit would illumine them for our neighbor. Our evangelism should also be undertaken as an act of worship as we rehearse the story of the Triune God and his redemption. It is in the context of Bible study and loving relationship that our Muslim neighbors encounter a powerful apologetic.

REFLECTION QUESTIONS

1. Why do Muslims argue that Jesus wasn't crucified? Why does Jesus not need to die according to Islamic theology?

2. How would you respond to a Muslim friend who contends that Jesus never clearly came out and said, "I am God?"

3. Where would you begin in the Bible to explain why Christians believe that God is triune?

4. Why are each of these issues important to biblically faithful Christianity?

5. Ultimately, what is the best way to overcome some of these objections? Where in Scripture might be a helpful place to begin studying the biblical teaching on these issues?

---

12. Carlos Madrigal, *Explaining the Trinity to Muslims: A Personal Reflection on the Biblical Teaching in Light of the Theological Criteria of Islam* (Pasadena, CA: William Carey, 2011), 82.

Is the Gospel Incompatible with Islam?

*For I delivered to you as of first importance what
I also received: that Christ died for our sins in
accordance with the Scriptures, that he was buried,
that he was raised again on the third day in
accordance with the Scriptures, and that he
appeared to Cephas, then to the twelve.*
~1 Corinthians 15:3–5

In contemporary Western culture one encounters pressure to reconcile different faith systems to each other. Admittedly, many similarities do exist between Christianity and Islam. Out of a desire to promote religious tolerance and acceptance, many people downplay the distinctives between Christianity and Islam in order to highlight shared commitments.

Pressure to reconcile the teachings of these two world religions arises not only from outside of the Christian tradition, but also through certain missionary approaches to Islam. A number of recent publications argue for what has been called "Insider Movement" missiology.[1] Advocates for Insider Movements encourage Muslims who believe in Jesus to retain their Muslim identity and community, at times trying to synthesize biblical teaching with the Qur'an.

---

1. See William Dyrness, *Insider Jesus: Theological Reflections on New Christian Movements* (Downers Grove, IL: IVP Academic, 2016). See also Jan Hendrik Prenger, *Muslim Christ Followers* (Pasadena, CA: William Carey Library, 2017).

Such movements are not without their detractors, however, and the idea that the Qur'an can be reconciled with the Bible has been hotly debated.[2] Since Christian faith is centered upon the gospel, any such discussion must consider whether or not the message of Islam can be reconciled with it. By comparing the biblical presentation of the gospel with the teachings of Islam, this chapter argues that Islam and the Christian gospel are essentially incompatible.

Christ Died, Was Buried, Was Raised Again

In 1 Corinthians 15:3–5, Paul summarizes the gospel message, framing it with the historical reality of Jesus's death and resurrection. Later, in the same chapter, Paul states, "if Christ has not been raised, then our preaching is in vain and your faith is in vain. . . . But in fact Christ has been raised from the dead, the firstfruits of those who have fallen asleep" (1 Cor. 15:14, 20). Thus, for Paul, Christ's death and resurrection are linked inseparably to his gospel message.

Turning to Qur'an 4:157, however, one reads, "[The People of the Book say,] 'Surely we killed the Messiah, Jesus son of Mary, the messenger of God'— yet they did not kill him, nor did they crucify him, but it (only) seemed like (that) to them." Reading Islamic commentary on this passage reveals that nearly all Muslims agree that this verse teaches that Jesus was not crucified.[3]

Some writers argue, however, that the Qur'an does not inevitably lead to this conclusion.[4] Such authors propose that this verse can be interpreted in the same way as Jesus's words in John 10:18: "No one takes it from me, but I lay it down of my own accord." Insider Movement advocates capitalize on such atypical readings of the Qur'an in order to suggest ways that Muslims can believe in Jesus while also appealing to their holy book for guidance.

It remains the fact, however, that as the Qur'an is usually interpreted by Muslims themselves, Jesus was not crucified. Consequently, Islam denies the historical events that Paul tethers to the gospel message. Not only is the historical event of Christ's crucifixion denied, but the connection with prophetic expectation of these events is also rejected.

---

2. See Gary Corwin, "A Humble Appeal to C5/Insider Movement Ministry Advocates to Consider Ten Questions," *IJFM* 24, no. 1 (Spring 2007): 5–21. In fact, the archives of the *IJFM* include many exchanges between those who advocate for insider movements and those who oppose them.

3. Gabriel Said Reynolds, "The Muslim Jesus: Dead or Alive?," *Bulletin of School of Oriental and African Studies* 72, no. 2 (2009): 237.

4. Reynolds, "Muslim Jesus: Dead or Alive?," 237. Reynolds acknowledges that this view has achieved near-consensus in both popular and scholarly opinion. However, Reynolds argues that the Qur'an alone does not require this conclusion. See also the argument for the literal death and resurrection interpretation of the Qur'an as offered by Mark Anderson, *The Qur'an in Context: A Christian Exploration* (Downers Grove, IL: IVP Academic, 2016), 253–54. One more resource that presents the argument that the Qur'an does not require denial of the resurrection is Gregory Lanier's, "'It Was Made to Appear Like That to Them:' Islam's Denial of Jesus' Crucifixion," *Reformed Faith and Practice* 1, no. 1 (2016): 39–55.

In Accordance with the Scriptures

A second component of Paul's gospel connects the historical events to the prophetic expectations fulfilled by Jesus's ministry. First, by using the title "Christ" to refer to Jesus in this passage, Paul establishes his belief that Jesus is the consummation of Jewish messianic hopes. These hopes were formed by the Hebrew Scriptures, which predicted a divine king and a suffering servant who would save God's people.[5] Therefore, when Paul twice includes the phrase "according to the Scriptures," he is linking gospel history with messianic expectation.

At first, the Qur'an seems to agree with the basic premise that 'Isa and his ministry were connected to the Jewish scriptures. By endorsing the "People of the Book" and the revelation entrusted to them, the Qur'an links Moses and 'Isa as those who proclaim a singular message. In fact, the Qur'an even refers to 'Isa as the messiah (*al-Masih*).[6] Yet, *al-Masih* in the Qur'an functions not as an indication of 'Isa's expected role; rather, it simply attaches itself to him as a mysterious last name without further explanation.

Likewise, the Qur'an merely mentions the Jewish scriptures as the book given to Moses. The details of these scriptures that prepare the reader to encounter Jesus as the fulfillment of the Levitical sacrificial system, however, are nowhere to be found in the Qur'an. In other words, the Qur'an claims to uphold the authority of the Old Testament and uses the messianic title for 'Isa while failing to connect them with the scriptural anticipation of the gospel events.

Thus, as Mark Anderson concludes, "the Qur'an radically diverges from the Bible on Jesus in two basic ways: it both dehistoricizes him and marginalizes him."[7] Thus, the biblical preparation for the gospel is nowhere to be found in Islam. Instead, 'Isa is disconnected from the Old Testament expectations, and is co-opted by the Qur'an as a spokesperson for Islam.

For Our Sins

Finally, Paul connects the gospel events to the effect the gospel has on those who believe: atonement for sins. As Mark Anderson compares the biblical teaching on atonement with the Qur'an's teaching on forgiveness, one sees a stark contrast:

> Biblically, believers please God solely on the basis of their present-tense salvation, united with Christ in his death, resurrection and ascension and adopted into God's family. Qur'anically, to claim such a relationship with God is deemed preposterous, since Jesus is only a prophet and believers can

---

5. Bruce Waltke, *An Old Testament Theology* (Grand Rapids: Zondervan, 2007), 888–89.
6. See Qur'an 3:45 as an example of the clear designation of 'Isa as the messiah.
7. Anderson, *Qur'an in Context*, 317.

neither know God intimately nor have any assurance concerning their fate on the Last Day.[8]

Thus, the Christian gospel views Jesus as a substitutionary sacrifice who makes forgiveness available, thus reconciling God and those who believe in Christ. Not only do Muslims deny the substitution, but they also deny the divine-human relationship it restores.

Furthermore, in the Qur'an, sins are not forgiven by the presentation of sacrificial blood. God simply forgives those who repent, as indicated by Qur'an 40:3, which states, "[God is] Forgiver of sin and Accepter of repentance, harsh in retribution, full of forbearance. (There is) no god but Him." Yet, the Qur'an nowhere indicates why God forgives sins or withholds forgiveness.[9] Neither is there any reconciliation of God's just wrath against sin and his extension of forgiveness.

Ultimately, then, the Qur'an denies the biblical concept of atonement.[10] In the words of Anderson, "Just as the Qur'an implicitly subverts the biblical notion that human beings cannot save themselves, it also implicitly denies the biblical teaching that our salvation is found in God's revelation of himself in Jesus."[11] Thus, the concept of Jesus as the messiah whose death, burial, and resurrection removes the sins of believers is irreconcilable with Islamic teaching.

Summary

Paul's gospel message is centered on the proclamation of Jesus as the anticipated Jewish messiah, whose substitutionary death and victorious resurrection extend forgiveness for the sins of those who believe. In that the Qur'an and Islamic teaching contradict every point of this message, they contradict the central components of the biblical gospel.

While there certainly exists a superficial layer of similarity between Islamic and Christian teachings, at the core the two faiths are irreconcilably different. Those who argue for Insider Movement approaches among Muslim peoples must always keep in mind that the Qur'an tells a story that is fundamentally in conflict with the central teaching of the Bible. Whatever contextual components of a Muslim's culture may be retained, the Qur'an cannot be made to compliment the Bible. At its core, the Qur'an is unfaithful to the biblical teaching that is of first importance.

---

8. Anderson, *Qur'an in Context*, 313.

9. Anderson, *Qur'an in Context*, 313.

10. See Qur'an 35:18. This reality is obscured by the fact that both the Qur'an and the Arabic Bible use the same Arabic word that is often translated into English as "atonement." In fact, however, the word functions differently in the Qur'an than it does in the Bible. For those who are interested in a larger discussion about this, see Matthew Bennett, *Narratives in Conflict: Atonement in Hebrews and the Qur'an* (Eugene, OR: Pickwick, 2019).

11. Anderson, *Qur'an in Context*, 314.

REFLECTION QUESTIONS

1. Where is a clear, succinct place in Scripture to find the gospel message? How does this passage in particular clarify the distance between the biblical gospel and the message of the Qur'an?

2. In what way does the Qur'an claim to continue the story "according to the Scriptures?" How does the Qur'an's teaching on 'Isa contradict that claim?

3. If the Qur'an maintains that no one can bear the burden of another's deeds, what does that tell us about its compatibility with the gospel?

4. If we want to explain Jesus's death, burial, and resurrection as the mechanism of human salvation, what categories do we need to explain first that our Muslim friends have not encountered in the Qur'an?

5. Beyond Paul's summary statement of the gospel, what places in the Bible might be most helpful in explaining how Jesus's ministry and gospel fulfills the whole story of Scripture?

How Should a Christian Use Islamic Texts?

> *If you are in doubt about what We have sent down to you, ask those who have been reciting the Book before you. The truth has come to you from your Lord, so do not be one of the doubters.*
> *~Qur'an 10:94*

Quoted above is a favorite Qur'anic verse for Christian missionaries. Here, the Qur'an not only endorses previous revelation as the truth from God, but it also recommends that when Muslims encounter doubts about the Qur'an, they should consult with the People of the Book. Citing this verse, then, a Christian can implore a Muslim conversation partner to read the Bible.

Fu'ad 'Accad refers to this approach as "a bridge to faith," whereby a Muslim is invited to study the Bible by reference to the Qur'an.[1] Following 'Accad's lead, Kevin Greeson has developed a model known as "the Camel Method." The Camel Method uses proof texts from the Qur'an with a Muslim audience to engender confidence and expose curiosity regarding the person of Jesus. Then the evangelist is encouraged to cross the textual bridge into the Bible.[2]

These bridge approaches are not the only endeavors to use the Qur'an in mission to Muslims. Another missiological camp views the Qur'an even

---

1. Fu'ad 'Accad, "The Qur'an: A Bridge to Faith," *Missiology* 4, no. 3 (July 1976): 332.
2. See Mark Snowden's adaptation of Greeson's method in *The Camel Method* (2006) http://www.brigada.org/wp-content/uploads/2016/09/PEACE-Camel-Training-Final.pdf, 2.

more positively, building upon the ideas of missiologist Kenneth Cragg, who writes, "The nature of the gospel is such that the impact of Christ is not totally to displace, but paradoxically to fulfill what is there."[3] Developing this idea further, some have begun to argue that Christ fulfills both the Old Testament and the Qur'an.[4]

Two problems arise when analyzing these approaches to Islam's holy book. First, the proof texts recommended for use are often wrenched out of context and interpreted by Christian missionaries in ways that run counter to Islamic interpretation. For initiated and educated Muslims, then, the manner in which these missionaries use their holy book is inadmissible, offensive, and unconvincing.

Second, for those who take a more positive view of Christ's fulfillment of the Qur'an, does it follow that the Qur'an is viewed as authoritative revelation? And for both approaches, Sam Schlorff's question must be addressed: "What kind of status are you according the Qur'an, whether explicitly or implicitly, when you quote it in support of a Christian position?"[5] Posed differently, "Does your reference to the Qur'an grant it revelatory authority?"

Responding to these theological dangers, some evangelicals have lost motivation to read the Islamic sources. This chapter, however, argues that those ministering to Muslims should read the Qur'an, the *Sunnah*, and Islamic theology, while recognizing that using it as a bridge to evangelism is usually misguided.

Read the Islamic Texts for Connecting

One of the oft-repeated claims of Muslims is that the Bible has been changed.[6] When pressed to produce evidence of where such changes occur, however, the accusers often reveal that they cannot specifically identify changes, nor have they ever read the Bible for themselves. One could be forgiven for dismissing such an accusation out of hand, due to the fact that the accuser has no experience with the Bible but is merely parroting an inherited assumption.[7] Yet this same approach to the Qur'an is often taken by Christians. Believing the Qur'an to be false religious teaching, Christians refuse to pick it up, despite the fact that it is foundational to the faith of billions of people around the world. A Christian thus dignifies their Muslim friend by considering the text that he or she takes to be authoritative.

---

3. Kenneth Cragg, *Sandals at the Mosque* (London: Oxford University Press, 1959), 92. See the discussion of Cragg's work as paradigmatic for dialogical models of contextualization for Muslims in Sam Schlorff, *Missiological Models in Ministry to Muslims* (Upper Darby, PA: Middle East Resources, 2006), 20–21.
4. Schlorff, *Ministry to Muslims*, 75–78.
5. Schlorff, *Ministry to Muslims*, 72.
6. See Question 28 and the discussion of the Islamic doctrine of *tahrif*.
7. Mark Anderson, *The Qur'an in Context: A Christian Exploration* (Downers Grove, IL: IVP Academic, 2016), 322.

Alternatively, one of the proofs given for the veracity of the Qur'an is its inimitable beauty. According to Seyyed Hossein Nasr, "The miracle of the Qur'an lies in its possessing a language which has the efficacy of moving the souls of men now, nearly fourteen hundred years since it was revealed . . . . A Muslim is moved by the very sound of the Qur'an."[8] Thus, if a Christian has read the Qur'an and deemed it to be wanting, it can cause a Muslim to consider how a person could encounter its message and be unmoved.

Read the Islamic Texts for Understanding

A second reason that a Christian should engage with the Islamic sources is to begin to truly understand how their Muslim friends view the world. One is often tempted to read a non-Christian religious text from a posture of skepticism, or from a desire to find and exploit dubious material. While such an approach has its place, it is far more important to utilize this material to gain an understanding of the Islamic worldview.

For example, it is well known that the Qur'an contains stories recounting events in the lives of biblical prophets. In fact, often times one might hear a Muslim comment to a Christian that they cannot be Muslims without believing in all of the prophets from the Bible. But until one reads the stories of the prophets in the Qur'an, one does not know how to make sense of such a claim. In fact, the Qur'an references prophets that bear resemblance to their biblical counterparts, but the Qur'an often utilizes these characters to endorse its own religion.[9]

Furthermore, the Qur'an utilizes concepts that appear to be shared in the Bible. The ideas of God, sin, forgiveness, and salvation appear in the Islamic texts and are often translated as such in the English versions of the Qur'an and *Sunnah*. However, as seen throughout this book, these concepts function very differently as they appear in the Qur'an.[10]

Beyond familiarity with the Qur'an, a Christian should also attempt to engage the *Sunnah*.[11] While the Qur'an is ubiquitous within Islamic society, its density and opaque style of communication causes the average Muslim to draw much more instruction and understanding of Islamic life from the

---

8. Seyyed Hossein Nasr, *Ideals and Realities of Islam*, rev. and updated ed. (San Francisco: Aquarian, 1994), 49. These sentiments only apply to the Qur'an as it is recorded in Arabic. Thus, one might encounter the claim that unless it is read in its original language, a foreigner reading a translation cannot apprehend the depth of beauty inherent in the Arabic meter and rhyme.

9. Sidney Griffith, *The Bible in Arabic* (Princeton, NJ: Princeton University Press, 2013), 63.

10. Question 35 addresses the significant differences between the way that the Qur'an understands the word "God" and the way the Bible understands it. Questions 16–18, likewise, address the understanding of sin in Islam, showing it to lead to biblically incompatible ideas of forgiveness and salvation.

11. An incredibly helpful, searchable resource for accessing the *Sunnah* in English, referenced throughout this work, can be found here: https://sunnah.com.

relative clarity of the *Sunnah*. Regarding the influence the *Sunnah* has in shaping the worldview of Muslims, Edward Hoskins writes,

> The only way to completely understand and apply the Qur'an to their lives is to follow every action and word of their prophet Muhammad. Because the traditions are so important to Muslims, they hear these teachings daily from family members, schoolteachers, and mosque leaders. . . . They become the foundation of a Muslim's life.[12]

Without an awareness of the Islamic texts, a Christian will lack an understanding of how their Muslim friends view the world, its origins, and its purpose. Without such an understanding, the process of communication will be frustrated by the assumption that shared words—such as God, sin, and salvation—indicate shared ideas.

Read the Islamic Texts for Communicating

A Christian seeking to dialogue with a Muslim faces the unique communication barrier of Islam's influence on the Arabic language. Because the Qur'an emerged as the first complete book-length text written in Arabic, the Arabic language has been indelibly shaped by the Qur'an's influence. Thus, even though Arabic-speaking Jews and Christians likely existed prior to the rise of Islam, the manner in which the written Qur'an standardized the language bears influence on the way that Arabic words communicate today.[13]

This influence has ramifications on one's ability to communicate Christian theological concepts in Arabic. For example, the Qur'an and the Arabic Bible both use the same word *kaffara* in divergent ways. When it appears in the Qur'an, it means "covering" or "expiation." When a Muslim hears the word *kaffara*, there is no sense of requisite substitution, blood, or propitiation of divine wrath at all. However, when *kaffara* appears in the Bible, it is translating the Hebrew and Greek words for atonement. This problem is not resolved when using English, as the Bible and the English rendering of the Qur'an both use the word "atonement." Thus, a Christian communicating with a Muslim cannot merely use the word "atonement." Rather, one must explain that biblical atonement involves substitutionary sacrifice and the presentation of blood.[14]

For the Muslim audience, the Qur'an purports to provide a means of atonement without reference to substitutionary sacrifice. Using it in

---

12. Edward Hoskins, *A Muslim's Mind: What Every Christian Needs to Know about the Islamic Traditions* (Colorado Springs: Dawson, 2011), 20.

13. Griffith, *Bible in Arabic*, 23, 43.

14. See chapter 5 in Matthew Bennett, *Narratives in Conflict: Atonement in Hebrews and the Qur'an* (Eugene, OR: Pickwick, 2019).

conversation as a shared word will only obscure the fact that the two faiths do not share its meaning. Christians will go on speaking of Jesus's atoning death, and Muslims will remain unmoved, believing that atonement requires no substitution and can be acquired in multiple other ways. Ultimately, then, if one does not engage the Islamic texts themselves in order to know how they shape theological words and ideas, one will inevitably remain ignorant of the conceptual difference hidden within lexical similarity.

Summary

The Qur'an claims to be a book of divine revelation, and the *Sunnah* is thought to be authoritative explanation thereof. Some Christian missionaries have attempted to use this material to support the Christian message or to demonstrate longings and expectations latent in the Qur'an that can only be fulfilled in Christ. Such attempts are problematic in that they either distort the Qur'an's teaching and offend its adherents, or they lend authority to the Qur'an and begin considering it to be revelatory.

Christians who want to respect their Muslim friends and who believe in a closed canon should not engage in either of these approaches. And yet, to attempt to communicate meaningfully with a Muslim, a Christian must consider how the Islamic texts have shaped the language, concepts, and worldview of their conversation partners. For that reason, if one is going to minister among Muslims, one should also read the texts that are forming the worldview of their Muslim friends.

REFLECTION QUESTIONS

1. What are some ways that Christians attempt to use the Qur'an as a bridge to discuss the gospel? Why is this an appealing route to gospel proclamation for some?

2. What is the theological difference between using the Qur'an as a bridge to the gospel and contending that Christ fulfills both the Bible and the Qur'an?

3. In what ways are the attempts to use the Qur'an to lead to gospel proclamation theologically dangerous? How are they disingenuous? How might they be offensive and counterproductive?

4. With the previously mentioned reasons to be wary of using the Qur'an in evangelism in mind, why should a Christian still read the Qur'an and the *Sunnah*?

5. What does a Christian learn about his or her Muslim friends by engaging their sacred writ? What does such engagement demonstrate about your concern and love for Muslim friends?

How Should a Christian Share the Gospel with Muslims?

Surely it is indeed in the scriptures of those of old.
~Qur'an 26:196

Over the last century, increased globalization, global terrorism, and global connectivity have brought Islam into the thoughts, politics, and neighborhoods of many Westerners. One result of this increased attention is that Christian interest in missions to Muslims has grown. Consulting the shelves of a local Christian bookstore, one finds multiple books about Islamic ideology, conversion stories of those who left Islam, and ways to share the gospel with Muslims.

I believe that most of the books and training materials for evangelism among Muslims have their place and should be considered helpful. Islam presents unique challenges to gospel communication, and people whom God has used to lead many Muslims to faith in Christ have much to teach about best practices. I praise the Lord for his faithfulness to use their efforts. Yet, I find myself skeptical when I see one method or another that claims to be *the* method that God is using to bring Muslims to Christ in the twenty-first century.

At the risk of undermining even this present project, I want to urge the reader of this book not to overcomplicate the process of sharing Jesus with their Muslim friends. Before one should consider any method of evangelism that is custom-built for Muslim audiences, it is far more important to consider a few basic issues about evangelism in general. In this chapter I want to unpack three simple aspects of sharing the gospel, using some of the background material you've hopefully gleaned from this book to do so.

Asking Questions

Of all the books that I have read on evangelism, the one that I recommend most highly is Randy Newman's *Questioning Evangelism*.[1] In it, Newman argues that evangelism is a process involving both listening and speaking. Well-formed questions get people speaking. If you listen well to the answers, you can begin to understand some of your conversation partner's concerns, aspirations, and ways of viewing the world. Such is the case with most Muslims.

My prayer is that the material in this book has not led you to believe that you now understand Islam, or that you know the answers that your Muslim friend will give to these questions. Instead, my prayer is that the material presented in this book would help you to form better, more informed questions to ask of your Muslim friends. Once you ask those questions, it is vital that you prayerfully listen to the answers as your Muslim friends articulate them.

One of the joys of ministry among Muslims is that it is often much harder to get a Muslim to stop speaking about spiritual things than it is to begin a spiritual conversation. Furthermore, Islam, being a faith that exerts influence on every aspect of life—private and public, sacred and secular—allows even the most mundane aspects of life to serve as gateways to spiritual conversation. Well-framed questions, then, are often the catalyst for transforming an everyday conversation into an opportunity to speak about faith.

Eventually, you will have an opportunity to respond to your Muslim friend, either with further questions or with a Christian perspective on the matter. As we have seen, for Muslims, much of their religious practice and ethic is tied to Muhammad's precedent-setting teaching and example as he perfectly lived out the Qur'an.[2] In other words, it is not tied to the story of the universe, but to the *story* of a religious exemplar. Therefore, rather than merely giving a Christian opinion on a matter, one should present how it fits within the story of the Bible.

Telling the Story

As we have seen throughout this project, Islam tells a story that is fundamentally different than the story of the Bible. Therefore, before we immediately jump into the argument about *whether* or not Jesus died on the cross, we need to set the cross within the biblical metanarrative that prepares us to see *why* it matters for Christians that Jesus died and rose again.

If you recall the Islamic perspective on creation, fall, forgiveness, and end times discussed in part 3, each of these teachings reinforces a story that diverges from the biblical account. The universe was not created in order that God might dwell with his creation, so even though sin needs to be forgiven,

---

1. Randy Newman, *Questioning Evangelism* (Grand Rapids: Kregel, 2004).
2. Edward Hoskins, *A Muslim's Mind: What Every Christian Needs to Know about the Islamic Traditions* (Colorado Springs: Dawson, 2011), 20.

perfection is not required. Forgiveness can be accomplished by divine fiat, so substitutionary atonement is unnecessary.

The Qur'an tells a story that is fundamentally at odds with the biblical story. As a result, the Qur'an forges an alternative worldview, creates a divergent set of expectations and values, and paints a different picture of God and his purposes than does the Bible. The differences between the Qur'an and the Bible are thus not superficial, but essential.

Thus, one should capitalize on any opportunity to tell the whole story of the Bible. The Bible presents a Muslim with an alternative view of the whole universe, from creation to new creation, fall to salvation. Likewise, it is helpful to specifically show the passages of Scripture that delineate the various developments in the storyline.[3] This allows the Muslim to encounter the story in the text itself, and it demonstrates the Christian's high view of Scripture rather than relying on creative storytelling.

Exalting Jesus

'Isa in the Qur'an is a highly revered character. Our Muslim friends are often quick to remind us that they would not be true Muslims if they failed to afford him respect and devotion. Even so, it is important that our love for Jesus, our gratitude for Jesus, and our desire to live so as to please Jesus be the driving factors in our presentation of the gospel.

In fact, perhaps the most important lesson that I have learned about evangelism in general is that it is best done as an act of worship. When sharing the gospel, we publicly invite someone to receive the message that we proclaim. Yet as we publicly proclaim it, we likewise can't help but respond in grateful worship as those who have been graciously changed by it. Rather than presenting the gospel in the context of an argument to be won, it should be extended as an invitation to join the worship of the only one worthy of it.

One place that might be fruitful for starting a conversation that would allow us to lift Jesus high while inviting further study would be in Luke 24, as the risen Jesus accompanies the two disciples along the road to Emmaus.

---

3. Genesis 1–2 can be consulted to discuss creation, pointing out God's intentionality and the resulting good creation. Genesis 3 should be read to discuss the fall and the effects of sin. Genesis 12 and 15 introduce Abram and God's covenant promises to bless Israel and the nations. Exodus 20 can be used to introduce the law, and Leviticus 16–17 should be discussed as it provides a foreshadowing of Christ's atonement in the sacrificial system. Second Samuel 7 helps to show that the messiah would be an anointed king who would reign forever. Isaiah 53 can be used to predict Christ's role as a suffering servant. When selecting a gospel to begin with, the Gospel of Luke comes recommended by Colin Chapman, *Cross and Crescent: Responding to the Challenge of Islam* (Downers Grove, IL: InterVarsity, 2003), 314–15. We will look further at this preference for Luke below. However, I also highly recommend an extended study of the book of Hebrews in that it serves to view the entire Old Testament story through the lens of the gospel. Finally, consulting Revelation 21 shows that God's intent is to dwell amid his people in a new creation.

Here, Luke states that Jesus explained his role as the messiah, his crucifixion, his resurrection, and his glory using the whole Old Testament (Luke 24:26–27). Later in the same passage, Jesus appears to his disciples and similarly opened their minds to understand the Scriptures and how they related to his death, resurrection, and the forgiveness of sins (Luke 24:45–49).

This passage elevates Jesus beyond 'Isa in multiple ways. Not only has he risen from the grave, but he explains that his death and resurrection fulfill the Scriptures. Here Jesus claims that all the Scriptures are in fact pointing to him, and specifically to his death, resurrection, glorification, and ability to forgive sins. All of these claims need to be investigated, and this passage can provide an opportunity to invite a Muslim friend to study the Bible to see if it does in fact point to Jesus.

Inviting Study

I believe evangelism should be conducted in such a way as to naturally lead into discipleship when a person believes. In fact, it might be helpful to stop speaking of evangelism and discipleship as if they are such radically distinct processes. Instead, if our Great Commission task is making disciples, then even before someone professes faith in Jesus and repents of their sins, our preparation for their faith should anticipate the manner in which that faith will develop.

Such a process, then, should begin with learning to study the Bible. Indeed, as we have seen throughout this project, Muslims will often need to spend long hours wrestling with the Bible as it both overlaps with and diverges from their holy text. What better way to share the gospel with someone than to walk them through the very pages of Scripture in order to explain it? One question that arises, however, is where to start.

Author and professor Colin Chapman suggests that the best place to begin with Muslims is the Gospel of Luke.[4] In Luke's gospel, one finds the parable of the prodigal son, which has been identified as helpful in explaining God's love to Muslims.[5] Likewise, Chapman highlights Luke's Christology and attention to Jesus's birth narrative as additional reasons that this gospel might be uniquely helpful in exposing Muslims to the biblical story of Jesus.

In addition to Luke, the book of Hebrews presents itself as a uniquely appropriate point of entry for introducing a Muslim audience to the biblical worldview and to Christ as the focal point of the biblical narrative.[6] In Hebrews the author explains the Old Testament law and sacrificial system, faith, redemption history, and atonement as they find their fulfillment in

---

4. Chapman, *Cross and Crescent*, 311–15.
5. See Kenneth Bailey, *The Cross and the Prodigal* (Downers Grove, IL: InterVarsity, 2003).
6. Matthew Bennett, *Narratives in Conflict: Atonement in Hebrews and the Qur'an* (Eugene, OR: Pickwick, 2019).

Christ. In some ways, one could read Hebrews with a non-Christian and see in its pages a sort of transcript of what Jesus might have said that day on the road to Emmaus.

Summary

There is no shortage of material available today purporting to be the best model for ministry to Muslims. Many of these offerings provide encouraging accounts of great harvests coming from among Muslim peoples, and to the degree that they represent reality, we should be enthusiastically praising the Lord of the harvest.

However, rather than devising new schemes or methods, we do well to realize that evangelism, discipleship, and church planting all emerge from the soil of prayerful gospel proclamation, exegetical Bible study, and grateful cultivation of worship. No method will supplant these essential components.

If one is faithful to develop relationships and engage in thoughtful conversations with Muslims derived from reading the Bible together, methodology will take a back seat to the power of the Word of God and the illumination of the Holy Spirit. Fortunately, many Muslims will gladly agree to talk about their faith and even to regularly read the Bible together.

REFLECTION QUESTIONS

1. With all the methods for reaching Muslims with the gospel on offer, what are the dangers in adopting any given approach? What can be lost in the process of searching for best practices in missiology?

2. Why is it important to tell the biblical story? Doesn't the Qur'an lean on the biblical narrative?

3. What kinds of questions might provoke meaningful conversation? Having read the previous chapters and considered some of the teachings of Islam, what places seem to be the most fruitful points of contact for asking meaningful questions?

4. How does the Old Testament biblical story exalt Jesus in a way that is fundamentally different from the way that the Qur'an portrays 'Isa? What aspects of the biblical narrative explain Jesus most clearly?

5. What might be the advantage of responding to Muslim objections to the gospel with an invitation to consider the answer by reading Scripture together?

How Can One Develop a Love for Muslims?

But he, desiring to justify himself, said to Jesus,
"And who is my neighbor?"
~Luke 10:29

As Islam becomes an increasingly present reality in contemporary Western culture, responses to Muslims exhibit an underlying ideological polarization. The news media in the United States has illuminated the deep fissures between political parties, portraying various reactions to issues related to Muslim immigration, religious freedom, and Islamic terrorism.

The academy has divided over whether to speak about Islam respectfully and on the basis of its own claims, or dismissively by citing contemporary critical scholarship that undercuts the essential historical claims Islam builds itself upon. Neighborhoods in which increased immigrant populations are settling also find themselves divided over whether to welcome refugees or to view them as a threat to the community.

Unfortunately, the same polarization often exists within the church as well. In fact, a *Christianity Today* article was published in response to a Pew Research study that revealed that white evangelicals express more concern about Muslims in the United States than any other group.[1] Rather than viewing our Muslim neighbors through the lens of the gospel, many of us find it

---

1. Kate Shellnutt, "Most White Evangelicals Believe Muslims Don't Belong in America," *Christianity Today*, July 26, 2017, https://www.christianitytoday.com/news/2017/july/pew-how-white-evangelicals-view-us-muslims-islam.html.

difficult to shed the skepticism and suspicion we've inherited from society around us or which we've incubated in our own hearts. This final chapter will suggest four basic ways to cultivate a loving response to our Muslim neighbors. It begins with a personal reflection on the gospel itself, develops in prayer, takes root in relationships, and bears fruit in community.

The Gospel

In Question 37 we compared the message that Paul declared to be of first importance with the teachings of Islam and concluded that Islam is incompatible with the gospel. However, if we who are saved by the merciful grace of the gospel withhold the same grace from others—Muslims included—our lives and attitudes also demonstrate incompatibility with the gospel.

Jesus indicates this untenable posture in the parable of the unforgiving servant recorded in Matthew 18:21–35. There, a servant is forgiven an unpayable debt by his sovereign, only to demand repayment of a small debt from a colleague. It is unthinkable that we whose sins against the eternal God have been forgiven would then turn and hold other humans ransom to their debts to us.

Likewise, Paul writes in Ephesians that before the gospel transformed us, "[We] were dead in the trespasses and sins in which [we] once walked" (Eph. 2:1). He goes on to write, "But God, being rich in mercy, because of the great love with which he loved us, even when we were dead in our trespasses, made us alive together with Christ—by grace you have been saved" (2:4–5). As if to make sure that we don't miss his point, he concludes, "For by grace you have been saved through faith. And this is not your own doing; it is the gift of God" (2:8).

Therefore, if we consider the gospel and its effect on us despite our undeserving condition, we cannot help but respond in gratitude. The gospel will not allow us to maintain a posture of superiority nor to withhold its saving power from any that we, in our unmitigated hubris, would deem to be unworthy of it. If there is any hint in us or in our churches of prejudice against Muslims, the gospel demands that such a posture be laid at the foot of the cross where our own sins have been forgiven. In the light of the gospel, prejudice melts into love.

Prayer

A second step to cultivating a loving approach to Muslims is by intentionally engaging in prayer on their behalf. Particularly during Ramadan, many Christian organizations develop prayer plans for how to beseech the Lord on behalf of billions of Muslims worldwide who are fasting and praying in search of God's forgiveness and guidance.[2]

---

2. For example, see "Thirty Days of Prayer for the Muslim World," https://www.30daysprayer.com.

Likewise, throughout the year one can integrate prayer for different Muslim peoples by consulting resources like the Joshua Project.[3] On this website one can use filters to find information on Muslim people groups around the world, along with specific ways to pray for them.

On an even more daily basis, one might consider downloading a Muslim prayer times application on a smartphone. Though Question 13 showed that the five daily Islamic prayers differ from Christian prayer, a regular reminder throughout one's day to pray that Muslims would hear and respond to the gospel is certainly a good practice.

If we regularly engage in bringing Muslims before the throne of grace in our prayers, it will be increasingly difficult to harbor prejudice against them. In fact, as we petition the Lord to save our Muslim friends, praying for them by name, we will only deepen in our love for them. Likewise, as we ask the Spirit to do the preparatory work in their hearts, we will be poised and ready to speak a word of hope to them as we spend time together.

Relationship

While gospel reflection and intentional prayer pave the way for love to characterize our approach to Muslims, such love will only develop roots in actual relationship with Muslims. It is right and good to pray for Muslims in general to come to faith, but when we begin to pray for our specific Muslim friends in the context of meaningful friendships with them, love for them as humans manifests tangibly.

In fact, when we have real relationships with Muslims, their humanity becomes much more central than the religious descriptor we attach to them. In isolation and without meaningful contact, it is much easier to simply deem this whole classification of humans as one monolithic group, and in so doing, to treat them conceptually rather than personally.

In North America, Australia, or Europe, it may initially seem more difficult to naturally befriend Muslims than it might in the Middle East or Southeast Asia. However, such difficulty is largely the product of assumption rather than reality. Most large cities in the United States have a Muslim population and mosques or Islamic centers. Many of these locations also have visitor's centers that will host community nights whereby the Muslim community invites interaction with the non-Muslim community. Scheduling a visit to one of these places can be an excellent starting point for striking up friendships with the local Muslim population.

Other options for natural engagement with Muslims could include visiting Mediterranean or Middle Eastern restaurants. Oftentimes these

---

3. See www.joshuaproject.net. This website collects up-to-date data regarding gospel engagement around the world. It is not limited to Muslim populations, but if one so desires, it is possible to use the website and mobile applications to filter for specific demographic criteria.

restaurants are operated by expats from Muslim majority regions. Just as McDonalds around the world attracts North American clientele, so too do these restaurants usually attract Middle Eastern patrons. Not only will you enjoy a delicious culinary experience, but if the staff are not too busy, you can easily strike up conversation about the dishes, decor, and country of origin, which can provide natural connections that can lead to budding friendships.

Community

One beautiful thing about working with Muslim populations is that typically they hold their social networks in high esteem and their lives are intimately intertwined. From nuclear and extended family to fellow Muslims with whom they attend mosque services, the community life of most Muslim populations often puts Christian fellowship to shame. Once a friendship has been established with a Muslim family, it is likely that opportunity to engage the broader Muslim community will also arise.

Becoming familiar and comfortable in the Muslim community may take some time. Despite the investment of time and energy, however, interactions with the Muslim community will develop a deep-seated love in you for your Muslim neighbors and is well worth the effort.

Likewise, it is important that your Muslim friends are also privy to your Christian community. Despite what one might initially think, inviting your Muslim friend to church is a nonoffensive idea, and probably far less awkward than it would be to invite your nonreligious neighbor. Including your Muslim friends in gatherings of Christians in your home for dinner, barbecues, and block parties is also a great way to demonstrate Christian community.[4]

Again, such integration of your Muslim friends into your life encourages depth in your love for them, and progress in no longer seeing them as your *Muslim* friend, but merely as your friend. In this context, they cease to be specific projects for evangelism and simply become part of your community with whom you naturally share your faith.

Summary

The gospel changes everything. It reconciles the enemies of God with their creator. It forgives the vilest of sinners. It causes cold, dead hearts to beat afresh with the infusion of an alien love. This gospel that has awakened life in us also awakens in us a new way of living.

No longer do we live as those who are estranged from God. Rather, with the very presence of God living in us, we are guided by the Holy Spirit to

---

4. You will want to be sure to avoid serving pork products or alcohol at such events. In order to help alleviate the potential concerns of your Muslim neighbors in accepting a dinner invitation, it will help to ask them to help you prepare a *halal* meal according to Islamic dietary code.

extend gospel-driven love to a world filled with those who have yet to encounter it. This gospel leaves no room for prejudice.

Furthermore, when we begin to pray gospel-driven and gospel-shaped prayers for Muslims, not only do we begin to put any potential prejudice to death, but we also make investments in love. Finally, as we develop relationships with our Muslim friends and integrate our communities, our love can flourish and opportunities to embody, demonstrate, and proclaim the gospel present themselves in manifold ways.

At the end of this project, my prayer is that this book helps in some small way to give you confidence to befriend Muslims. Also, I pray that through those relationships, the Lord would be pleased to bring Muslims into a meaningful encounter with his endless mercy in the gospel of Jesus the Messiah. Because the one, triune God of creation is worthy of the praise of all peoples.

REFLECTION QUESTIONS

1. What was your initial impression of Muslims before reading this book? Has anything changed?

2. Where are the places in your heart that you still need the Lord to work in order to see an abiding love characterize your posture regarding your Muslim neighbors?

3. What does the gospel have to do with your posture toward your Muslim neighbor?

4. What ways seem most readily available for you to engage with Muslims in your community? Do you have any friends who would likely join you in getting to know your Muslim neighbors?

5. How are you praying that the Lord would deepen your love for your Muslim neighbors?

Glossary of Select Arabic Terms[1]

bid'a   Innovation in theology or practice that contradicts tradition principles of Islam.

bismillah   Invocation of the name of God; often a reference to the first chapter of the Qur'an.

fatwa   Rulings regarding the application of Islamic law, usually issued by qualified scholars of Islam (see *mufti* and *qadi* below).

fiqh   The process of Islamic jurisprudence and determining Islamic law.

hadith   A saying about the actions or teachings of Muhammad.

hajj   The pilgrimage to Mecca to be performed during the Islamic month Dhu al-Hajja.

hanif   A righteous or upstanding person. Abraham is named as a *hanif* in Qur'an 3:67.

isnad   The chain of transmitters associated with the retelling of each *hadith*.

jihad   Lit.: struggle; variously interpreted as internal spiritual struggle, defensive physical warfare, or aggressive holy war.

Ka'ba   The cube-like structure at the center of the Great Mosque in Mecca; the *hajj* ritual begins with pilgrims making seven circuits around this building, which is believed to have been built by Ibrahim and Ismail as a temple of monotheistic worship.

madhhab   Schools of Islamic jurisprudence distinguishable by their approach to the process of determining Islamic law and the tools permitted for the task. There are four major Sunni schools: *Hanafi, Shafi'i, Maliki,* and *Hanbali*.

mufti   A trained judge of Islamic law, endowed with the capacity to issue *fatwas* (rulings regarding the application of Islamic law). Usually the *mufti* serves as a consult with the State to ensure proper governance and legislation. The Grand Mufti (also known as the Sheikh al-Islam) is the State's chief advisor on all matters of Islamic law.

---

1. Many of these definitions are distilled from the helpful glossary found in Clinton Bennett, ed., *The Bloomsbury Companion to Islamic Studies* (New York: Bloomsbury, 2015), 327–74.

qadi   A trained judge of Islamic law, endowed with the capacity to render *fatwas* (rulings regarding the application of Islamic law). Ideally this position is independent of the state or political rulers.

qibla   The orientation to Mecca—specifically toward the Ka'ba—toward which *salat* prayers are to be directed.

Rashidun   According to Sunni Muslims, the first four caliphs were known as the Rightly Guided (Rashidun) Caliphs.

salat   The five daily ritual prayers offered by Muslims.

sawm   Fasting; often associated with the thirty-day fast during Ramadan.

Shahadah   The Islamic confession of faith: "There is no god but The God and Muhammad is His messenger."

Sharia   Usually understood to mean the sum total of Islamic law; literally referring to a path of guidance to an oasis.

shirk   The grave sin of associating partners with God; polytheistic worship.

Sira   Shorthand for *Sirat Rasul Allah*, the biography of Muhammad's life apparently written by Ibn Ishaq, but only available through the edited recollection thereof by Ibn Hisham, written two hundred years after Muhammad died.

Sunnah   The traditional material regarding Muhammad's life, teaching, and embodiment of the principles of Islam. This includes the *Sira*, the collections of *hadith*, and can even include early commentaries.

tahrif   The accusation that Christians and Jews have corrupted their scriptures, changing parts so as to render their texts unreliable.

tawhid   The absolute oneness of God; a monadic commitment to the transcendent uniqueness and singularity of the Islamic conception of God. Arguably the most formative concept in Islamic theology.

'ulama   The body of recognized scholars of Islamic law.

Ummah   The worldwide community of Muslims.

ummi   Variously understood to mean illiterate, uneducated, or something more akin to a commoner or Gentile.

zakat   Alms given to charity; traditionally understood to be two and a half percent of a person's income.

Select Bibliography

Anderson, Mark. *The Qur'an in Context: A Christian Exploration*. Downers Grove, IL: IVP Academic, 2016.

Bennett, Clinton, ed. *The Bloomsbury Companion to Islamic Studies*. New York: Bloomsbury, 2016.

Bennett, Matthew. *Narratives in Conflict: Atonement in Hebrews and the Qur'an*. Eugene, OR: Pickwick, 2019.

Chapman, Colin. *Cross and Crescent: Responding to the Challenge of Islam*. Downers Grove, IL: InterVarsity, 2003.

Cuypers, Michel. *The Banquet: A Reading of the Fifth Sura of the Qur'an*. Miami: Convivium, 2009.

Droge, A. J., trans. *The Qur'an: A New Annotated Translation*. Bristol, CT: Equinox, 2015.

Fries, Micah and Keith Whitfield, *Islam and North America: Loving Our Muslim Neighbors*. Nashville: B&H Academic, 2018.

Griffith, Sidney. *The Bible in Arabic: The Scriptures of the "People of the Book" in the Language of Islam*. Princeton, NJ: Princeton University Press, 2013.

Guillaume, A., trans. *The Life of Muhammad: A Translation of Ibn Ishaq's "Sirat Rasul Allah."* Oxford: Oxford University Press, 1982.

Hoskins, Edward. *A Muslim's Mind: What Every Christian Needs to Know about the Islamic Traditions*. Colorado Springs: Dawson, 2011.

Kaltner, John and Younus Mirza. *The Bible and the Qur'an: Biblical Figures in the Islamic Tradition*. New York: T&T Clark, 2018.

McAuliffe, Jane Dammen, ed. *The Cambridge Companion to the Qur'an*. New York: Cambridge University Press, 2006.

Nasr, Seyyed Hossein. *Ideals and Realities of Islam*. New York: Aquarian, 1994.

_____. *The Heart of Islam: Enduring Values for Humanity*. New York: HarperOne, 2004.

Ohlig, Karl-Heinz, ed. *The Hidden Origins of Islam: New Research into Its Early History*. Amherst, NY: Prometheus, 2010.

_____. *Early Islam: A Critical Reconstruction based on Contemporary Sources*. Amherst, NY: Prometheus, 2013.

Qureshi, Nabeel. *No God but One: A Former Muslim Investigates the Evidence for Islam and Christianity*. Grand Rapids: Zondervan, 2016.

Rahman, Fazlur. *Major Themes of the Qur'an*. Chicago: University of Chicago Press, 2009.

Reisacher, Evelyne, ed. *Toward Respectful Understanding and Witness among Muslims: Essays in Honor of J. Dudley Woodberry*. Pasadena, CA: William Carey Library, 2012.

_____, ed. *Dynamics of Muslim Worlds: Regional, Theological, and Missiological Perspectives*. Downers Grove, IL: IVP Academic, 2017.

Renard, John. *Islamic Theological Themes: A Primary Source Reader*. Oakland: University of California Press, 2014.

Reynolds, Gabriel Said. *The Qur'an and Its Biblical Subtext*. New York: Routledge, 2010.

_____, ed. *New Perspectives on the Qur'an: The Qur'an in Its Historical Context*. Vol. 2. New York: Routledge, 2011.

_____. *The Emergence of Islam: Classical Traditions in Contemporary Perspective*. Minneapolis: Fortress, 2012.

Schlorff, Sam. *Missiological Models in Ministry to Muslims*. Upper Darby, PA: Middle East Resources, 2006.

Wu, Jackson. *One Gospel for All Nations: A Practical Approach to Biblical Contextualization*. Pasadena, CA: William Carey Library, 2015.

Bible and Qur'an Index